Feeling Faint

Rethinking the Early Modern

Feeling Faint

Affect and Consciousness in the Renaissance

Giulio J. Pertile

Northwestern University Press
Evanston, Illinois

Northwestern University Press
www.nupress.northwestern.edu

Printed in the United States of America

10 9 8 7 6 5 4 3 2 1

Library of Congress Cataloging-in-Publication Data

Names: Pertile, Giulio J., author.
Title: Feeling faint : affect and consciousness in the Renaissance / Giulio J. Pertile.
Other titles: Rethinking the Early Modern.
Description: Evanston : Northwestern University Press, 2019. | Series: Rethinking the Early Modern | Includes bibliographical references and index.
Identifiers: LCCN 2018039108 | ISBN 9780810139190 (cloth : alk. paper) | ISBN 9780810139183 (pbk. : alk. paper) | ISBN 9780810139206 (ebook)
Subjects: LCSH: European literature—Renaissance, 1450–1600—History and criticism. | European literature—Early modern, 1500–1700—History and criticism. | Consciousness in literature.
Classification: LCC PN720 .P47 2019 | DDC 809.8940903—dc23
LC record available at https://lccn.loc.gov/2018039108

For my parents

Locke sank into a swoon

—W. B. Yeats, “Fragments”

CONTENTS

ACKNOWLEDGMENTS

Research for *Feeling Faint* was aided by generous grants from the American Council of Learned Societies and the Huntington Library in California. The book would not have been possible at all without the conversation, encouragement, and advice of many people—too many to name here. I am, however, especially grateful to advisers, friends, and colleagues at Princeton University, the Claremont Colleges, and the University of St. Andrews. Leonard Barkan, Jeff Dolven, Daniel Heller-Roazen, and Nigel Smith were shaping the project before it was so much as a tremor in consciousness. Helen Vendler read through the whole manuscript and provided invaluable comments on matters both large and small. The anonymous readers at Northwestern University Press gave me generous, thoughtful, and incisive feedback on the manuscript, while Gianna Mosser, Anne Gendler, and their colleagues at the Press have shepherded it through the production process with scrupulous patience and care. My greatest debts are to my parents, Lino Pertile and Anna Bensted, who have been a constant source of support and encouragement, and to the love, patience, wisdom, and computer expertise of Katerina Stergiopoulou.

Feeling Faint

Chapter 1

Swoons: Fainting in the First Person

At least if we can judge by its words, the early modern period lacked a concept of consciousness. The word "consciousness" itself existed, but it referred primarily to "internal knowledge or conviction; the state or fact of being mentally conscious or aware of something" (*OED* def. 1). Since the knowledge involved was usually of "something" in particular—more often than not one's guilt or moral weaknesss—"consciousness" in this sense almost always took a prepositional phrase or clause, as in the *OED*'s earliest example: "consciousness of his owne worthlesness" (from Sir Edwin Sandys's *Relation of the State of Religion*, 1605). Meanwhile, to be "conscious" meant primarily "having awareness of one's own wrongdoing, affected by a feeling of guilt" (*OED* 1); it meant, in other words, to feel the stings of that "internal witness" which we would now distinguish from consciousness as "conscience."[1] "Conscious" could also mean "having knowledge or awareness; able to perceive or experience something" (*OED* 2), but in this sense, like "consciousness," it almost always took a clause or a prepositional phrase: the OED's earliest examples include "conscious of my love" (from John Marston's *What You Will*, 1607) and, crossing over into the moral sense, "conscious of an upright and unspotted life" (from Robert Bolton's *A Discourse about the State of True Happinesse*, 1611). Early modern usage of both "conscious" and "consciousness" was more or less directly modeled on that of the Latin words *conscius* and *conscientia*, which typically took a preposition and referred to knowledge of something specific, and not widely known, that was shared with select others (hence the prefix *con*). It is with this sense in mind that John Denham can speak of "the conscious groves, / The scenes of his past triumphs," and that John Milton can describe Satan's army as working "under conscious night" (6.521).[2]

Today, in contrast, the words "conscious" and "consciousness" are used above all, in a sense we might characterize as "intransitive," to describe our underlying state of awareness as such: "having the faculty of consciousness; characterized by the presence of consciousness" (*OED* 8); "aware of and responding to one's surroundings; having one's mental faculties in an active and waking state" (*OED* 10). In these senses, which depart from the meanings of the Latin *conscius* and *conscientia* as well as from their early modern English equivalents, and which do not take any kind of object, "conscious" is only attested in the early eighteenth century. "Consciousness" itself, when defined as "the faculty or capacity from which awareness of thought, feeling, and volition and of the external world arises" (*OED* 2a), is first attested in the late seventeenth century, in Ralph Cudworth's *True Intellectual System of the Universe* (1678). Earlier usages of "consciousness," like those of "conscious," always refer to consciousness of an object, event, or idea.

Until the seventeenth century, in other words, "conscious" and "consciousness" do not designate the activities of a distinctive faculty; they do not refer to a state of awareness as such. Rather, they refer to states of knowledge, and in particular that moral self-knowledge which today we associate exclusively with the word "conscience." Of course, the absence of the word's modern sense does not tell us anything about how people experienced their own inner workings. Lyric poetry from the period, as well as dramatic monologues from the stage, have long served as testimony to the richness of early modern interiority, even when we have sought to situate that interiority in social and political contexts. And other words often expressed notions which we would today describe in terms of conscious experience or awareness. When John Webster's Duchess of Malfi says, "I will plant my soul in mine ears, to hear you," or when John Donne bids "good morrow to our waking souls / Which watch not one another out of fear," or when Julius Canius (as Montaigne tells his story in the *Essais*) wonders whether his dying soul "will shew some feeling of her sudden departure" (III, 6; 185), in each instance the "soul" seems to feel and sense of its own accord, suggesting not an immaterial substance, but rather a form of conscious perception.[3] In each of these cases, the "soul" itself is what feels: it is a power of sentience tied to the five senses. Yet in none of them can the soul be fully identified with one sense in particular or even with all five. Rather, like our modern concept of consciousness ("the faculty or capacity from which awareness of thought, feeling, and volition and of the external world arises"), it involves a more general form of awareness *of* the senses which cannot be reduced to any of the senses themselves.

At the same time, all of these examples also bear witness to a major difference from our contemporary notions of consciousness. The Duchess's "I" manipulates her soul as if it were an instrument independent of her;

Donne bids good morrow to the lovers' watching souls as if the people speaking and the souls watching were separate entities; and Canius speaks of his soul in the third-person feminine. The "soul" in all of these passages, in other words, is described in terms which render it oddly distinct from the person speaking of it or experiencing it. Where consciousness today is often seen as fully coterminous with first-personness, with an "I" whose sense of self indelibly imprints everything we think, say, or do, in each of these examples the "soul," while fully sentient and closely linked to the first person who speaks of it, remains fundamentally distinct from that person. In this regard, the "soul" in these passages evokes Aristotle's notion of the sensitive soul rather than the modern idea of consciousness. A faculty responsible for sensing and feeling and which human beings shared with animals but not plants, the sensitive soul was a potential for sensory experience by virtue of which each sense organ could temporarily take on the qualities of an external object; it was clearly distinct from the intellectual soul, which was a uniquely human power of reasoning and logical thinking.[4] In the same way, in the three examples I have cited, "soul" is treated as a sentient power that is temporarily actualized by specific stimuli. Thus, while the sensitive soul has sometimes been identified with the modern notion of consciousness, unlike that notion, it cannot be characterized by first-personness, by a thoroughgoing sense of self.[5] Like the "soul" in Montaigne, Donne, and Webster, it is sentience in a fundamentally impersonal guise.

Since the nineteenth century, the early modern period has often been seen as a crucial moment in the history of the notion of consciousness—whether to be celebrated as a turning point in the emergence of the autonomous individual, or lamented as the origin of the alienated modern self.[6] Yet starting with Jacob Burckhardt, consciousness itself—in his words, "that which was turned within as that which was turned without"—has always been immediately subsumed by another concept, in Burckhardt's case by individuality.[7] Perhaps the historical mutations of the word "consciousness" have made us reluctant to look for evidence of it in early modern texts, before the emergence of the word's distinctive modern meanings—what C. S. Lewis describes as its "dangerous" (i.e., anachronistic) sense.[8] Or perhaps we have followed Enlightenment philosophical assumptions in identifying consciousness with self-consciousness, treating it as effectively identical with ideas of selfhood, individuality, autonomy, and Cartesian separation from the body. Indeed, most of the critics who have addressed their attention to questions of subjectivity in the Renaissance regard consciousness as fully synonymous with a form of selfhood whose bases, for better or for worse, are political, social, and historical. Catherine Belsey's assertion that "this interiority, this consciousness which is also being, defined the humanist subject, the author and origin of meaning and choice," expresses assumptions about subjectivity that have been shared even when Belsey's claims have been critiqued;[9] the editors of *Passions and Subjectivity in Early Modern Culture*, for example, trace back to Burckhardt a "bias towards the study of consciousness and the subject as self-fashioning agent."[10] Statements such as these seamlessly identify a series of terms which, as we have seen in the examples cited above, early modern texts might well warrant carefully keeping apart. The notion of a specifically *sentient* consciousness in the early modern period—as distinct from notions of selfhood and individuality—has not received sufficient attention.

Feeling Faint attempts to remedy this omission by drawing together four moments from Renaissance literature in which the nature of consciousness is acutely at stake. They are all scenes of fainting: Montaigne's swoon on falling from a horse in book 2 of his *Essais*, Guyon's faint in book 2 of *The Faerie Queene*, Othello's trance at the beginning of act 4 of *Othello*, and Hermione's deathlike coma in *The Winter's Tale*. It may seem odd to study consciousness by focusing on moments when it is lost. Yet in each of these cases, the transition from consciousness to its absence enforces close scrutiny of what, exactly, is lost. And as we shall see, the transition involved is, in fact, in each case more complex: it is not simply a passage from consciousness to oblivion, but rather a rich, albeit brief, experience unto itself—something like what Milton calls, in a phrase which blurs early modern senses of the word with later ones, "conscious dreams" (9.1050).[11] As his phrase suggests, at this moment of flux in its history the word "conscious" could be more capacious than its modern counterpart, extending below the threshold of first-personness and waking awareness which define the word today. Rather than cutting consciousness off, the early modern swoon gives us unique access to a dimension of conscious experience which we might otherwise simply characterize as un- or non-conscious, exposing a layer of being in which, as in the examples cited above, the "soul" appears to do and think and feel of its own accord—in which it is conscious and yet at least partially uncoupled from a self who might lay claim to that consciousness.

Consciousness is notoriously difficult to define, in part because it is so difficult to pin down what we are talking about in the first place. In his *Essays on Psychology*, William James describes the difficulty of capturing the "rush of thought" in its movement: "Let anyone try to cut a thought across in the middle and get a look at its section," he writes, "and he will see how difficult the introspective observation of the transitive tracts is."

Doing so would be like "seizing a spinning top to catch its motion, or trying to turn up the gas quickly enough to see how the darkness looks."[12] Both of these things are impossible: whether you are seizing the top or turning on the light, you destroy what you are trying to see in the very effort to make it visible. While all of us probably feel that we know what consciousness is, we tend to be conscious *of* other things rather than of consciousness itself, which we mostly take for granted; it can be almost impossible to sift our awareness from its objects and turn its focus upon itself. Yet the swoon accomplishes exactly what James characterizes as impossible: just as modern neuroscience learns about consciousness by studying patients in whom it is absent or impaired, so, as a character's consciousness falters into blankness, he or she has a transient yet intimate encounter with consciousness itself. In such moments, as we will see, the power of a specifically sentient consciousness is disclosed, consciousness as an ongoing felt experience rather than as a detached faculty of representation grounded in a self. By tracing carefully the contours of such moments, we readers too may have a brief encounter with such consciousness—with that impersonal, background feeling whose retreat from our grasp is what makes everything palpable in the first place.

"We Feel That We See": Consciousness beyond the Cogito

In a brief but profound essay on the work of Michel de Montaigne, Maurice Merleau-Ponty argues that Montaigne's writing puts "not self-satisfied understanding but consciousness astonished at itself at the core of human existence."[13] This statement may well seem paradoxical. Astonishment is a state in which consciousness becomes suspended, fixated on a particular object or idea. For consciousness to be astonished at itself, therefore, would be for consciousness to be overpowered by an apprehension of its very own operations. Yet as we will see, this description is apt not only for Montaigne, who loses consciousness upon falling from his horse in one of the most famous episodes from the *Essais*, but for all of the other swoons I will consider in this book. In each case, the suspension of consciousness involves not its termination but rather its intensification, a temporary condition in which consciousness grasps nothing but itself—nothing, that is, but its own constitutive movement. Indeed, Merleau-Ponty's phrase describes exactly that conjunction of motion and stasis which James describes as seizing a spinning top to catch its motion. As Merleau-Ponty describes it, astonishment can be like an instantaneous anatomy or X-ray of consciousness, achieving the paradoxical goal of capturing in stasis something whose essence is change and movement. In Montaigne himself, in Spenser, and in Shakespeare, astonishment is what enables consciousness to turn its gaze toward itself. Consciousness is on the one hand utterly transformed: no longer attentive to the world of objects and people around it, it may also seem to lack self-awareness; that is, attention directed inwards to the flow of thoughts and feelings. And yet, when the mind is cut off from the world around it and when even its own powers of self-reflection have been hampered, it is not arrested altogether but rather plunged into a layer of itself which normally remains invisible: the place where it intersects with the body, the passions, and the senses—with, in a word, life.

In the early modern period, it was René Descartes who most fully explored the mind's powers of awareness.[14] Many of the functions which for Aristotle comprise the sensitive soul are ascribed by Descartes to *res extensa*, the soulless world of mechanized matter over against which he posits the *res cogitans* or "thinking thing" of mind.[15] *Res cogitans* is defined by a power which Descartes, adapting the Latin term, refers to as *conscientia*, and indeed it is in the wake of Descartes that the term "consciousness" takes on its modern association with the activities of a disembodied faculty of awareness seated in the mind alone. Descartes's notion of *conscientia*, however, is both more complex and more capacious—more closely connected to sensation—than is often assumed. *Conscientia* emerges from the radical doubt to which Descartes subjects all of his own thoughts and sensations in the *Meditations*. Since even the seemingly most certain thoughts—"that I am here, sitting by the fire, wearing a winter dressing-gown, holding this piece of paper in my hands"—may be deceptive, Descartes is forced to seek certainty outside the content of any particular ideas.[16] He arrives at it by means of an ingenious twist: even if every thought and sensation is deceptive, he argues in the "Second Meditation," the sheer experience *of* thinking and sensing cannot be denied. Even when he is deceived, Descartes argues, he must have an awareness of the deceptive experience itself, which cannot be doubted: "For example, I am now seeing light, hearing a noise, feeling heat. But I am asleep, so all this is false. Yet I certainly *seem* to see [*videor videre*], to hear, and to be warmed. This cannot be false; what is called 'having a sensory perception' is strictly just this, and in this restricted sense of the term it is simply thinking."[17]

Videor videre, "I seem to see," Descartes writes: the emphasis in this "seeming" is not (as so often in Renaissance literature) on the possibility that seeming and reality may differ, but rather on the unquestionable phenomenological reality of the experience of seeming itself. I may not actually be seeing anything at all, but I cannot doubt the experience of seeing. For in order to call my seeing into doubt in the first place, I must have experienced it—I must, at any rate, have experienced something. It is this explicitly sensory and undeniably real experience of our own inner states which, in the *Principles of Philosophy*, Descartes defines as *conscientia*: "By the term 'thought' [*cogitationis nomine*], I understand everything which we are aware of as happening within us [*illa omnia, quae nobis consciis in nobis sunt*], insofar as we have awareness [*conscientia*] of it. Hence, *thinking* is to be identified here not merely with understanding, willing, and imagining, but also with sensory awareness [*sentire*]."[18] Unlike the Latin *conscientia*, therefore, the Cartesian use of this term refers not to knowledge states, but rather to our ability to be aware of what is happening in our mind at any given time. In Descartes's words, *cogitatio* is not simply what is *in nobis* but what is *nobis consciis in nobis*—an inward state that transpires "with our awareness of it" or more literally "with us [being] aware." While *conscientia* here certainly looks much more similar to "consciousness" in its modern sense than to *conscientia*'s traditional Latin senses, it is also clear that the power of self-awareness it describes is first and foremost a power of feeling, *sentire*.

Especially in literary scholarship of the early modern period, Descartes is frequently seen as an uncompromising mind-matter dualist who inaugurated a newly disembodied concept of mind. Yet from these descriptions, it is not clear that such a characterization is entirely accurate. As Michel Henry has argued, Descartes's account of the cogito actually puts sensation and feeling at the center of the picture: "Descartes continuously affirms that we sense our thought, sense that we see, that we hear, that we warm ourselves."[19] Even the mind of an infant, Descartes argues in response to an objection raised by Antoine Arnauld, "is immediately aware of its thoughts."[20] Clearly, Descartes's notion of *conscientia* is far removed from a power of conscious *reflection* on our own thoughts, which is hard to attribute to infants. Instead, as Descartes tells us several times, *conscientia* is first and foremost a feeling: "we feel that we see [*sentimus nos videre*]," he writes.[21] The *videor* in Descartes's formula *videor videre* does not, therefore, relate to seeing specifically, but rather stays the same across the range of our sensory, intellectual, and emotional experiences. Expanding on Descartes's argument, Henry argues that this power of sensing is built in to all of our experience as such, and that it is first and foremost a power of *self*-sensing, by virtue of which all subjective experience feels itself before it relates to its object, and without which it would experience nothing at all—"a power other than its own, a power in which it is auto-affected so that it feels its seeing and feels itself seeing."[22] In order to doubt our own perceptions we must have experienced them in the first place: there must be a capacity for *self*-experience which is intrinsic to all perception and to sensory life in general.[23] Descartes's *videor videre*, therefore, describes a "fashion of being in us" and a "mode of interiority"[24] which is what makes all of our experiences subjective in the first place, "the self-sensing that originally presents thought to itself and makes it what it is."[25] Its existence is self-evident in a way that is entirely independent of truth-value if the latter is conceived in terms of correspondence to external reality. Far from contaminating vision or the other senses with doubt and uncertainty, "seeming" in the sense of *videor* possesses a truth-value unique to it and unavailable to any of the senses proper.

Michel Henry's analysis of the *videor videre* turns on its head the notion of "Cartesian" dualism: rather than severing mind from body, Descartes's discovery of the power by means of which thinking thinks itself instead serves to explain consciousness as affectivity and a mode of sensory life.[26] For if before apprehending anything outside itself, consciousness grasps itself—grasps that it is happening, and that therefore it exists—it must do so by virtue of feeling rather than by representation or perception. As Jean-Luc Marion has shown in a reading of Henry, there is no other way in which consciousness could perceive itself, since in order to represent itself to itself it would have to become something other than what it is, namely, an object. Instead, it feels its own activity by a power of self-feeling which Marion follows Henry in calling "auto-affection": "Consciousness thinks, and thinks of itself, fundamentally by auto-affection. Before any other operation consciousness experiences itself, with an absolute immediacy, without which it could never experience anything else."[27] In *The Inner Touch*, Daniel Heller-Roazen traces this power of self-feeling back to Aristotle: not to the sensitive soul but rather to what Aristotle calls the "common sense" (*koine aisthesis*). Described in book 3, chapters 1 and 2 of Aristotle's *De Anima*, the common sense is a capacity which enables us to sense common sensibles—qualities that do not pertain to any one sense in particular, such as motion, number, or magnitude—as well as to sense the fact that we are sensing in the first place.[28] In terms close to those with which Henry describes the *videor videre*, Heller-Roazen writes: "No sense can be considered the sense of its sensible object alone. It must also be 'of itself,' receptive, in other words, to the second degree. Capable of perceiving that which lies outside it, every sense must, at the same time, be capable of being affected by its own pure power to do so."[29] Where other readers of Aristotle have found in the sense of sensing a precursor to the modern idea of consciousness, Heller-Roazen argues that the two should be kept distinct.[30] In his account as in Henry's, the sense of sensing is not necessarily a separate power over and above the senses, as it usually is for Enlightenment and post-Enlightenment philosophy; rather, it is a capacity for being affected by itself which is intrinsic to each sense. Consciousness is not, in this account, a central cognitive faculty whose separate existence is always implicit in acts of awareness, but rather a power distributed across the senses whereby they are each made capable of feeling their own activity.

Henry's version of the Cartesian cogito perceives itself because it is, always already, fully inside itself, because it perpetually encounters itself through an intimate self-touching that is bypassed by every form of reflection and representation. As Henry, Marion, and Heller-Roazen all show, this sense of sensing is in the first place a form of affect, fundamentally distinct from the forms of self-perception and representation which so often define consciousness in the Enlightenment and afterwards and thus from the self which that consciousness defines in turn. Whereas to know things by these latter means is to know them, even when they are within us, from a distance, to experience them affectively is to know them by means of immediate contact and felt change.[31] The objectifying processes of representation simultaneously presume such contact (inasmuch as we cannot represent an object to ourselves without being affected by it first) and dispel it (inasmuch as representation introduces a distance which separates what touches). Perception and representation, in other words, presuppose affect, but not all affect can be made subject to representation: we cannot represent experiences of hunger or anger to ourselves without losing what is essential about those experiences, the way in which they are felt. To say that consciousness is fundamentally a form of "auto-affection," therefore, is to say that it is an "affect" which is at once self-induced and self-experienced, generated by nothing outside itself and feeling nothing beyond itself, and always localized in acts of feeling rather than supervening on them. Defined in this way, auto-affection can become synonymous not only with consciousness but also with life itself, insofar as life is defined in terms of spontaneous, self-engendering change (e.g., growth)—in Aristotle's words, as the "capacity for self-sustenance, growth, and decay," and in Derrida's words, "as . . . a spontaneity that is capable of movement, of organizing itself, marking, tracing, and affecting itself with traces of itself. This *auto-motricity* as auto-affection and relation to itself is the characteristic recognized as that of the living and of animality in general."[32] When it is understood as the power to affect itself, consciousness is nothing other than life.

Henry's account of the cogito entails an important claim about intellectual history more broadly. Subsequent accounts of consciousness, Henry argues, mistakenly limit consciousness to acts of representation; thus, when Freudian psychoanalysis discovers an "unconscious" comprised of invisible affective energies, it is operating within the terms of this false, post-Cartesian delimitation. In Descartes's early accounts of the cogito, by contrast, Henry locates a concept of consciousness which is deeply implicated in our affective life and does not admit of a distinction between conscious and unconscious. Henry's version of the Cartesian cogito can thus help us to understand that more capacious concept of consciousness which is glimpsed in Milton's "conscious dreams"—a phrase which seems almost intentionally to transgress the central distinctions of Freudian psychoanalysis—and which is also revealed, I will argue, in the "conscious" swoons and trances of Montaigne, Spenser, and Shakespeare. Instead of simply destroying consciousness, swoons and trances can disclose this immanent power of self-sensing which constitutes life itself—consciousness as affect rather than perception.

Is it not enough simply to turn our attention inwards and pay closer heed to our own internal states? As Michel Henry suggests, the feeling of feeling is harder to grasp than we might assume. For the immanent feltness of all experience is intrinsically invisible and intractable to representation in the mind: "Our life is never and cannot be seen,"[33] he writes, and thus "as soon as I try to see this reality, it disappears."[34] Catherine Malabou describes the workings of such "life" in terms of what she calls "cerebral auto-affection," a feeling which feels itself and yet paradoxically remains unfelt:

> As I write these lines, I see myself write them, but this vision is only the distantly derived and thoroughly elaborated form of a primary auto-affection—cerebral auto-affection, constant but invisible, which forever keeps me from experiencing the wealth of energy that it contains and that makes it possible for me to write in the first place. *Cerebral auto-affection is the unconscious of subjectivity.*[35] (emphasis in original)

Beneath Malabou's conscious self-awareness ("I see myself write them") lies a different and deeper form of self-awareness which is dimly implied at best, a biological self-feeling which she knows to be present and yet cannot bring to the surface; she is aware of it only to the extent that she is aware of something which eludes her awareness as soon as she tries to pin it down. Malabou identifies this feeling with what Antonio Damasio calls the proto-self, an unconscious neural map that represents the state of the organism to itself at all times and that underlies both motion and feeling.[36] Only if we lose our subjectivity altogether—as happens in cases of neural damage—does this stratum of consciousness come to the surface: "Autoaffection becomes sensible only when we lose it or at least when its fundamental mechanism is impaired. Autoaffection, which is the root of all other affects, is subjectively invisible."[37] If the self-sensing of sensing is what gives rise to subjectivity rather than the other way around, the subject cannot grasp that sensing as long as she conceives of herself as separate from the act of sensation itself. A pure experience of sensing's self-immanence would therefore require total self-loss.

The sense of sensing, in other words, can only be apprehended in its ongoing evanescence: as Brian Massumi has argued, our "continuous, non-conscious self-perception" can only be perceived in its "escape from perception."[38] Massumi sounds surprisingly similar to Montaigne when he writes (as John Florio's Elizabethan translation of the *Essais* has it) that "at every minute me thinks I make an escape [from myself]" (I, 19; 31); "a chaque minute il me semble que je m'eschape." Montaigne's phrase captures the perception of a feeling which is perpetually in the process of escaping, and which is only detected in a wavering, non-definitive seeming (*il me semble*) that is analogous to Descartes's *videor*. For Malabou and Massumi—and, as we will see, for Montaigne too—this self-perception of feeling is the self-perception of life, and it eludes the grasp of ordinary first-person consciousness. But perhaps, in that temporary stunning of consciousness we call astonishment—in other words, in a faint which approximates the brain damage described by Malabou—we are granted a momentary exemption from this law. Perhaps, in moments of phenomenological crisis when the being of the living organism as a whole is under threat and its powers of feeling are fundamentally shaken, the sheer capacity for self-sensing as such comes to the fore—not as a particular mood, passion, or sensation, nor as the property of a particular organ or limb, but rather as the ability to feel which they all presuppose. In the absence of any particular form of affect—in a state which we might well be tempted to describe as blank or as insentient—what we discover instead is the power of affectivity as such. The analysis of this power, however, will lead us down a road very different from the one opened up by Burckhardt: away from selfhood, and towards a form of experience which only becomes available when everything that defines such selfhood is left in abeyance, a form of experience which is at once utterly universal and impersonal and at the same time so profoundly private that it is hardly available even to consciousness itself.

"This Sensible Warm Motion": Fainting between the First and Third Persons

For scholars of Renaissance literature who have focused on questions of the body and the senses—including Michael Schoenfeldt, Gail Kern Paster, David Hillman, and others—it is Descartes who "begins the gradual epistemic process towards abstraction that overtakes early modern discourses of body and mind,"[39] producing "a pronounced dissociation of essential self from body, a dissociation from which we are still trying to recover."[40] For these critics, the Cartesian cogito signals with particular clarity the end of an era in which subjective experience took place in and through the body, and in particular through the four humors. Correspondingly, these critics all conceive of themselves as engaged in a project of what Bruce Smith first dubbed "historical phenomenology," and what Hillman refers to as "an excavation of the visceral dimensions of the Shakespearean texts":[41] recovering an account of what conscious experience was like in a "pre-Cartesian" world, when it was fundamentally different from what the term indicates today. These critics all argue that the theory of the four humors comes with an account of consciousness which, unlike the purportedly disembodied cogito, is as it were "built-in" to bodily life. For the referents of melancholy, bile, choler, and blood can be both objective things in the world (i.e., fluids coursing through the body) as well as the subjective experience to which those things give rise. Schoenfeldt writes: "Indeed, when one gets over the initial unfamiliarity of a particular description of a bodily process, one is struck by the fact that this is indeed how bodies feel as if they are behaving. So different from our own counterintuitive but more effective therapies, these accounts describe not so much the actual workings of the body as the experience of the body."[42] Likewise for Gail Kern Paster, the study of the humors opens up "the possibility of historical differences in modes of emotional self-experience,"[43] and thus of "discover[ing] the phenomenological character of early modern experiences of emotion—what passions of many sorts might have felt like."[44]

More recent work on early modern subjectivity, however, has pointed to a significant gap in these accounts, one which is highlighted by Paster's passive construction. Surely someone or something feels—and is even, we might say, aware of—the movements of the humors and the pressures of the passions: as Drew Daniel points out, a full account of a humor such as melancholy would have to include not only "an entire theatrical dynamic of signifying emotional behaviors to be recognized externally" and "an entire passionate repertoire of affective states to be recognized internally," but also "a notional self or consciousness to do the recognizing."[45] Along similar lines, James Knapp observes, in reference to Schoenfeldt's *Bodies and Selves*, that "the idea that the humors could be regulated suggests that something . . . was doing the regulating," just as Brian Cummings and Freya Sierhuis, arguing against "assumptions about bodily performance that are reductively separated from the cognitive," insist that "by the body we mean the body as felt to exist by a first-person subject."[46] As all of these criticisms suggest, much of the foundational work on the early modern body implicitly relies on a fairly conventional notion of subjectivity while never quite spelling it out. By doing so, it risks upholding those oppositions between the body and consciousness, between the self and its affects, and between the first and third person which are associated with the Cartesian framework that is ostensibly under critique. Meanwhile, the central question of phenomenology—the question of how and under what conditions subjective experience takes place—is left unaddressed.[47]

For scholars of the early modern period who are working with the insights of affect theory, the apparent impersonality of the early modern body is a virtue rather than a shortcoming.[48] Rather than reintroduce the first-person subject, these scholars use affect theory's "conceptual distinction between emotions, feelings that a subject is aware of and claims as his own, and affects, intensities that generate physiological and environmental effects beyond the boundaries of a singular subject" to do away with selves and subjects altogether, instead drawing our attention to dynamic moments of flux, becoming, and exchange which do not feed back into first-person cognition.[49] Thus, where much of the original work on humors still emphasizes the qualitative, emotional, and subjective dimension of early modern embodiment, affect theory, which focuses on "early modern explorations of those phenomena that fail to register as emotion," asks us to rethink embodiment in thoroughly nonsubjective terms, replacing questions about early modern selfhood (whether humanist or humoral) with an emphasis on a decentered assemblage of impersonal intensities. Such an approach is, perhaps inevitably, even more liable to charges of covert dualism: in an influential critique, Ruth Leys writes that affect theory "operates at once with a highly intellectualist or rationalist concept of meaning and an unexamined assumption that everything that is not 'meaning' in this limited sense belongs to the body. This too is a false dichotomy, one that—in spite of a professed hostility to dualism—threads its way throughout much of the new literature on affect."[50] Benedict Robinson has Leys's critique in mind when he "contrasts affect as a non-cognitive bodily response with a premodern understanding of passion as a kind of cognition," reminding us that "in virtually every premodern theory of the passions, the passions are forms of intentionality, ways of seeing, and therefore also perceptions and modes of cognition."[51] When it comes to Renaissance literature, then, affect theory draws our attention to moments like those with which I started this chapter—moments in which the soul seems to feel and experience of its own accord—but in doing so, affect theory risks not only a reaffirmation of dualism, but also a considerable simplification of early modern subjectivity itself. Affect theorists speak of consciousness exclusively in its Enlightenment and post-Enlightenment senses, and thus, to the extent that the word in these later meanings itself encodes dualistic assumptions, it causes them to carve up early modern experience into categories by which (as Milton's "conscious dreams" suggests) it does not necessarily abide. Gregory Seigworth and Melissa Greg define affect as "the name we give to those forces—visceral forces beneath, alongside, or generally *other than* conscious knowing, vital forces insisting beyond emotion," yet as we have already begun to see, at least in the early modern period "conscious" and "knowing" do not necessarily go hand in hand. Montaigne's swoon in particular explores the possibility that consciousness itself might become other than knowing.

Fainting is, in many ways, a paradigmatic example of affect's power to disrupt and overturn ordinary first-person cognition, and in the following pages we will encounter several situations in which the body's autonomous powers of feeling supplant consciousness altogether. But crucially, each instance of fainting I will consider in *Feeling Faint* is also an experience unto itself: the dissolution of consciousness is something which each character I consider actually feels. Fainting puts pressure on the first person without simply undoing it; at least briefly, it opens up a space for consciousness between the first person and the third, forcing us to think about how far what Massumi calls the "autonomy of affect" overlaps with, and does not merely displace, conscious experience. The very absence in the early modern period of a clearly defined concept of consciousness—a word which encodes dualistic assumptions starting from the early eighteenth century—means that there is less impetus to categorize experiential states as conscious or unconscious, and hence that more attention is paid to states which do not clearly abide by this division. On the basis of such states, we can begin to fill in that subjective space implicitly left open by humoral and embodied accounts of early modern experience, moving beyond the impasse that dualism continues to pose for such accounts—not, however, by simply reintroducing a notion of self, but rather by reimagining subjectivity in terms of that vital self-sensing which, for Michel Henry, is what truly comprises consciousness even as it remains invisible. Indeed, if we understand Descartes himself in terms of the evanescent discovery, briefly glimpsed by "beginning Cartesianism" though subsequently obscured, of the senses' self-sensing,[52] we might understand Renaissance literature as participating in Descartes's "philosophy of radical subjectivity and life" rather than as resisting it.[53]

The fundamentally transitional quality of the swoon is what distinguishes it from sleep, which is the subject of an important recent study by Garrett Sullivan Jr. In Sullivan's reading, early modern sleep testifies to "a specific conception of humanness—a specific relation—which foregrounds connections between forms of life," namely between the vegetable, animal, and human components of the Aristotelian tripartite soul.[54] Yet the three souls to whose interrelation sleep bears witness remain at least notionally distinct, and thus to the extent that sleep can be clearly ascribed to the animal and vegetable souls, what it marks is the temporary "ascendance of the animal and vegetable souls" over the intellectual soul.[55] In contrast, in the liminal space opened up by the swoon, the sensitive soul does not merely supersede the intellectual; rather, at least for a brief moment, the capacities of the two are thoroughly mingled and we become, as Montaigne puts it, "intellectually sensible and sensibly-intellectual" (III, 13; 570). As a transitional state between first-person cognition and third-person sensing, in other words, the faint partakes of both—so that, paradoxically, we are made aware of awareness's displacement. Studying the faint can therefore give us a more vivid picture of *how*, in Sullivan's words, "humoral physiology sutures cognition to embodiment": of how consciousness extends beyond the mind and inheres in the self sensing of bodily life. To put it differently, the faint gives us a picture of affect not as an alternative to inner life but rather as a fundamental form of it—and, conversely, of consciousness as a form of affect rather than as its contrary.

All of the figures whom I will consider in the next four chapters approach a condition of total insentience, yet in proximity to it their inner life is not effaced but enriched. With the possible exception of Montaigne, none of these figures displays that searching self-awareness, that "capacity for instantaneous, self-conscious analysis" which for some critics still defines early modern interiority, and which has been associated above all with Hamlet.[56] But it is, in fact, Montaigne who provides the clearest articulation of the inner life as I intend it here. Especially in his later essays, Montaigne's "inwardness" is not that of detached self-analysis, but rather an immanence to corporeal self-experience which does not simply replace consciousness but rather, in moments of illness, sleeping, and above all swooning, transfigures it through immersion in the stream of sentient life. Among Shakespearean characters, it is not Hamlet but Claudio, faced with the prospect of his execution in act 2 of *Measure for Measure*, who discovers Montaigne's form of inwardness and, in a simple phrase, best expresses it: "This sensible warm motion" (3.1.123).[57] What is suddenly and heartbreakingly "sensible" to Claudio is nothing other than the circulation of the spirits and the humors which, in the Renaissance, defines and drives life and gives consciousness its being. Yet it must be *this* sensible warm motion, for it is not ultimately its sensory and embodied qualities but rather its sheer thisness, in a here and now which can neither be prolonged nor repudiated, that gives this motion its pathos and reality—that same irreducible reality and certainty which Descartes attains in his *videor*. Crucially, however, Claudio's deictic does not indicate an object from the point of view of a consciousness that stands outside it, but rather testifies to a "warm motion" which is fully consubstantial with the experience of it. The ambiguity of the word "sensible" is essential in this regard. Is "this warm motion" sensible (*OED* 1: "That can be perceived by the mind or intellect, or by the senses") *to* a subject who perceives it, or is the warm motion—like those impersonal "souls" with which we started—itself sensible, a locus of experience unto itself (*OED* 2: "Capable of perceiving or responding to a stimulus; having senses"; *OED* 4: "Aware, conscious")? The answer is both: the deictic "this" which is at the heart of perceptual consciousness becomes fully sensible, in both senses, only when we relinquish our distance from it, only when the first person is absorbed into the warm medium of affect through or rather as which we are rendered susceptible to the material world. Invisible to consciousness when it is conceived in terms of the first-person representation of objects, the "this" of Claudio's sensible warm motion becomes palpable only when such consciousness is suspended in a swoon or (for Claudio) when its permanent effacement looms—in an experience which, refusing the distinction between first and third person, is both intimate and alienating at once.

For if life is what lies at the heart of subjective experience, it is also what resists our efforts to transmute that experience into something transparent, continuous, and self-identical.[58] Moments of phenomenological crisis allow us to glimpse the proximity of two poles which the very structure of our thought otherwise impels us to keep apart: consciousness and life, consciousness and vital matter.[59] In Joseph Campana's words, "vitality cannot be perceived as an object, as something separate from experience; it can be known only when felt materially as the pain of animation that produces sympathetic resonance."[60] Yet the swoon, by suspending consciousness without destroying feeling, allows us to briefly overcome this impasse and to grasp consciousness and matter as two sides of a single underlying sentient and vital substance. From the waves and clouds to which Montaigne likens his reawakening state, to the "vital air" which intermingles with Guyon's "living breath" on the outskirts of Mammon's Cave and Guyon's own body, to the pervasive "infirmity" which "shakes the island" as well as Othello himself, in every swoon that I consider, consciousness is transformed into an atmospheric phenomenon even as the atmosphere itself comes alive as energy, mood, or affliction. In each of these cases, fainting thus represents "the conversion of the materiality of the body into an *event*" by virtue of the same process which converts consciousness, in a way which is always more than metaphorical, not simply into matter or body, but rather into the sensible palpitations of a vital element.[61] In chapters 3 and 4 we will find contextual support for this environmental dimension of consciousness in the Galenic concept of *spiritus* and in the Paracelsian theory of epileptic aura: both ideas reveal how, especially in moments of cognitive failure, perception and sensation emerge from sensible matter. To the extent that we can conceive of consciousness itself in terms of the third-person states of materiality, then fainting offers not merely the clearest instance of such states, but also a moment in which, suspended on the boundary between first-person awareness and its third-person material counterpart, both are grasped simultaneously as one.

In the only major study of the swoon as a broad cultural phenomenon, Catherine Clément draws on European Romanticism and Eastern philosophy to find in fainting, epileptic seizures, trances, mystical raptures, and a range of similar experiences an alternative to what she characterizes as our Western "obsession" "with the autonomous and aware Subject."[62] Connecting faints and fits to the syncope in music and dance—"an element of rhythm and of accentuation [that] begins on a weak beat and carries over onto a strong beat"—Clément unsurprisingly opposes such experiences to Cartesian certainty, which represents, she says, "the opposite of syncope: everything is eclipsed, except for the subject who remains, the only fixed and sure point."[63] In a sense, a similar agenda drives the work of Paster, Hillman, and other scholars of the early modern body: in the presumed alterity of early modern culture, all of these critics locate a form of human being fundamentally different from that which is, in their eyes, inaugurated by Descartes's cogito. Michel Henry, too, opposes material phenomenology and the self-experience of life to what he understands as "Greek" models of subjectivity, with their privileging of vision and representation.[64] And yet to proceed in this way, to treat the Cartesian subject or Western culture itself as monoliths while pursuing alternative forms of experience in the archives of European literature or beyond Europe altogether, is to leave those monoliths fully intact. By contrast, in its early modern guise the swoon does not merely anticipate Romantic and non-Western moments of liberation in which "the mooring ropes that hold fast the subject—consciousness, its *cogito*, its history, and through that everyone's history—are cast off at last."[65] The swoon offers us not merely an alternative to the Cartesian or Western subject, but rather a transformation which opens up *inside* that subject, allowing us to reconceive consciousness rather than simply cast it off. For where modern notions of consciousness identify it with selfhood and individuality, in swooning consciousness is revealed, as we will see in the final chapter and as the etymology of the word itself suggests, as an intrinsically intersubjective condition. In swoons we find our consciousness to be connected to the experience of others before it becomes fully available to ourselves.

"Feeling Life to Fayle": Syncopes, Swoons, and Swounds

Fascination with swoons and trance-states goes back to both the classical and the early Christian worlds. In Plato's *Symposium*, Socrates stops motionless on the porch of Agathon's house and does not respond to slaves calling his name, whereupon Aristodemus explains that "it's one of his habits: every now and then he just goes off like that and stands motionless, wherever he happens to be" (175b). Indeed, in his speech later on in the dialogue, Alcibiades describes an occasion on which, during a military campaign in Thrace, Socrates stood outside "glued to the same spot" for twenty-four hours "thinking about some problem or other" (220c).[66] The idea of falling into a contemplative trance remained a fixture of the Platonic tradition until the Italian Renaissance, figuring prominently in the work, for example, of Marsilio Ficino.[67] It was in close proximity, moreover, with a Christian tradition that took as its starting point Saint Paul's description, in the Second Epistle to the Corinthians, of "a man in Christ above fourteen years ago (whether in the body, I cannot tell; or whether out of the body, I cannot tell: God knoweth) such an one caught up to the third heaven"—a man usually assumed to be Paul himself.[68] Paul's *raptus*, as it came to be known, remained influential for mystical and contemplative traditions throughout the Middle Ages, often in close connection with its Neoplatonic versions, providing visionary poetry such as Dante's *Paradiso* with its governing principle.[69] Explicitly alluding to Paul, Dante describes his own ascent to Paradise in terms of a similar uncertainty: "Whether I was there in that part only which you / created last is known to you alone, O Love who rule / the heavens and drew me up there with your light" (1.73–75).[70]

For both Dante and Saint Paul, the trance is not simply the out-of-body experience which it often becomes in both Neoplatonic and mystical writings, but rather a state in which the difference between the body and the soul becomes difficult to discern—in this regard, both writers anticipate closely the questions about consciousness which are raised when characters swoon in the Renaissance. More often in medieval literature, however, we find swoons used as narrative or emotive devices. Dante's *Divine Comedy* itself features swoons as means of transition between cantos as well as expressions of heightened emotion (Dante's faint at the end of *Inferno* 5 is both). In this guise, fainting is always a relatively transient phenomenon, and never entails a deeper exploration of consciousness or the soul per se. In a wide survey of medieval swooning, Barry Windeatt concludes that the medieval swoon is part of an apparatus of tropes which belong to a "more emotionally demonstrative medieval culture," and therefore constitutes "nothing more remarkable than one among prevalent conventions for representing powerful feelings";[71] rarely, he argues, does a text "make a swoon's larger implications a focus for contention."[72] The major exception in medieval English literature is Troilus's swoon in book 3 of Chaucer's *Troilus and Criseyde*. Pandarus has deceived Criseyde into believing that Troilus is jealous of the fictitious Horaste; when Troilus arrives at Pandarus's house and discovers a distraught Criseyde, he swoons:

> Therwith the sorwe so his herte shette
> That from his eyen fil there nought a tere,
> And every spirit his vigour in knette,
> So they astoned or oppressed were.
> The felying of his sorwe, or of his fere,
> Or of aught elles, fled was out of towne;
> And downe he fel al sodeynly a-swowne. (3.1086–92)[73]

For Jill Mann, Troilus's swoon plays a crucial role in the evolving power dynamic between the couple.[74] For us, the swoon's interest lies in this "sorwe" so powerful that, paradoxically, it causes the "*felying* of . . . sorwe" to go numb—in other words, in a phenomenological crux in which feeling is raised to such a pitch that it is pried apart from itself. Whereas, as Windeatt argues, in the Middle Ages detailed literary accounts such as that offered by Chaucer remained the exception rather than the rule, early modern versions of the "swowne" would probe much more deeply the consequences for consciousness of a "sorwe" so intense that it hampers our capacity to have "felying" of it.

If not quite to the same extent as in medieval romances, the swoon nevertheless continued to feature prominently in Renaissance literature, and in particular in early modern plays. According to Alan Dessen and Leslie Thomson, as stage directions "*swoon* and its variant spelling *sound* each occur about a dozen times" in early modern plays ranging from Shakespeare's *Henry VI, Part 2* to Tourneur's *The Atheist's Tragedy* and Fletcher's *The Humorous Lieutenant*; by one count there are eighteen instances of swoons from strong emotion in Shakespeare alone.[75] In many of these works, however, the swoon remains "nothing more remarkable than one among prevalent conventions for representing powerful feelings," just as in medieval texts. As Michael Screech has argued, moreover, the emergence of skepticism in the sixteenth century tended to undermine the authority of ecstatic states such as those described by Saint Paul and Dante. He sees Montaigne in particular as having "ousted ecstasy, rapture, and revelation from the privileged place they had occupied in philosophy, the natural sciences and the humanities as ultimate guarantees of certainty."[76] Yet if early modern skepticism tended to call into question the metaphysical pretensions of ecstatic states, this did not necessarily deprive such states of their exploratory potential. Indeed, in the texts I consider, swoons come closer than medieval examples to reflecting "modern assumptions that swooning is something extreme and exceptional."[77] As we will see in the next chapter, although Montaigne does not ascribe transcendent meaning to his swoon, it is a rich and complex experience unto itself, one which he uses to meditate in depth on the entanglement of selfhood, sensory experience, and bodily life. Like Montaigne, characters who swoon in Renaissance literature are not merely deprived of consciousness; their experiences can be revelatory even if they are not "visions and revelations from the Lord" (2 Corinthians 12:1). Swooning, so to speak, in the opposite direction from that of late antique and medieval mystics, early modern characters travel down into the depths of the body and the senses rather than up into a supersensible world, and explore what happens there in the absence of a controlling first person. In the early modern period, the trance becomes a means not of resisting or escaping life, but of entering more deeply into its flow.

Scenes of swooning in this period can thus often be better understood through physiology than through metaphysics or theology (though in some cases, particularly that of epilepsy, these discourses could go hand in hand). Medical accounts of swooning in the Renaissance were still deeply indebted to the Greek medical tradition, in which it is termed *syncope* and defined by Galen as "an acute collapse of capacity"[78] and explained as a weakening of the vital spirits. Derived from the Greek prefix meaning "together" (*syn*) and the verb meaning "to cut" (*kopto*), the word "syncope" suggests a linear thread that has been cut in at least two places at once, creating a rupture which both joins and separates them. The word's etymology is perhaps most evident in its rhetorical and musical meanings: in rhetoric the figure of syncope is defined by "cutting letters or syllables from the middle of a word," while the musical syncope, bridging an unaccented beat with an accented one, creates the effect of a missed beat, a delay which is simultaneously an anticipation. The medical syncope has a similar effect, blurring the boundary between two moments in experience which would normally be separated, and creating the experience of a slurred or missed beat which consciousness subsequently tries to fill in. Both meanings are cited together in Sir Thomas Elyot's Latin dictionary, the *Biblioteca Eliotae*: "*Syncopa*, or *Syncope*, a fygure, where a letter or syllable is taken awaye, as *compostus* for *compositus*. It is also a soundynge for debilitie of the vitall spirites."[79] The physician Philip Barrough offers a more thorough gloss on Galen's definition in the chapter of his *Methode of Phisicke* (1583) dedicated to the problem "Of Swounding":

> SINCOPE is a swift falling of the strength (as Galen saith). It is caused through much excretion and avoyding of bloud or through vnmeasurable emptying of the belly, or vehement moving, or through great paine, or much and often washinges. Also through aboundant swetts, and all other immoderate vacuations, also feare, dread, and all such like perturbations of the mind. Moreover through abounding of crude & raw humours, through great inflammacion or through vicious and thinne humours, or els by taken breath in a stincking ayer. The *sincope* is knowen by these tokens, the pulse is rare and obscure, the extreme partes, as the hand and feete be cold, swete about the face, the taking away of the brightnes of the skinne that is in it, and as it weare a palsey of the whole body. Moreouer to these ther commeth desperation, vexation of the mind, & shaking of the body.[80]

Treating "perturbations of the mind" such as "fear" and "dread" as fully equivalent to "aboundant swetts, and all other immoderate vacuations," Barrough's vivid description speaks to the way in which swooning involves both body and mind. Despite its matter-of-fact medical approach, Barrough's account also bears witness to the felt dimension of the swoon—including "desperation, vexation of the mind, & shaking of the body"—and thus to a characteristic shared by Troilus's swoon and all of the swoons I will consider: loss of feeling often follows a sudden heightening of it, as if feeling itself, paradoxically, all of a sudden became too acute to be felt, and enforced a transition into insentience.

More than their medieval forebears, early modern poets were fascinated by how this transition might feel, by the shadow that unconsciousness seems to cast on the states which immediately abut on it. In the third book of his *Arcadia*, for example, Philip Sidney describes a "forsaken Knight" "who had fainted so long till he had lost the feeling of faintnesse"—isolating, between first-person consciousness and its loss, a specific "feeling of faintnesse" which fainting serves to disclose.[81] The "forsaking" of personal identity goes hand in hand here with loss of consciousness (Windeatt speaks of the "self-absenting that occurs during swooning"), but not without bringing to the surface a "feeling of faintness" felt on that loss's threshold. Another liminal moment, this one from book 4 of Spenser's *Faerie Queene*, offers an especially pointed example of what the philosopher Alva Noë calls "consciousness outside the head."[82] In canto 3, the brothers Priamond, Diamond, and Triamond line up one after another to fight the knight Cambell for his sister Canacee. Though the first two brothers are killed one after the other, by a special decree of the Fates each brother is able to transfer his life and strength to the next sibling when he dies. Thus it is not altogether surprising when, at the end of the second duel, Diamond's decapitated torso briefly discovers an autonomous sentience of its own:

> The headlesse tronke, as heedlesse of that stower,
> Stood still a while, and his fast footing kept,
> Till feeling life to fayle, it fell, and deadly slept. (4.3.20)[83]

Spenser's laborious pun makes what would seem to be an obvious point—how can we heed without a head?—until we discover that the "headlesse trunk" continues to feel. Although Diamond's "stower" necessarily renders him unconscious, it also activates (as "till" suggests) the momentary experience of a new form of feeling discovered on the brink of permanent insentience—"feeling life to fayle." Lingering on the border between personhood ("his") and the impersonal life force "it" shares with Priamond and Triamond, Diamond's headless body exhibits a nonsubjective and yet sentient vitality that can be shared across multiple bodies but that does not belong to any singular subject. Juxtaposing the "feeling of faintness" and "feeling life to fayle" with feeling's total loss, the gap opened by the "together-cut" of the "syncope" thus exposes the existence of a feeling which extends beyond the forsaken first person.

When, in his *True Intellectual System of the Universe* (1678), the Cambridge Platonist Ralph Cudworth uses the word "consciousness" to denote a distinctive faculty of self-awareness for the first time in the language (*OED* 2a), he cannot do so without simultaneously bearing witness to everything which this newly restrictive meaning leaves out, and displaces to states of insentience: "the souls of men in all profound sleeps, lethargies, and apoplexies," he writes, are not merely blank, but rather shot through by "vital energies without express consciousness."[84] The notion of *express* consciousness leaves open the possibility that these alternate states might still be characterized by a consciousness which remains somehow implicit—that more capacious notion of consciousness to which Milton testifies when he uses the phrase "conscious dreams." Along similar lines, in his *Natural History of Nutrition, Life, and Voluntary Motion* (1659), Walter Charleton argues that

> in palpitations, tremblings, syncopes, swooning fits, and other Cardiacal symptoms or affections, the *Heart* doth variously move, and agitate it self; as being offended with something preternatural and noxious to it, and irritated to resist and repell the same: and this in respect only of some sense or feeling, by which it discerneth what is incommodious and harmfull.[85]

Rather than simply cutting awareness off, "syncopes" and "swooning fits" expose a special kind of "sense or feeling" which Charleton goes on to call the "Natural sense." As Timothy Harrison shows, Charleton clearly distinguishes this natural sense from consciousness. Yet by doing so he also acknowledges the ways in which sentient life can persist even when we "have . . . no particular cognisance of any such sense."[86]

"Vital energies without express consciousness" are also at the heart of swooning for Margaret Cavendish in her *Ground of Natural Philosophy* (1668), written just before Cudworth's *True Intellectual System*. At first Cavendish suggests that we have no feeling of our own swoons: "a Human Swound is somewhat like Sleeping without Dreaming; that is, the Exterior Senses do not move to Human Exterior Perception."[87] And yet in her fullest discussion of swooning, Cavendish offers a more nuanced account of what happens to us when we lose consciousness:

> In a Man in a Swound, some of his Corporeal Motions are only altered from the property and nature of a living Man; I say, some

> of his Corporeal Motions, not all: Neither do those Motions quite alter from the nature of a living Man, so as the alterations of the Fundamental Motions do: but they are so alter'd, as Language may be alter'd, *viz.* from *Hebrew* to *Greek, Latin, French, Spanish, English*, and many others; and although they are all but Languages, yet they are several Languages or Speeches; so the alteration of the Corporeal Motions of a Man in a Swound, is but as the altering of one sort of Language to another; as put the case, *English* were the Natural Language or Speech, then all other Languages were unknown to him that knows no other than his Natural: So a Man in a Swound is ignorant of those Motions in the Swound: but, when those Motions return to the Nature of a living Man, he hath the same knowledge he had before.[88]

Cavendish's surprising analogy between fainting and the speaking of a foreign language may at first bring to mind the spiritual phenomenon of glossolalia—speaking in tongues. But when we realize that she is specifically thinking of translation *between* languages, we see that her analogy suggests not so much the prophetic kind of possession celebrated by mystics and Neoplatonists—a vertical transformation in which the subject is lifted above him or herself into a divine order—as a horizontal dislocation between parallel dimensions that are both located within subjective being. When we are in a swoon, she thus suggests, our typical "motions" are not simply absent or diminished, but rather altered to a state which stands in relation to it as one language does to another: equivalent and parallel and yet fundamentally non-fungible. We may have no idea of what happens to us in a swoon, but there *is* something to be understood, a state of sensory being which, if only we had the language, we could decipher. That event is constituted by a different and new set of "corporeal motions": Cudworth's "vital energies without express consciousness," and what Malabou describes as a "wealth of energy." For a moment—that unit of time and affect which Spenser calls a "stound"—we straddle two parallel worlds of motion which are at once linked and sundered by this phenomenological stutter or syncopation that we are briefly permitted to inhabit. Each of the characters who swoons seems almost to understand something essential, and yet falls short or fails to articulate what exactly that something is—as if it had been disclosed to them in a language they did not understand. Those who do attempt to translate it—Othello and Leontes—will fall into tragedy.

John Locke's *An Essay Concerning Human Understanding* (1689) might seem in retrospect to have banished decisively the specter of those "vital energies without Express consciousness" which, for Cudworth, Charleton, and Cavendish, swooning still serves to expose. Defining consciousness as the "perception of what passes in a man's mind,"[89] Locke installed an equation of consciousness and selfhood that remains deeply rooted in both popular and philosophical thinking today. In his famous example, a prince who wakes up in the body of a cobbler will still be a prince due to the continuous presence of "consciousness of the prince's past life": "For should the soul of a prince, carrying with it the consciousness of the prince's past life, enter and inform the body of a cobbler, as soon as deserted by his own soul, every one sees he would be the same person with the prince, accountable only for the prince's actions."[90] Consciousness's persistence across changing bodily states and even changing bodies is what assures us of always being ourselves. It is specifically the continuity of consciousness, its ability to extend to the past and the future, that makes a person self-identical:

> For it is by the consciousness it has of its present thoughts and actions, that it is self to itself now, and so will be the same self, as far as the same consciousness can extend to actions past or to come, and would be by distance of time, or change of substance, no more two persons, than a man be two men by wearing other clothes today than he did yesterday, with a long or a short sleep between: the same consciousness uniting those distant actions into the same person, whatever substances contributed to their production.[91]

In its very absurdity, Spenser's fable of the three brothers may seem to anticipate Locke's argument here by demonstrating just how fanciful it would be to suppose that multiple people could share a single consciousness. And yet Spenser also naturalizes that sharing, comparing the life distributed between the three brothers to a single vital substance: "[l]ike three faire branches budding farre and wide, / That from one roote deriu'd their vitall sap" (4.2.43). Locke himself, on the other hand, cannot fully put behind him the problem raised by swoons and sleeping. On the contrary, as Yeats perhaps recognizes in the epigraph to this book, it is only by imagining a syncope, "a long or a short sleep in between" two states of consciousness, that Locke fully demonstrates how consciousness ensures continuity and personal identity. The persistence of personal identity depends on the continual possibility of syncopation—of assimilating to self-awareness in the present other self-aware states separated from it across time—and thus Locke must both acknowledge and suppress those intermediate states in which such awareness is absent or hampered (not to mention cases of permanent memory loss or other brain damage). Insisting on a clean separation of consciousness and its absence, with no mingling possible, Locke must also both entertain and dismiss the possibility that we could somehow be conscious while sleeping, for "if a sleeping man thinks without knowing it, the sleeping and waking man are two persons"[92]—a preposterous conclusion, he suggests. But early modern writers were not so sure: Spenser, Shakespeare, and Montaigne all explore the possibility that, at or beyond the boundaries of the first person, thinking lingers on in the flickerings of an impersonal, self-sensing vitality.

Although Descartes, Cudworth, Cavendish, and Locke all came after the authors I will consider in this book, anxious questions already surrounded the soul's nature at the end of the sixteenth century.[93] Notions of the soul's materiality—and even more so, of its potential mortality—threatened not only philosophical but also religious orthodoxies. It is against the background of this uncertainty that so much attention is lavished on these swoons in early modern texts.[94] The swoon becomes a way of exploring these issues surrounding the nature of the soul on stage or in the imagination. Its medicalization in several of these works bears witness, therefore, not to a movement of demystification, but on the contrary to the opening of a new terrain for exploration and discovery. Montaigne, who had long maintained that the soul felt nothing in death or states of extreme duress, instead discovers in his swoon the soul's extraordinary power to produce and to feel sensory states outside of its own volition; he compares it to "the paines that our feet or hands feele whilst we sleepe [which] are not ours" (II, 6; 187). It is this discovery, I will maintain, which leads him to his subsequent notion of *expérience*. Guyon's swoon in book 2 of Spenser's *Faerie Queene* serves him as a portal to the voyage through his own body he undertakes in canto 9, where he discovers that the ongoing process of self-regulation which sustains the virtue of temperance is fundamentally physiological in nature, and is premised on the body's continual acts of balanced self-sensing. The movement of "Alma" throughout her house speaks to a third-person consciousness that is neither seated in any particular organ nor severed from the rest of the body, but rather immanent to the self-feeling vitality of each and every bodily process. In Othello's swoon in act 4 of *Othello*, the vibration of an unstable macrocosm ripples across his body in the shaking of an epileptic fit. Othello's belated consciousness of this process speaks to a power of cerebral and corporeal self-sensing which is entirely independent of subjectivity, and whose workings Othello tragically misrecognizes as offering certainty about the world around him. *The Winter's Tale* too concerns a noble man who mistakes the vividness of his self-feeling for certain knowledge about the world around him—a mistake which he shares with Descartes himself. But in Shakespeare's late romance that mistake is, finally, corrected by being inscribed into a sequence of swoons. The "chain-reaction" fainting around which *The Winter's Tale* centers will allow me to conclude by demonstrating that the intersubjective dimension of sensing is not an objective knowledge on which all subjects can agree (as in Enlightenment empiricism), but rather a layer of shared vulnerability and openness to affectivity which grounds communal life in sentient life and vice versa.

My question, then, will be less one of how Montaigne, Spenser, Shakespeare, and Descartes himself express a shared culture (in which case it is hard to justify privileging just these figures) than of how they take that culture to its limit, testing some of its fundamental assumptions through experiments lived, staged, and imagined—a question which is, in its way, equally historical if necessarily more speculative. When characters faint in works of Renaissance literature, authors are afforded an exploration of consciousness's material contours which brings them into close proximity with Descartes and the project of "material phenomenology," and in particular with his exploration of that biological power of self-feeling he captures in the phrase *videor videre*; that power, they reveal, is only exposed at the limits of first-person awareness. The techniques of literary language give these authors a unique purchase on such states: essays and dramatic monologues capture fainting's irreducibly experiential dimension; dramatic performance highlights that embodied dimension of consciousness which comes to the fore during swoons; and metaphors and other rhetorical tropes such as hypallage speak to the strange ways in which, during the faint, consciousness is displaced onto both material and social environments. For it is, finally, less a philosophical theory of consciousness—whether ancient or new—that the moments I consider bear out than the continual impetus to investigate our own inner workings, and in the study of our own experience the best medium, as Montaigne suggests, is experience itself. What the discourses of medicine, of philosophy, or of affect theory ultimately help us to understand is not a meaning which literature is incapable of expressing in its own terms, but rather why there remain certain experiences which literature remains our *only* means of grasping. While many of the works I consider take an implicitly medical approach to a state which had previously been seen in metaphysical terms as a state of ecstasy and transcendence, in doing so they do not simply demystify it. Rather, they unveil the mystery of consciousness itself, which is the mystery not of something that transcends matter, but rather of the fact that matter itself can feel, think, and live.

CHAPTER 2

Slippings: Learning How to Die in Montaigne's *Essais*

Montaigne's *Essais* have often been assigned a privileged position in the history of the self. In his prefatory address "The Author to the Reader," Montaigne himself announces that "myselfe am the groundworke of my booke," and thus it is hardly surprising to find his *Essais* mentioned as a turning point in several recent histories of subjectivity.[1] And yet if the *Essais* can be said to comprise, indeed to "inaugurate," a "search for the self," it is at least partly because that self is so difficult to pin down.[2] At the beginning of the essay "Of Repenting," Montaigne tells us once again that his principal task is to "represent a particular" man—that is, himself—but he soon confesses just how difficult he finds it to keep this "object" fixed:

> I cannot settle my object; it goeth so unquietly and staggering, with a naturall drunkennesse; I take it in this plight as it is at the instant I ammuse my selfe about it, I describe not th' essence but the passage; not a passage from age to age, or as the people reckon, from seaven yeares to seaven, but from day to day, from minute to minute. My history must be fitted to the present. I may soone change, not onely fortune, but intention. It is a counter-roule of divers and variable accidents and irresolute imaginations, and sometimes contrary; whether it be that myselfe am other, or that I apprehend subjects by other circumstances and considerations. (III, 2; 409)

It is he himself whom Montaigne cannot "settle": it is he and his ideas which change so rapidly that, in attempting to capture them, he can at best offer a momentary snapshot of what, in "Of Experience," he calls "certaine inconstant and unknowne motions in us" (III, 13; 567). In that essay as in others, Montaigne's self is not only the subject but also the object of his "experience"—a "constant movement of thought" which he struggles to keep still—and thus like all experiences it is subject to uncertainty, something he can report on only tentatively and provisionally.[3]

No moment better exemplifies the challenges of recording the fluctuations of self-experience than Montaigne's fall from his horse, which is described at length in the sixth essay of the second book, "Of Exercise or Practice." Montaigne's first-person description of this event abounds in uncertainty and obscurity, starting with the date of the event itself:

> During our second or third troubles (I doe not well remember which) I fortuned one day, for recreation sake, to goe forth and take the ayre, about a league from my house, who am seated even in the bowels of all troubles of our civill warres of *France*, supposing to be most safe, so neere mine owne home and retreite, that I had no need of better attendance or equipage. I was mounted upon a very easie-going nag, but not very sure. At my returning home againe, a sudden occasion being offered me to make use of this nag in a peece of service whereto he was neither trained nor accustomed, one of my men (a strong sturdy fellow), mounted upon a young strongheaded horse, and that had a desperate hard mouth, fresh, lusty and in breath, to shew his courage, and to out-goe his fellowes, fortuned with might and maine to set spurrs unto him, and giving him the bridle, to come right into the path where I was, and as a *Colossus* with his weight riding over me and my nag, that were both very little, he overthrew us both, and made us fall with our heeles upward: so that the nag lay along astonied in one place, and I in a trance groveling on the ground ten or twelfe paces wide of him: my face all torne and brused, my sword which I had in my hand a good way from me, my girdle broken, with no more motion or sense in me than a stocke. It is the only swowning that ever I felt yet. (II, 6; 185–86)

Jean Starobinski points to this moment as offering "a good example of Montaigne's ability to articulate the singular uniqueness of physical experience," while for Géralde Nakam it is the first time in which "he speaks of himself with such intensity."[4] And yet there is something paradoxical in treating this moment as a characteristic example of what Montaigne will call *expérience*. How can Montaigne be said to experience a moment in which he loses consciousness and lies on the ground "with no more motion or sense in me than a stocke"? He may have "felt" all of this, but if he did so it was in the absence of any self-aware "self," as Montaigne himself shortly suggests: "I was cleane distracted from it" (II, 6; 187), he says, or as the French has it, "Je n'y estois aucunement" ("I was not there at all").

Florio's translation, adjusting a state of absence into one of distraction, captures the difficulty we have in comprehending Montaigne's assertions: how can he say that he "felt"—and then describe in such detail—a swoon during which he "was not there at all"?[5] Distraction offers a less counterintuitive example of how this might be possible: when we are too caught up in our own thoughts, for example, to notice something going on outside us—or even, for that matter, inside us. But it also skirts some of the fundamental questions which the episode raises. If what Montaigne "feels" and proves by "experience" is something from which he himself was completely absent, then we must think carefully about what those terms might actually mean, and about "whom" they might refer to. Starobinski argues that for Montaigne, the notion of experience refers above all to felt "'personal' or 'inner' experience, wherein each individual feels the unique quality of his own existence" as opposed to the "'objective' experience of modern science, with its insistence upon sophisticated methodology."[6] And yet if Montaigne's fall is to serve as its paradigmatic instance, the feeling which defines this experience cannot, as Starobinski suggests, belong to "the domain of *mine*, of *possession*";[7] it cannot, as other influential readers have put it, be "entirely first-person" in nature, or the property of "unconditional subjectivity."[8]

Taking my cue from what happens to Montaigne in his swoon, in this chapter I will argue that in his *Essais* selfhood and experience are not fully coterminous, and that indeed it is only when selfhood falls short that Montaigne truly realizes what experience means.[9] Prying experience apart from selfhood, Montaigne's swoon allows him to identify the former as something apart from himself, as much a property of his body and its own private movements and feelings as of his own, first-person consciousness. In the swoon Montaignean *expérience* grasps precisely what first-personness cannot: the flux of subjective feltness with regard to which intentional awareness is always belated. This flux is the obscure element in which physiological life experiences nothing but itself, what Montaigne describes as "unknown motions in us." These motions, he discovers, contain a world of feeling of their own, but it is a feeling that normally goes unfelt, at least by us. To try, as much as possible, to tune in to that feeling is what Montaigne ultimately means by *expérience*.

Montaigne's blurry and yet vivid account of his swoon reveals to us that he has briefly crossed that barrier separating him from the "obscure apparence and shadow" that, as he says in his "Apologie of Raymond

Sebond," comprises "every human nature" (II, 12; 309). It is not that he has shed light on the shadow or dispelled the obscurity. Rather, in a radical transformation of his sensorium, he has experienced in and of themselves that obscurity and shadow in which life—that in us which, as Michel Henry puts it, "is never and cannot be seen"—normally moves.[10] For Montaigne, in other words, genuinely experiencing the self, overcoming what Hugo Friedrich calls "the difficulty of self-analysis," does not mean finding a stable point of view outside the flux of sentience, a secure position from which we can observe experience without being affected by it.[11] On the contrary: it means bridging, however briefly, the gap that separates us *from* that flux, that separates consciousness from life—the invisible vital stream of "sensible warm motion." If, as Merleau-Ponty argues, the "paradox of a *conscious being*" means in Montaigne's case that "at each instant, in love, in political life, in perception's silent life, we adhere to something, make it our own, and yet withdraw from it and hold it at a distance, without which we could know nothing about it," here I will suggest that, during and after the swoon, Montaigne overcomes this paradox by discovering the knowledge that is intrinsic to "perception's silent life" itself.[12]

As we will shortly see, Montaigne initially presents his swoon as an answer to a question about another kind of barrier to consciousness, one which has already been troubling him for a long time: what will death feel like?[13] But as he tries to prove, in line with the stoicism of his early essays, that it will not feel like anything at all, what he discovers is something else: a bodily self-sensing which exists beyond the domain of the conscious self. Rather than confirming a belief which Montaigne had long held, the swoon instead makes available a form of experience which Montaigne had not previously felt or even imagined. In the sensual English of Florio's translation, that newly discovered experience would in turn be made available if not to Spenser, then certainly to the Shakespeare of *Othello* and *The Winter's Tale*.[14] English Renaissance literature will continue and deepen Montaigne's exploration of that falling back of consciousness into affect which he discovers in the course of "the only swowning that ever I felt yet" (II, 6; 186).

"The Motion of an Instant"? Tasting Death in the *Essais*

At first, the significance of the swoon seems clear. As Montaigne tells us at the beginning of "Of Exercise or Practice," it offers him an answer to a problem which had long been preoccupied him: how to prepare for death.

A philosopher who puts all of his faith in knowledge drawn from lived experience, Montaigne faces in death a particularly acute challenge:[15]

> A man may, by custome and experience, fortifie himselfe against griefe, sorrow, shame, want, and such like accidents; but concerning death, we can but once feele and trie [*essayer*] the same. We are all novices and new to learne when we come unto it. (II, 6; 184)

The swoon, however, appears to offer Montaigne a way around this dilemma, a way to "die" and yet retain a lived sense, a "taste and savor," of what death is like: "such as by some violent accident are falne into a faintnes of heart, and have lost all senses, they, in mine opinion, have well-nigh beene where they might behold her [i.e., death's] true and naturall visage" (II, 6; 185). For Montaigne death constitutes a phenomenological crux, one which we can only resolve if a swoon in which we "have lost all senses" gives us a preview of it.

Montaigne had been concerned with the question of how death would feel from the very beginning of his autobiographical writing, and indeed, before he undertakes the exploration of his swoon in "Of Exercise or Practice," he treats death with more confidence. As an event which is either malleable or insensible, the early Montaigne argues, death will present no real challenge to the true stoic.[16] Once we recognize, as he puts it in the title of an early essay, "that the taste of goods or evils doth greatly depend on the opinion we have of them" (I, 40), then we ourselves, can take away death's sting by molding our opinion of it and thereby changing its taste.[17] We can start by considering how differently others have viewed the same object: "Now death, which some of all horrible things call the most horrible, who knowes not how others call it the only haven of this lives torments? the soveraigne good of nature? the only staie of our libertie? and the readie and common receipt of our evils?" (I, 40; 117). The point here is not that death *is* the "soveraigne good of nature"; the point is that, since it is subject to so many different interpretations, "we are very fooles to bandy for that partie which is irksome to us, and to give infirmities, indigence, and contempt, a sharp and ill taste, if we may give them a good" (I, 40; 117). In no case is this truer than for death, which does not have, as it were, any taste at all: "Death is but felt by discourse, because it is the motion of an instant" (I, 40; 120): "La mort ne se sent que par les discours, d'autant que c'est le mouvement d'un instant." We do not, Montaigne assumes, really feel anything at all through "discourse," and thus we will not feel death—we merely imagine what it "tastes" like in advance, and that taste is something we can control.[18] The notion that death is "but the motion of an instant" is intended to underscore this point—as in Zeno's paradox, the motion accomplished in an instant is infinitesimally small, and therefore insensible. It is not surprising, then, that Montaigne's first and fullest essay on death, "That to Philosophise Is to Learn How to Die" (I, 19), contains no reflections on how it will feel at all.

Yet despite Montaigne's assurance in "That the Taste of Goods or Evils" that death "ne se sent que par le discours" and can therefore be manipulated by the mind, other essays abound with conjectures as to what death is *really* like, implicitly undermining the logic of that earlier essay. In his essay "Cowardize the Mother of Cruelty," for example, Montaigne describes Mohammed II's cruel method of execution: slicing the condemned in half, "which caused them to die two deaths at once . . . both parts were seen full of life, to move and stirre long time after, as if they had been in lingring torment" (II, 27; 357). Despite this horrible spectacle, Montaigne is quick to reassure us and himself that they do not feel anything, or much: "I do not thinke [*Je n'estime pas*] they felt any great torture in that moving." Citing this passage, Timothy Harrison argues that "Montaigne minimizes the pain involved but refuses to claim that these parts lose the capacity to feel."[19] To read it in this way is to ignore Montaigne's use of litotes—his point is that the victims don't, in fact, feel anything. But Harrison's reading is justified inasmuch as Montaigne's use of rhetoric is itself symptomatic of an uncertainty that he wishes to conceal: his litotes both covers over and exposes the fact that although Montaigne wants to believe, and wants us to believe, that Mohammed's victims do not feel anything, he cannot in fact say so for sure—there may be some residual feeling after all. Although this claim seems at first to echo the belief in death's insensibility expressed in "That the Taste of Goods or Evils," what differs here, in addition to the litotes, is the qualifying phrase "I do not thinke" (which in turn necessitates the use of a rhetorical figure rather than a definitive statement of fact): an acknowledgment of uncertainty which qualifies this assertion as referring to an experience that Montaigne himself did not undergo, and did not even witness firsthand. Montaigne's commitment to the epistemological primacy of lived experience compels him to frame his thoughts about what these condemned souls may or may not have felt in terms of conjecture and belief.

The qualifications inevitably accompanying a living person's description of how death feels expose an underlying sense of uncertainty, and even anxiety.[20] Thus it is unsurprising when, in another essay, we find Montaigne taking a different view of the question. In "Of Judging of

Others' Death" (II, 13), he acknowledges that some people do maintain sentience as they die whereas others do not, singling out the former for distinction and implicit praise:

> But even of those who most undantedly have resolved themselves to the execution, we must consider (I say) whether it were with a life ending stroke, and that tooke away any leasure to feele the effect thereof. For it is hard to guesse [*c'est a deviner*] seeing life droope away little by little, the bodies-feeling entermingling it selfe with the soules [*le sentiment du corps se meslant à celuy de l'ame*], meanes of repentance being offered, whether in so dangerous an intent, constancie or obstancie were found in him. (II, 13; 312)

In some deaths, Montaigne now admits, the "bodies-feeling" does "entermingle" with the soul's, so that in these cases sentience is maintained as we are passing away. Though Montaigne does not describe what the "bodies-feeling" is like, he is presumably imagining it as painful and unpleasant, since most people, he tells us, would lack the "constancie or obstancie" needed to refuse "meanes of repentance" under such circumstances. No matter how much "constancie or obstancie" one may have demonstrated during life, the unknowable challenge faced in death may turn out to be too much. Death will distinguish the real stoics from the pretenders, but, due to the unknowability of the feeling of death, until it actually happens it is hard to know where the line will fall. If death can only be felt through discourse, in other words, perhaps this is not because death is impalpable, but because it is unknowable.

Thus, while on the one hand Montaigne is now entertaining a wider range of possible deaths than he had acknowledged before, on the other hand he is forced, somewhat self-consciously, to continue framing those possibilities in the language of uncertainty: "it is hard to guesse" whether those who experienced a quick death would have been as resolved had they been sensible of what was happening to them. In fact, as the essay unfolds, Montaigne begins to consider yet another possible version of death, based on the example of those, such as the philosopher Cleanthes, who are able to encounter and even savor it:

> It is farre from fearing death to goe about to taste and savour [*taster et savourer*] the same. The historie of *Cleanthes*, the Philosopher, is much like to this. His gummes being swolne, his Physitians perswaded him to use great abstinence. Having fasted two daies, he was so well amended, as they told him he was well, and might

> returne to his wonted course of life. He contrarily having already tasted some sweetnes in this fainting, resolveth not to drawe back, but to finish what he had so well begunne, and was so far waded into. (II, 13; 313)

Montaigne's language of taste recalls his earlier descriptions of death and adversity, but he now suggests not only that death may be something we can in fact feel, but also that the feeling may be pleasant. This belief—the third opinion of death which Montaigne has espoused—becomes more and more prominent as the essay winds up. Tullius Marcellinus, a Roman whose story is told in Seneca's *Epistles*, serves as a second example:

> [H]e undertooke to depart from this life, not by running from it: not to escape from death, but to taste it [*mais de l'essayer*]. And to have leisure to condition or bargaine with death, having quit all manner of nourishment, the third day ensuing, after he had caused himself to be sprinkled over with luke-warme water, by little and little he consumed away; and (as he said) not without some voluptuousnesse and pleasure. (II, 13; 313)

Again Montaigne suggests that death, far from being insensible or unpleasant, might in fact be characterized by "some voluptuousness." Florio's translation of "essayer" as "to taste" underscores a conclusion which is rapidly becoming inescapable: death *is* a sensory experience, and indeed it possesses a unique "taste" which Montaigne himself has not yet sampled. Yet even when, as in the case of Marcellinus, we do have the chance to hear about death firsthand, it is always another's version of it: the voluptuousness of Marcellinus's death is only "as he said." In combination with his frequent use of conjecture and opinion, Montaigne's reliance on anecdotes such as this one reveals the persistence of a gap between all human attempts at "judging of death" and the felt evidence of what death "tastes" like in person—a gap which only the swoon, he suggests, can help him overcome.

Towards a Phenomenology of Fainting

By the time he reaches "Of Exercise or Practice," then, Montaigne has abandoned the notion that death is merely a matter of "discours." On the contrary, it has now become a singular experience, unlike any other that we might know: "we can but once feele and trie the same" (II, 6; 185).

Others may have felt and tried it before us, but they are, of course, unable to communicate their findings: “There have, in former times, beene found men so good husbands and thrifty of time, that even in death they have assayed to taste and savor it [*de la gouster et savourer*]; and bent their minde to observe and see what manner of thing that passage of death was; but none did ever yet come backe againe to tell us tidings of it [*nous en dire les nouvelles*]” (II, 6; 184). There was, for example, Julius Canius, whose story Montaigne would have found in Seneca’s *De Tranquilitate Animi*:

> Canius Iulius, a noble Romane, a man of singular vertue and constancie, having beene condemned to death by that lewdly-mischievous monster of men, Caligula: besides many marvelous evident assurances he gave of his matchless resolution, when he was even in the nicke to endure [*comme il estoit sur le point de souffrir*] the last stroke of the executioner; a Philosopher, being his friend, interrupted him with this question, saying: “Canius, in what state is your soule now? what doth she? What thoughts possesse you now?” “I thought,” answered he, “to keepe me ready and prepared with all my force, to see whether in this instant of death, so short and so neere at hand, I might perceive some dislodging or distraction of the soule [*quelque deslogement de l’ame*], and whether it will shew some feeling [*ressentiment*] of her sudden departure; that (if I apprehend or learne any thing of her) I may afterward, if I can, returne and give advertisement thereof unto my friends.” (II, 6; 184–85)

Canius is about to be executed, but rather than fearing death, he is solely concentrated on seeing what the final moment of his life feels like—on answering that question which, as we have seen, so troubles Montaigne himself in the essays surrounding “Of Exercise or Practice.” Yet the anecdote itself does not actually extend to Canius’s death, for throughout Montaigne’s account, Canius remains “in the nicke to endure” his death. And he does not, presumably, return to “give advertisement thereof unto [his] friends.” The example of Canius thus undermines its own exemplarity: while we might be inspired, like Canius, to try to “taste” our own deaths, his precedent has brought us no closer to an understanding of what it will actually be like to do so. Montaigne does not tell us whether or not Canius perceives any “dislodging or distraction of his soul”; what he ends up admiring in the episode is something else: that Canius remained a philosopher “not only untill death, but even in death it selfe: what assurance was it, and what fiercenes of courage, to will that his owne death should serve him as a lesson" (II, 6; 185). But that lesson itself is one from which Canius alone can draw the fruit—if he does in fact succeed in his project.

While the story of Canius does not offer a clear answer to the question of what death is like, it nonetheless introduces an important new wrinkle into the discussion, one which is vital to understanding what Montaigne undergoes during his swoon. Most of us, Canius implies, will not in fact feel our deaths. For it is not enough, he suggests, merely to wait for death and see what it is like. He must tense his soul "with all his force," making absolutely sure that he does not let the experience of death pass him by without his awareness. This tensing and preparation represent a specialized attitude towards death, one which distinguishes Canius from non-philosophers and which is what Montaigne singles out for admiration. The need for these preparations implies that we *can* experience death, but if we are not focused enough, or if we are too distracted or unprepared, it is possible to miss out on the experience altogether. Earlier Montaigne had suggested that death is impalpable because it is "but the motion of an instant"; now, drawing on Canius, he implies that there may in fact be a brief window of time in which some feeling of death is perceptible. The instant of death may turn out to have a "motion" of its own, a movement which draws it out more than Montaigne had expected. But we must be especially attentive—and perhaps especially philosophical too—if we wish to notice it.

What kind of feeling is it which—unless we strain ourselves into a state of maximal attentiveness—slips by us altogether? The pronouns in Canius's account suggest that it is not he but rather his soul, as it were in the third person, which will feel his death: he wants to see whether "I might perceive some dislodging or distraction of the soule, and whether *it* [*elle*] will shew some feeling of *her* sudden departure; that (if I apprehend or learne any thing of *her*) *I* may afterward, if I can, returne and give advertisement thereof unto my friends." It is the soul which may or may not have "some feeling of her sudden departure"; Canius's perception of that feeling will be something over and above it, and will not follow from it automatically. He hopes for a lesson from his soul even as his friends hope for a lesson from him—neither is guaranteed. For death will not happen to him in the first person, but rather to his soul, to a center of perception and cognition that is not fully his, not completely coterminous with his "I." What Canius's account anticipates, then, is not how death feels—we do not get that far. Instead, it reveals that in death, the soul becomes a third person to itself, a condition in which sensory experience is severed from first-person awareness so that one must try much harder than usual to see if anything is perceived. Death becomes a prime example of unfelt affect—not unfelt, however, because we lack consciousness altogether, but rather because, in the moment of death, we become other to ourselves. In Canius's account, death is an auto-affection of the sensory soul, a state of "some dislodging or distraction" to which it alone, as the one that has been "dislodged," is privy.

This aspect of Canius's story prepares the ground for Montaigne's account of his own swoon—not because it anticipates what the swoon is actually like, but rather because it speaks to the difficulty, in the course of a "dislodging or distraction" of the soul, of coinciding with oneself long enough to have any consciousness of what one is undergoing. Yet in this very respect it reveals something crucial about the phenomenological structure which is shared by the experiences of both death and swooning. After his initial description of the fall and swoon, Montaigne tells us that "after I had for two houres space by all beene supposed dead and past all recoverie, I began to stir and breathe" (II, 6; 186), and he now describes, in careful detail, the gradual reawakening of his senses:

> Touching the functions of the soule, they started up and came in the same progresse as those of the bodie. I perceived my selfe all bloudy; for my doublet was all sullied with the bloud I had cast. The first conceit I apprehended was that I had received some shot in my head; and in truth, at the same instant, there were divers that shot round about us. Me thought my selfe had no other hold of me but of my lips-ends [*Il me sembloit que ma vie ne me tenoit plus qu'au bout des lèvres*]. I closed mine eyes to help (as me seemed [*ce me sembloit*]) to send it forth, and tooke a kinde of pleasure to linger and languishingly to let my selfe goe from my selfe [*à me laisser aller*]. (II, 6; 186)

The principal object of Montaigne's reawakening sentience is himself and his own conscious state; the faint thus isolates the self-perception of consciousness even as it induces a pleasant feeling of lightness and drifting. Yet Montaigne perceives himself not returning but rather, as it were, floating off: "Me thought my selfe had no other hold of me but of my lips ends." What kind of perception is this? If it is Montaigne's self that is on the verge of drifting off, how and from where does he perceive it? Does perception not imply a stable and fixed center from which that perception takes place—one which cannot be moved? But who or what perceives the drifting away of Montaigne's consciousness if not that consciousness itself? Montaigne's account is successful not because it conveys something that consciousness saw or felt, but rather something that *happened to* consciousness, a transformation in which the activities that normally define it—seeing, believing, thinking—are suspended, and its mode of apprehension is fundamentally changed. By substituting another "my selfe" for "ma vie," Florio emphasizes the self-reflexive quality of this state in which the soul feels nothing but the metamorphosis of its own powers; at the same time, his translation reveals just how close, in this moment of cognitive weakness, vitality and subjectivity have become.

Canius's account of his death as an auto-affection of the soul thus captures exactly what Montaigne undergoes here: the soul senses its own transformation, but since the soul is itself nothing but sensation, this means that, all of a sudden, sensing senses only itself. In doing so it necessarily excludes first-personness, which maintains its structure precisely in *not* being affected by what it perceives. The slippage of Montaigne's soul, in contrast, is indistinguishable from the blurry state ("me seemed") which perceives that slippage, for as we will see in Othello's trance as well, what is affected is one and the same as what perceives that affection: the dislodged, slipping soul itself. If to perceive an object as real is to perceive it as independent of our own consciousness (and hence available to other minds as well), then Montaigne merely "seems" not because his perception has been called into doubt, but because his consciousness has been turned on itself and perceives nothing but itself, and "seeming" is the only way it has of appearing to itself. "Seeming" is Montaigne's description of a state which does not refer to outside objects at all and which therefore cannot claim either truth *or* falsehood vis-à-vis the external world—it is his description of a single, fuzzy, and yet vivid act in which the soul perceives nothing but its own perceptual state. The word "seeming" closely anticipates Descartes's interpolation of a *videor* into every act of sensing, whereby that act senses and simultaneously senses itself; what Montaigne had previously imagined as an intense but one-dimensional sensory experience of something new and foreign—an unprecedented taste or flavor—is now reconceived as an immanent sense *of* sensing which he describes in terms of seeming and which Florio suggestively captures as "methought." What is lacking is any point of view over and above this seeming from which one might evaluate it as true or false and dispel its intrinsic fuzziness—the point of view, in other words, of a first-person self. There is no contrast, as there is for the Hamlet of act 1, between that which "seems" and "that within which passeth show": for Montaigne, "that within" is *pure* seeming, pure consciousness in absolute self-immanence.[21]

As we will see later, Montaigne is only able to reconstruct all of this through memory. In the moment itself, he is not fully conscious of what is happening to him—he does not see himself as we see ourselves in a mirror, standing at a distance from ourselves. Indeed, he does not *see* himself at all. If "an ability to detach himself from himself at the very moment of experience, which I shall call instantaneous self-reflexivity, characterizes Montaigne's self-consciousness," then that self-consciousness is either completely absent in this episode, or it is articulated not "at the very moment of experience" but only across an irremediable temporal gap.[22] Montaigne's state is one of total immediacy, in which his body apprehends itself in that entirely nonrepresentational fashion which Jean-Luc Marion has described in terms of auto-affection:

> Consciousness thinks, and thinks of itself, fundamentally by auto-affection. Before any other operation consciousness experiences itself, with an absolute immediacy, without which it could never experience anything else. This auto-affecting of consciousness is therefore accomplished before any reflexivity of representation, precisely because it precedes even nonreflexive representation.[23]

The self-thinking of consciousness, Marion suggests, is not merely devoid of representation—it is also presupposed by all forms of representation itself. And yet only in moments such as the swoon, when ordinary representation breaks down, can its underlying self-thinking be unveiled. As he continues his account, Montaigne describes consciousness's self-feeling as a form of exceptional pleasure:

> It was an imagination swimming superficially in my minde [*C'estoit une imagination que ne faisoit que nager superficiellement en mon ame*], as weake and as tender as all the rest: but in truth, not only exempted from displeasure, but rather commixt with that pleasant sweetnesse which they feel that suffer themselves to fall into a soft-slumbring and sense-entrancing sleepe. (II, 6; 186)

What is this "it," *ce*? The pronoun refers to the whole state articulated by the previous sentences, in which Montaigne takes pleasure to "let my selfe goe from my selfe." Like "methought" and "me seemed," the phrase emphasizes that this state is experienced only through the imagination and as something that happens to it—only as a state of pure appearance of which it is both subject and object at once, without reference to the standard of an external reality. As Marion argues and as Montaigne's metaphor so vividly conveys, that imagination apprehends itself not through the internal distancing of self-representation, but rather as immanently and invisibly as, when we are swimming, we perceive the water that surrounds us—by means of a gentle, all-embracing touch in which the boundary between subject and object is all but effaced. The idea of the sea encompasses both mind and body in a mobile, material, and tactile substance of which any given feeling is just a momentary state ("an imagination"). For the mind to perceive itself is, according to this metaphor, for it to float in the element of its own activity and bask in its own touch, feeling and felt by the very same act. This act, by which consciousness perceives itself, thus also transforms consciousness into something radically different from what it normally is, rendering it indistinguishable from vital flux itself: swimming in itself, consciousness is no longer an aspiration toward detached stasis, but rather an immersion in a state of gentle and yet ever-changing movement. The object as well as subject of a single, impersonal experience, Montaigne's "me" has been caught up in the self-sensing stream of third-person life.

Proving by Experience

Montaigne now digresses from his phenomenological account of the swoon itself to reiterate that question about death which preoccupies him so much throughout the first two books of the *Essais*, and which the swoon, in principle, should enable him at last to answer. To die is to experience a state, he can now conclude, just like that which he feels during his swoon:

> I beleeve it is the same state they find themselves in, whom in the agony of death we see to droop and faint thorow weaknesse: and am of opinion we plaine and moane them without cause, esteeming that either they are agitated with grievous pangs, or that their soule is pressed with painfull cogitations. It was ever my conceit, against the opinion of many, yea and against that of *Stephanus la Boetie*, that those whom we see so overwhelmed and faintly-drooping at the approches of their end, or utterly cast downe with the lingring tediousnesse of their deseases, or by accident of some apoplexie or falling-evill,
>
> ———*(vi morbi sæpe coactus*
> *Ante oculos aliquis nostros ut fulminis ictu,*

> *Concidit, et spumas agit, ingemit, et fremit artus,*
> *Desipit, exentat nervos, torquetur, anhelat,*
> *Inconstanter et in jactando membra fatigat),*
>
> (Some man by force of sicknesse driv'n doth fall,
> As if by thunder stroke, before our eyes;
> He fomes, he grones, he trembles over all,
> He raves, he stretches, he's vext, panting lyes,
> He tyr's his limmes by tossing,
> Now this now that way crossing),
>
> or hurt in the head, whom we heare throb and rattle, and send forth grones and gaspes, although we gather some tokens from them, whereby it seemeth they have yet some knowledge left and certaine motions we see them make with their body: I say, I have ever thought they had their soule and body buried and asleepe.
>
> *Vivit et est vitæ nescius ipse suæ.*
> He lives yet knowes not he,
> That he alive should be.
>
> And I could not beleeve that at so great an astonishment of members and deffailance of senses the soule could maintaine any force within, to know herselfe [*pour se recognoistre*]; and therefore had no manner of discourse tormenting them, which might make them judge and feele the misery of their condition, and that consequently they were not greatly to be moaned. (II, VI; 186)

After adding to these examples the state we fall into before sleep, in which we "apprehend as it were in a slumber, what is done about us, and with a troubled and uncertaine hearing, follow the voyces, which seeme to sound but on the outwards limits of our soule," Montaigne finally offers his conclusion: "which thing now I have proved by experience [*Or, à present que je l'ay essayé par effect*], I make no doubt but hitherto I have well judged of it" (II, 6; 187). In the marginalia to a 1632 edition of Florio's translation, we find an early reader of Montaigne spelling out what the episode purports to show: the chapter is "a discourse of the authoure prouinge by his owne experience, that there is but litle payne in death."[24]

And yet if Montaigne has now decisively settled his former doubts, "proving by his owne experience" that death is painless, why does he continue even here to frame his claim in terms of opinion and conjecture:

"I beleeve"; "[I] am of opinion"; "It was ever my conceit, against the opinion of many"; "I could not beleeve"? Does he not now have the experience necessary to make a firmer claim on our assent, leaving these qualifications behind? As we have seen, Montaigne's earlier belief about what we feel in death in fact oscillates a great deal, leaving it hard to say just *what* opinion the swoon should be confirming. His dominant notion seems to be that death does not feel like anything at all—or that if it does, then the feeling is a pleasant one. As we have already begun to see, however, Montaigne's own account of the swoon does not fully square with either of these lessons which he hopes to draw from it. If we look, for example, at the broader context of the passage that Montaigne excerpts from book 3 of Lucretius's *De Rerum Natura*, any support we might expect it to provide for Montaigne's point quickly evaporates. In book 3 of *De Rerum Natura*, Lucretius is actually arguing for the mortality and materiality of the soul, and the passage quoted by Montaigne, with its example of an epileptic fit, is used in order to demonstrate that even before death, when the body is in extreme distress due to a disease, the soul too is seriously affected. Given that the soul is so vulnerable when it is "in the body itself," it is highly unlikely, Lucretius concludes, that it could survive the body's death:

> haec igitur tantis ubi morbis corpore in ipso
> iactentur miserisque modis distracta laborent,
> cur eadem credis sine corpore in aëre aperto
> cum validis ventis aetatem degere posse? (3.506–9)

> Since, therefore, the mind and spirit are tossed about by so great diseases in the very body itself, and are miserably torn asunder and distressed, why do you believe that the same without body, in the open air, amidst the mighty winds, are able to live?[25]

For Lucretius, then, the states which Montaigne lists all go to show how easily the soul *is* affected even when it is "inside the body itself." In such states, the soul is "miserably torn asunder and distressed"; whether or not it has "some knowledge left," it seems to suffer greatly. Once we reinsert the passage culled by Montaigne into its original context, it is hard to be as reassured by it as Montaigne might hope. For Lucretius, the soul in a near-death state certainly can hardly be said to enjoy the "pleasant sweetness" that Montaigne claims for it here.

It would not, of course, be beyond Montaigne to challenge the authority of a classical thinker, and in any case, Montaigne and Lucretius concur in the broader claim that death is not something to fear. But Lucretius's agenda in the broader passage from which Montaigne quotes can actually serve to shed light on something about Montaigne's own condition during the fall, something which his own rhetoric distorts in order to vindicate his long-held beliefs. Montaigne's soul must, after all, have felt *something*, some "effect" ("je l'ay essayé *par effect*"), at some point during his fall: "C'est le seul esvanouisement que j'aye *senty*" (my emphasis), he writes. It would be of little use, in resolving the quandaries with which the essay begins, if he really felt nothing at all. And in fact, if we actually look at Montaigne's language in his description of people in extreme states, it reveals some discrepancies from the broader claims which he uses that description to advance. Although "it seemeth they have yet some knowledge left [*qu'il leur reste encore de la cognoissance*]," he "could not beleeve," he says "that at so great an astonishment of members and deffailance of senses the soule could maintaine any force within, to know herselfe [*pour se recognoistre*]." The exact nature of the view which Montaigne "could not beleeve" depends very much on how we understand *se recognoistre* and *cognoissance* in this passage, both of which are rendered in modern translations as referring to consciousness. *Se recognoistre*, which Donald Frame translates as "to be conscious of itself," can be used idiomatically to mean *reprendre conscience*, but since Montaigne specifies that people in extreme states could not *maintain* (*maintenir*) any force to know themselves, that does not seem to be its meaning here.[26] Frame thus treats *se recognoistre* as meaning simply to be conscious of oneself, but for Florio it means something slightly different: to know or recognize oneself. Self-consciousness and self-knowledge are not, of course, identical, and it is certainly possible to be conscious without having self-knowledge. It is just such a possibility, wherein consciousness persists without the presence of a self who might "know" it, which Montaigne's experience in his swoon bears out. Where contemporary affect theory draws a clear line between consciousness and impersonal affect, for Montaigne, at least in this scene, the two can overlap; it is knowledge, in his swoon, which drops out of the picture.

A similar conclusion may be drawn from Montaigne's use of the word *cognoissance* (i.e., *connaissance*), which may mean "knowledge" *or* "consciousness." Both Frame and M. A. Screech translate this term simply as "consciousness," but it is hard to say whether the difference between the two senses of *connaissance* was clear to Montaigne, or whether he was familiar with the second one at all.[27] *Connaissance* as "consciousness" probably did not emerge until some decades after Montaigne's writing: the *Le Petit Robert* dictionary gives "before 1650" as the origin of *connaissance* in the sense of the English term "consciousness," and *Larousse* dates its earliest usage in this sense to 1647. The French word *conscience* itself—the primary word for "consciousness"—did not start to take on this meaning until the mid-seventeenth century, just as the English word "consciousness" was not used in the sense of "faculty of awareness" until the later seventeenth century.[28] Again, it is possible to be "conscious" and not to have "knowledge," and thus it is not surprising that these two senses of *connaissance* came to be distinguished and defined differently. And when Montaigne was writing, it would seem that *connaissance* still just meant "knowledge" in the more specific sense. Florio's translation—"have yet some knowledge left"—confirms this view, as does Montaigne's own formulation of the belief he is disproving, "that their soul is pressed by painful cogitations" ("avoir l'ame pressée de cogitations penibles"): the absence of cogitations does not, of course, necessarily entail the absence of all feeling and affect. Montaigne's point, then, is not the one which modern translations tend to suggest: he has lost his capacity to know himself and what was happening to him, but his consciousness, at least in its sentient dimension, was not necessarily all gone. In this reading, what the stoic wishes to avoid in such states is not feeling pain, but *knowing* that one is feeling it; the quotation from Ovid reproduced earlier, "vivit et est vitae *nescius* ipse suae" (emphasis mine), bears out this idea as well. At the outer limits of experience, Montaigne discovers not the total absence of consciousnness but rather the possibility that consciousness might be transformed into affectivity without knowledge.

Thus, if Montaigne continues to frame his experience of the swoon in terms of opinion and conjecture, it is because it is an experience that is, by virtue of its very structure, impervious to knowledge—an experience in which feeling and cognition have come apart. Consciousness's self-experience is undergone as a total metamorphosis of its power in a moment of "auto-affection," a form of experience which, transpiring in a space between the first and third person, leaves open a gap between knowledge and experience and thus renders conjecture and opinion still necessary. In this regard, Montaigne's language of opinion is of a piece with the repeated displacements of first-person experience in his description of the swoon itself: "me thought," "as me seemed." Their purpose is less to describe a hypothesis which would be subsequently confirmed by experience—in which case presumably they should vanish now—than to describe an experience which does not feed back into knowledge at all. Rather, it changes the nature of experience altogether, making way for that state in which the soul, severed from its owner, feels only itself. Such self-feeling, which Montaigne refers to as "seeming," is radically different from the stability needed, as Reiss reminds us, for self-reflection—on the contrary, it involves yielding to the perpetual movement which makes such reflection impossible.[29]

Montaigne now returns to the description of his swoon, suggesting that its meanings were not in fact exhausted by the confirmation of his previously held opinions—otherwise the account would surely end with that. Instead he now shifts his emphasis slightly, away from the "pleasant sweetnesse" of the experience and towards the state of his soul, in particular its absence of volition:

> For, first lying as in a trance, I laboured even with my nailes to open my doublet (for I was unarmed), and well I wot that in my imagination I felt nothing did hurt me. For, there are severall motions in us which proceed not of our free wil.
>
> *Semianimesque micant digiti, ferrumque retractant.*
>
> The halfe-dead fingers stirre, and feele,
> (Though it they cannot stirre) for steele.
>
> Those that fall, doe commonly by a naturall impulsion cast their armes abroad before their falling, which sheweth that our members have certaine offices, which they lend one to another, and possesse certaine agitations, apart from our discourse:
>
> *Falciferos memorant currus abscindere membra,*
> *Ut tremere in terra videatur ab artubus, id quod*
> *Decidit abscissum, cum mens tamen atque hominis vis*
> *Mobilitate mali non quit sentire dolorem.*
>
> They say, sith-bearing chariots limbes bereave,
> So as on earth, that which cut-off they leave,
> Doth seeme to quake; when yet mans force and minde
> Doth not the paine, through so quicke motion, finde.
>
> My stomacke was surcharged with clotted bloud, my hands of themselves were still running to it, as often they are wont (yea against the knowledge of our will) where we feele it to itch. There are many creatures, yea and some men, in whom after they are dead we may see their muskles to close and stirre. All men know by experience, there be some parts of our bodies which often without

> any consent of ours doe stirre, stand, and lye down againe. Now these passions, which but exteriourly touch us [*ces passions qui ne nous touchent que par l'escorse*], cannot properly be termed ours; for, to make them ours, a man must wholy be engaged unto them: And the paines that our feet or hands feele whilst we sleepe are not ours. (II, 6; 187)

The uncontrolled motions of our bodies are, Montaigne tells us, "*passions*, which but exteriourly touch us." In the Renaissance, "passions" referred primarily to the passions of the soul—anger, fear, lust, jealousy, and so on—which were understood as movements in the soul wrought by an external agent (usually the body). What Montaigne's nonconscious motions have in common with the passions is their passive and involuntary quality: both are impervious to mind or volition. Yet Montaigne also distinguishes such movements from the passions, which Thomas Wright defines as "internal acts or operations of the soul,"[30] by specifying that they "touch" him only "exteriourly."[31] It is not merely that they happen on or outside the surface of our body; Montaigne puts "the paines that our feet or hands feele whilst we sleepe" in the same category. Montaigne's movements are not exterior, then, in a spatial sense, and it is not simply that they are unwilled; like the pains felt by the hands and feet and unfelt by the self, "they are not ours" primarily in the sense that they are not registered by a first-person self, the ego to whom Descartes would attribute all subjective states. Montaigne's description looks forward to Cavendish's account of "Exterior Senses [which] do not move to Human Exterior Perception," and yet which continue to move in the absence of a subject who senses that motion. The self-sensing of such "exterior senses" is what the swoon discloses, and without the presence of a passive self to register them, *to* whom they are happening, these senses necessarily take on the more active tinge we associate with movements, becoming impersonal flickers of life whose self-feeling is a form of motion entirely independent of representation. Whether these happen in the limbs or in the soul is irrelevant: both kinds of motion are auto-affections, at once producing and feeling themselves, which from Montaigne's point of view take place "exteriourly."

Thus, even as Montaigne finally hits on the most surprising element of the experience—the total absence of self—he simultaneously bears witness to the persistence of a different and deeper mode of sensory life:

> When I came neere my house, where the tidings of my fall was already come, and those of my household met me, with such outcries

> as are used in like times, I did not only answer some words to what I was demanded, but some tell me I had the memory to command my men to give my wife a horse, whom I perceived to be overtired, and labouring in the way, which is very hilly, foule, and rugged. It seemeth this consideration proceeded from a vigilant soule: yet was I cleane distracted from it [*si est-ce que je n'y étais aucunement*], they were but vaine conceits, and as in a cloud, were only moved by the sense of the eyes and eares: they came not from my selfe. All which notwithstanding, I knew neither whence I came nor whither I went, nor could I understand or consider what was spoken unto me. They were [*ce sont*] but light effects, that my senses produced of themselves, as it were of custome. Whatsoever the soule did assist it with was but a dreame, being lightly touched, and only sprinkled by the soft impression of the senses. (II, 6; 187)

For a brief moment, Montaigne has penetrated the mystery of self-sensing. What we might describe merely as a kind of low-level consciousness—awareness without an accompanying, second-order knowledge of that awareness—turns out to conceal a self-affecting structure of its own. Montaigne's sensory activities, he tells us, do not merely shut down or grow dimmer. Rather, what distinguishes them from ordinary, conscious sensation is that they are no longer fully passive, but instead now seem to be taking place of their own accord, as movements analogous to the unconscious gestures that Montaigne's body produces on its own. If a moment ago Montaigne reduced his bodily motions to the status of mere "passions," here he performs the inverse operation, describing what would normally be seen as passive sensations in terms of self-producing *activity*. The senses are now capable of inducing movement out of themselves: his "vaine conceits . . . . were only moved by the sense of the eyes and eares. . . . They were but light effects, that my senses produced of themselves."

As we have seen, this feeling which at once feels and produces itself is synonymous with life itself, for it exhibits that "spontaneity that is capable of movement, of organizing itself and affecting itself" which for Derrida is life's most distinctive feature: it is a current of perpetual flux whose changes and movements are entirely self-generated.[32] Such a feeling, however, can only be experienced in a state of pure seeming or in what Montaigne now metaphorically describes as a "dream"—a description which refers not to correspondence with (or discrepancy from) reality, but to phenomenological self-sufficiency, to a sentient state which refers to nothing outside itself. Where earlier this state was described as a swimming in the sea, now instead Montaigne compares it to a different sort of elemental state: "they were but vaine conceits, and as in a cloud." The metaphor of the "cloud" captures the felt experience of these thoughts which Montaigne cannot clarify to himself—cannot represent for himself in the reflexive, self-detached manner that, for thinkers such as Locke, defines consciousness itself. For his thoughts in the swoon do not appear to him as distinct objects or propositions—things that the mind is "about" or "of"—but rather affect him in the manner, at once more proximate and more indistinct, of an atmosphere, an encompassing material element which is always there even if we usually are only rarely aware of it. These thoughts have the fuzziness and the indistinct outlines of a cloud because they are what Descartes would call "obscure and confused"—the opposite of clear and distinct. But we should think of them not as indistinct and unresolved representations of objects subject to further, clarifying analysis, but rather as the constantly shifting states of a mobile affect that feels and is felt in the same act, and which clarification or distinction into subject and object would dissipate entirely: this cloud, in other words, is a description of "thought's affectivity," of what thought feels like to itself, a feeling which "can only adopt a visible appearance on the condition of setting aside its own reality."[33] What such metaphors express is just how difficult it is to arrest or to capture the felt movement of our own thinking without betraying its essence: consciousness necessarily holds its object at a distance (the distance of representation), making it impossible for consciousness to know what it itself is like. Thus Montaigne's analogies: just as we perceive the state of the sea or cloud which surrounds us by virtue of a contact too immediate for consciousness, so we perceive consciousness itself only by virtue of a feltness which is immanent to it, and which cannot be represented *for* consciousness. To stand outside this feltness and attempt to perceive it as such is to miss out on precisely the kind of self-perception that is intrinsic to it.[34]

Montaigne's own report of this experience cannot, therefore, come directly from the heart of it, and indeed, as he concludes his account, he explains that he had to reconstruct it primarily by means of memory:

> But a while after and the morrow next, when my memorie began to come to itselfe againe, and represent [*representer*] the state unto me wherein I was at the instant, when I perceived the horse riding over me (for being at my heeles, I chanced to espy him and helde my selfe for dead: yet was the conceit so sudden that feare had no leasure to enter my thoughts) me seemed it was a flashing or lightning that smote my soule with shaking, and that I came from another world. (II, 6; 188)

The key word here is *represent*. Representation is exactly what Montaigne is barred from doing during the event itself—he is able to feel his state, or rather his feelings are able to feel their change, but the structure of representation, in which an image is registered in the mind as simultaneously apart from and yet present for a self that sees it, has broken down. For a brief moment consciousness feels itself not effaced, but rather transformed into a state of unconditioned affectivity and immediacy, without the extended and distancing structures of representation.[35] Those are only supplied, at a remove, by memory later on. It has been suggested recently that Montaigne did not in fact experience anything at all during the swoon—that he reconstructed it entirely based on the reports of his servants and his wife.[36] But while such a claim usefully calls attention to the paradoxes of this foundational *expérience*, it greatly underestimates the phenomenological sophistication of Montaigne's account. It is true that Montaigne "himself" is not present during the swoon, but it does not follow, as we have seen, that feeling is not present at all. What Montaigne, when he returns to himself, can draw on is not merely the reports of others, but also the transformed state of those feelings which, just as in a dream, were briefly permitted to experience their own autonomous life without the intervention of the first-person self. At a distance from the event, Montaigne is then able to convert these feelings into representations, but what he has discovered is that representation is not the only form of experience: it is based on the "flashing or lightning" of an affectivity which always precedes it.

A few essays later, at the end of his essay "Of Judging the Death of Others" (II, 13), Montaigne again insists on his belief that death will be pleasurable, and he draws on the experience of those who have swooned as evidence: "verily, such as have had these faintings and sownings of the heart, which proceed from weaknesse, say that they feele no paine at all in them, but rather some pleasure, as of a passage to sleepe and rest" (II, 13; 313). Earlier, in "Of Exercise or Practice," Montaigne described his own swoon in great detail, insisting on its value precisely as a form of personal, lived experience. Why does he now refer this experience to others, third persons, as though he was not one of them himself—as though he did not have "experience" of it himself? Perhaps, though it is unlikely, he wrote the later essay before he swooned. But perhaps the swoon simply does not tie up the problem of death's epistemology, crossing the gap from opinion to experience as clearly as Montaigne suggests in "Of Exercise or Practice" itself. As we have just seen, if Montaigne manages to recollect the fragments later on, it is in the manner of a flash memory, "a flashing or lightning, that smote my soule with shaking"—of an experience that is all the more vividly personal in having, for all intents and purposes, befallen another. Perhaps even after the experience, then, the soul has remained a third person to itself, and its encounter with its own depths in the swoon was possible only on the condition that it remain permanently beyond the boundaries of what Montaigne can draw on as his own.

Unfelt Feeling, Feeling the Unfelt: From "Exercise" to "*Expérience*"

In his last round of revisions to the *Essais*, Montaigne added to the end of "Of Exercise or Practice" a new reflection on his writings and on their relationship to himself which resonates with the passage from "Of Repenting" with which I began:

> Some may peradventure suppose that by deeds and effects, and not simply by words, I witnesse of my selfe. I principally set forth my cogitations [*Je peins principalement mes cogitations*]; a shapelesse subject, and which cannot fall within the compasse of a workman-like production; with much adoe can I set it downe in this ayrie bodie of the voice [*ce corps aeré de la voix*]. (II, 6; 189)

It would seem that Montaigne wished retrospectively to justify his inclusion of the experience he has just related to us—which, as he had already admitted in the conclusion to the earlier version, is "so slight" that it would be "but vaine and frivolous were not the instructions I have drawne from thence for my use" (II, 6; 188). But there is more at stake in this coda than Montaigne's wish to defend his focus on his own experience. Montaigne gives us a revelatory account of what he understands himself to be writing *about*, explaining that he "principally sets forth his *cogitations*"—it is they which form his "shapeless subject." Montaigne compares himself to a painter here (*Je peins*): like a painter, he must observe and "set downe" his "subject" from without, and he must train his perceptions in order to capture details which the layman would miss or misconstrue.[37] But where a painter is able to impose on his subject a fixed and finished form, the best Montaigne can hope for is to capture his "cogitations" in their natural, perpetually unfinished state of flux. Montaigne's description of his writing here thus accords with what he experiences in his swoon, in which, as we have seen, his thoughts and sensations take on a life of their own, participating in an impersonal affectivity that is independent of the self. Far from being anomalies, then, what Montaigne describes as "vaine conceits, and as in a cloud . . . moved by the sense of the eyes and eares" and as "but light effects, that my senses produced of themselves," actually become prototypes for the subject of Montaigne's *Essais*. And those *Essais*, in turn, become the record of Montaigne's *efforts* to feel and to capture sensations which might otherwise go unfelt, at least by him: of his essay at bridging the temporal gap between first-person consciousness and life. But the very blurriness of those sensations also makes them delicate, susceptible at the very most only to the "airy body of a voice." In order to accommodate them, language must be transformed into a semi-corporeal atmospheric medium—much like the cloud and sea in which, during his swoon, his cogitations appear to float.

This approach to his own cogitations marks a notable change in Montaigne's philosophy, and as he set about making his final revisions, he must have realized that "Of Exercise or Practice" marked that change most clearly.[38] For where in his earlier essays he seeks to mold his floating cogitations in order to give them the "flavor" that suits him most, in "Of Exercise or Practice" and subsequent essays he is increasingly willing to let them float in the airy element of their own happening, content enough if he can get an occasional glimpse. The cognitive condition which Montaigne has come to see as man's natural one is no longer a mental battle against adversities, but rather a state of "naturall drunkennesse" which "goeth unquietly and staggering" ("troublé et chancelant, d'une yvresse naturelle"). He uses similar terms to describe old age later in book 3, in "Of Vanitie": "it is the motion of a drunkard, stumbling, reeling, giddie-brain'd, formeles, or of reedes, which the ayre doth casually wave to and fro, what way it bloweth" (III, 9; 492). A natural drunkenness is, of course, something of a contradiction in terms, but Montaigne's point is not that our judgment and perception are perpetually off-kilter, as if there were some outside standard by which we could know this (Montaigne's Pyrrhonic rather than Academic skepticism excludes such a standpoint). Rather, his point speaks to the ways in which, just as the reeds are perpetually swayed by the "ayre," our body is always already altered by its openness to an intoxicating physical world—altered in ways of which that state itself, whether or not it is a conscious one, whether or not it belongs to a self, is our best and only measure. Montaigne's "natural drunkenness" thus bears a close resemblance to the state in which he finds himself when he reawakens from his trance—"with so dim and so troubled [*troublé*] a sight, that I could not discerne anything of the light" (II, 6; 186). In book 3, then, the "troubling" of Montaigne's perception during the swoon is reevaluated: more now than merely an opportunity to prepare for death, the state he enters becomes a metonymy for the human condition at the broadest level, for the inarticulate and instinctual feltness of those sensory cogitations in which the final essays rest all of their confidence. Rather than the trance interrupting consciousness, it now begins to look as if consciousness itself were an extension of the trance, as if the whole rest of Montaigne's life were comprised of the unshakable but not unpleasant stupor of his reawakening. His sensations, during the swoon, of swimming in a mind-sea and floating amidst thought-clouds represent the first stirrings of what he will call, in his final essay, *expérience*.

The concept of *expérience* is itself a slippery one. At the beginning of his essay on the subject, "Of Experience," it is defined in opposition to the abstractions of theoretical knowledge and of inherited dogma. The fields of law and medicine come in for particularly harsh scrutiny, for no matter how much lawyers extend and refine the laws, Montaigne argues, the proliferation of individual cases will always outpace them: "What have our lawmakers gained with chusing a hundred thousand kinds of particular cases, and adde as many lawes unto them? That number hath no proportion with the infinite diversity of human accidents" (III, 13; 546). To have experience in this sense means to work with the details of particular cases and examples rather than relying on broad generalities; such experience may well be sensory in nature, but it is particularity rather than sensuousness which Montaigne has in mind at this point. As the essay progresses, however, "Of Experience" reveals that Montaigne privileges a particular form of such experience above others. No experience of the outside world, Montaigne tells us, can compensate for a defective experience of ourselves: "Whatsoever then the fruit is we may have of experience, the same which we draw from forraine examples will hardly stead our institution much; if we reape so small profit from that wee have of ourselves, which is most familiar unto us, and truely sufficient to instruct us of what we want. I study myselfe more than any other subject. It is my supernaturall metaphisike, it is my naturall philosophy" (III, 13; 550). If this claim sounds conventionally Platonic in nature, Montaigne quickly clarifies that his self-knowledge is above all concerned with the body rather than the soul: "But concerning bodily health, no man is able to bring more profitable experience than myselfe" (III, 13; 553). Montaigne now proceeds to set the knowledge he has derived from observation of his own body—knowledge of his habits and customs, his proclivities and aversions, his weaknesses and strengths—against the authority of medical knowledge. Doctors, after all, can draw on no principle higher than experience themselves. They have treated a number of different patients whereas Montaigne is only familiar with one, but the underlying source of their knowledge—experience—is the same.[39]

Montaigne, however, does not rest satisfied with the idea that his knowledge of the body is as reliable as that of any doctor. Ultimately, it is not knowledge at all that Montaigne draws from his body, but rather a different kind of wisdom. What Montaigne derives from his own experience—and what distinguishes his relationship to such experience from that of medical professionals—is an awareness of the extent of his own ignorance: "It is by my experience I accuse humane ignorance, which, in mine opinion, is the surest part of the world's schoole. Those that will not conclude it in themselves by so vaine an example as mine or theirs, let them acknowledge it by Socrates" (III, 13; 552). There is, of course, a sense in which Montaigne knows his body very well—he proceeds now to report, in stunning detail, on its habits, appetites, pleasures, tendencies, and so on. As he sets out on his discussion, he speaks almost boastfully of his familiarity with his own inner movements:

> Would every man pry into the effects and circumstances of the passions that sway him as I have done of that whereunto I was allotted, he should see them comming, and would somewhat hinder their course and abate their impetuousity; they doe not always surprise and take hold of us at the first brunt; there are certaine forethreatnings and degrees as forerunners. (III, 13; 551)

Yet Montaigne knows these passions only because he has studied them, in other words because he has studied himself—as if to suggest that his body was, to begin with, essentially opaque to him. And he always keeps the limitations of even this acquired knowledge in view: at any point, he acknowledges, the body may unexpectedly change its ways, for there are "certaine inconstant and unknowne motions in us" (III, 13; 567) of which the swoon offers the most dramatic illustration. Even when it comes to those passions into whose "effects and circumstances" he has "pried," he is not able to control, understand, or even foresee them. He is merely able to know, when they are already irreversibly underway, *that* they are happening by means of "certaine forethreatnings and degrees as forerunners," while the process which gives rise to them itself remains deeply foreign and unpredictable. At best, those passions may predict themselves, may announce their coming to the body by means, presumably, of certain changes, and what Montaigne prides himself on is his attunement to *that*—to the knowledge which is built in to the body's own power of self-sensing. The knowledge that Montaigne draws from his body is thus a knowledge of ignorance in a richly specific sense: it has taken years for his body to teach him just how independent and unknowable its immanent sensory life really is. To know that life well is to know that it is subject to unknowable processes, and perhaps, at best, to be aware of those processes as they are happening.

From the outset, then, Montaigne's celebration of his own experience presents the same paradox as his swoon: the experience in question is as much that of another as it is his own, as much a feature of his body's rapport with itself as of Montaigne's rapport with his body. Indeed, as he suggests in a later passage, his relationship to his own bodily changes is by no means a privileged one; others may have better access to them than he does: "[m]y visage and eyes doe presently discover me. Thence begin all my changes, and somewhat sharper than they are in effect. I often move my friends to pitty ere I feele the cause of it" (III, 13; 564). These are changes, in other words, which touch him "but exteriourly," and are felt by themselves and by others before they are felt by him. Montaigne, in other words, cannot and does not take the transparency of his experience to himself for granted, and thus like Canius he must "keepe me ready and prepared [*bandé*] with all my force" to see what it will teach him. This aspect of experience becomes especially apparent when he begins to describe the gradual decline of his body, from the weakening of his sight to the loss of his hearing. Unless he makes an effort, Montaigne tells us, he will not feel its changes at all: "Yet am I in doubt that my hearing is about to become thicke, and you shall see that I shall have lost it halfe when yet I shall finde fault with their voyces that speake unto me. The minde must be strained to a high pitch to make it perceive how it declineth [*Il faut bien bander l'ame, pour luy faire sentir, comme elle s'escoule*]" (III, 13; 569).[40] Failing to perceive his own loss of perception, Montaigne like Canius must keep himself "bandé de toute ma force" in order to perceive a layer of affect which normally remains unfelt.

Both Canius and Montaigne must *bander* their souls in order to perceive something which ordinarily lies outside the bounds of conscious perception altogether: the nonvisual, affective life of embodied process. Montaigne again recalls Canius—as well as his own swoon—when, offering another example of his commitment to *expérience*, he speaks of his desire to feel sleep (a state which he had likened to swooning in "Of Exercise or Practice"). Again, he insists on the effort necessary to feel the inner workings of our own body—the effort necessary, we might say, to feel ourselves feel:

> According as the possession of life is more short, I must endeavour to make it more profound and full. Other men feele the sweetnesse of contentment and prosperity. I feele it as well as they, but it is not

> in passing and gliding; yet should it be studied, tasted and ruminated [*estudier, savourer, et ruminer*], thereby to yeeld it condigne thanks, that it pleased to grant the same unto us. They enjoy other pleasures, as that of sleep without knowing them; to the end that sleepe should not dully and unfeelingly escape me [*ne m'eschappast ainsi stupidement*], and that I might better taste and be acquainted with it [*que je l'entrevisse*], I have heretofore found it good to bee troubled and interrupted in the same. (III, 13; 573)

Here Florio's translation emphasizes and extends Montaigne's sensory language, translating not only "savourer" as "tasted" but including this meaning in his translation of "entrevoir" (which he renders as "taste and be acquainted") as well. As with Canius's death, however, the sensory experience in question is so subtle that it will pass us by completely unless we make an effort to pay attention at the right moment. And in fact Florio emphasizes this dimension as well, translating *stupidement* not merely as "dully," but as "unfeelingly." Other men do feel pleasures, and yet they feel them only "in passing and gliding"—only, as it were, unfeelingly. Sleep metonymically encompasses all of these experiences whose intrinsic self-feeling must be redoubled in order to be felt at all: as Florio sees, Montaigne wants to feel them feelingly.

This passage thus presents a set of paradoxes similar to those raised by the swoon. What might it mean to "taste," to experience not "unfeelingly" a state which for Aristotle was defined precisely as "an affection of the sensitive part of us—a kind of fetter or immobilization"?[41] How could Montaigne criticize those who enjoy sleep "unfeelingly"—is this not the very definition of sleep, and indeed precisely what makes it so enjoyable? When it comes to swooning, Montaigne insists, as we saw, that such states are generally unfelt, and he describes his own swoon in this way as well: "we do also in yawning, before sleep fully seize upon us, apprehend as it were in a slumber, what is done about us" (II, 6; 187). Like the swoon, sleep provides a signal example of the soul's third-personness: of its susceptibility to states and transformations which normally go unfelt. More than a mere privation of sensation, sleep is also a complex physiological state unto itself, depending on a set of internal, physiological changes which produce and feel themselves without involving the first-person self (Aristotle himself calls it an affection or *pathos*). But like the Canius anecdote, Montaigne's description of trying to feel sleep acknowledges this unfelt dimension while simultaneously opening the possibility that we might, if we make an essay at it, succeed in feeling what is normally unfelt, in grasping pains such as those "that our feet or hands feel while we sleep" (II, 6; 187). *Expérience* thus refers both to a sensory world whose operations, though grounded in feeling, are normally unfelt by us, and at the sime time to the effort—which Montaigne commends to us—to bridge that gap, to bring those feelings up to the surface and feel them fully. As Montaigne reminds us in another essay from book 3, "even sleeping [the soul] is mooving and doing" (III, 10; 516), just as the feet can feel pains without our knowing, and it is presumably this "moving and doing" which, though it normally exceeds the boundaries of the first-person self, he is anxious not to have escape him "unfeelingly." Sleep too may possess "certaine forethreatnings and degrees as forerunners," but they are palpable only for as long as we can linger on the threshold between consciousness and its absence. And such lingering is by no means to be taken for granted: it is possible only in exceptional states such as swoons, or if we make a special effort to feel our own feelings on the brink of slumber. All of these states are versions of the "motion of an instant" which comprises death: a movement which is intrinsically imperceptible, and yet which Montaigne now recognizes as a substantial one. He struggles to perceive it precisely because he finally recognizes that, despite its fleetingness, it *is* a motion. Like Massumi's "missing half-second," this moment of life's self-feeling *is* a movement, but it can only be perceived in moments of what both Montaigne and Massumi call escape—in falling asleep, in swooning, in dying.

"Our life is nothing but motion" (III, 13; 563), Montaigne famously says in the midst of this final essay (a much apter place for such a claim than the essay's beginning or conclusion). "Motion" has by now become much less metaphorical than it was for Montaigne when he dismissed death as the motion of an instant: what he now has in mind is the ongoing series of literal movements that comprise the body's life in a fully biological sense of that term, the possibility of spontaneous change that distinguishes vital from dead matter, but which may not be fully available to the first person. And yet whether Montaigne is reflecting on the "flowing out" of his mind from his body or on the melting away caused by his illness ("[t]hus I sinke and scape from myself" [II, 6; 567]: "C'est ainsi que je fons et eschape à moy"), what he speaks to in his last essay is not merely the mutations inherent in human embodiment, but also our own shifting, nebulous experience of those mutations, which in turn his writing attempts to capture. Something "flowing" and "melting," is, of course, something material, but it is also something which it is difficult to grasp firmly—thus, near the conclusion of his "Apologie of Raymond Sebond," Montaigne writes: "[a]nd if perhaps you fix your thought to take its being, it would be even as if one should go about to graspe the water" (II,

13; 309).[42] Montaigne's writing itself, as we have seen, is nothing but a struggle to "grasp the water," to fix, for a moment, the "shapelesse subject" so that we might have a glimpse of it—a subject which is none other than the movement inherent to bodily life itself. Hovering between the felt and the unfelt, that life eludes us as soon as we try to grasp it—unless, that is, we can understand that our efforts to feel life's flux are themselves already a part of it. For what may seem to be Montaigne's detachment both arises from and folds back into his immanence to life: "everything," as Michel Henry puts it, "falls back into life."[43]

If the above account makes Montaignean selfhood seem more dualistic than is often assumed, we are losing sight of the fact that, for Montaigne, consciousness is itself part and parcel of this flux, losing its immanence only when we try to step outside and grasp it from without (i.e., as the object of an intentional thought). What Montaigne urges us to do in "Of Experience" is not to stand apart from our changes and watch them, but rather to yield ourselves fully to them, becoming one with the perpetual slippings that, in this final essay, define life itself. As for his swoon in "Of Exercise or Practice," while the nature of the "lesson" which Montaigne professes to draw from it is ultimately ambiguous, what is clear in that episode is the sense that *some* important wisdom is contained in it. The best way to capture that wisdom, however, is not to generalize about the experience or even reflect on it, but rather, as Montaigne's experiments with sleep late in his life suggest, simply to try repeating it: to try swooning again. As Montaigne's own life begins to slip away, as his senses begin to weaken, and as his *Essais* themselves draw near their terminus, all three of these "movements"—life, experience, and writing—begin to converge in an ever fainter flowing which Montaigne, as he approaches his final swoon, can at last begin to feel.

Chapter 3

Stounds: Physiology and Experience in Spenser's *Faerie Queene*

Although the final two versions of Montaigne's *Essais* were published in close proximity to the two installments of Spenser's *Faerie Queene*—the so-called B- and C-texts of the *Essais* came out in 1588 and 1595, while the first three books of *The Faerie Queene* appeared in 1590 and the second three in 1596—the two works might seem to have little else in common.[1] As we have just seen, Montaigne's *Essais* insist on the primacy of corporeal self-experience, valorizing the autonomous life of the senses over the abstractions of knowledge. Spenser, meanwhile, is much more firmly committed to the Neoplatonism which Montaigne rejects, and which moves in the opposite direction from Montaigne: away from personal experience to transcendent forms. As Andrew Escobedo points out in his studies of Spenser's characters, because it is so grounded in Neoplatonic metaphysics, Spenserian allegory has a tendency to exclude both "deliberative contemplation" and "psychological complexity" from *The Faerie Queene*,[2] so that the characters who populate its six books are driven by the concepts they are supposed to represent as if by a kind of demonic possession. "Subordinating consciousness to essence, persons to personification," Spenserian allegory, with its drive toward ideas, obviates the need for the reflective monologues that so often precede action in Shakespeare or Milton, and with which Montaigne's writerly practice in the *Essais* can seem almost identical.[3]

Certainly in comparison to Shakespearean or Miltonic characters, consciousness in the sense of inner awareness and reflection seems in *The Faerie Queene* to be largely absent. Yet one would be hard-pressed to make the same claim about the notion of *experience* in the poem. On the contrary, the poem abounds in states of pain, fear, shock, and anger—moments in which, in other words, experience is wrought to its very highest pitch, and cognitive categories break down in the face of something unknowable or overwhelming.[4] Such moments, which Spenser often calls "stounds," may not be reflective or self-aware, and yet they certainly entail consciousness—at times so violently that they threaten to shut it down altogether, leading to the swoons and stupefied states that are common in the poem. Perhaps—much as neuroscientists today study consciousness from its absence—these "stounds" are where we ought to look for an implicit account of Spenserian subjectivity.

The word "stound" derives from the same root as the German *stunde*, or "hour," and it means "a time, while; a short time, moment" (*OED n.*, 1a; see Chaucer's *Troilus and Criseyde*: "Now lat us stinte of Troilus a stounde"). By extension of this meaning, it can also refer to a "time of trial or pain" (*OED n.*, 1.2a) or to "a sharp pain, a pang; a fierce attack, a shock" (*OED n.*, 1.2b), while as a verb it can mean "to be acutely painful; to smart, throb" (*OED v.*, 1.2b). Its second major definition—"a state of stupefaction or amazement" (*OED n.*, 2)—is not unrelated to the first, but derives not from German but from the Latin word for amazement, *attonitus*, or thunderstruck. On the basis of its Latin root, then, "stound" suggests a sudden suspension of conscious experience, while in its Anglo-Saxon derivation it points to both time and painful affect. Being "in a stound" may mean being on the brink of unconsciousness, but a "stound" is simultaneously a period of time in which consciousness is dramatically heightened, whether by pain or some other intense feeling. The kind of affect involved in a stound is in fact not always easy to specify, or to trace to a particular humor or passion—instead, what it seems to involve is a sheer intensity of feeling as such. That feeling is experienced by way of a rupture in the fabric of time, in which a "short," unspecified stretch appears to stand out. Describing the stound will therefore mean, in Catherine Clément's words, "describing the inside of ravished time."[5]

Brian Massumi defines affect as a temporal disruption which consciousness subsequently smooths over—"a suspension of action-reaction circuits and linear temporality in a sink of what might be called 'passion,' to distinguish it both from passivity and activity"—and in this sense the stound might be understood as affect's primordial unit.[6] As "a time of trial or pain," the "stound" is also a window of decision—"the time for doing something; one's 'hour' or opportunity" (*OED* 1f)—and yet more often than not, that window is closed before we can even become aware of it, a decision having been made with or without our assent; it is thus a state in which we are on the border between the active and the passive. Massumi's analysis shows how affect is concentrated in that "missing half-second" that elapses between sensation and its conscious perception, during which "what we think of as 'free,' 'higher' functions, such as volition, are apparently being performed by autonomic, bodily reactions occurring in the brain but outside consciousness, and between brain and finger."[7] This half-second "stound"—an interval of time which also disrupts time's passage, a missing beat or syncope in consciousness which bridges two separate moments in time by blurring the interval between them—is also what Montaigne has in mind as he contemplates death. In his initial essays, we saw, he insists that "death has no feeling, because it is the motion of an instant" (I, 40; 120). But as he comes to understand the range of affective movements which are constantly taking place without our full awareness or participation, so his understanding of death changes, and he reimagines it as comprised by the movement of an unfelt "stound" which, if we pay close enough attention, we may in fact discern. Death may be an instant, but that instant turns out to have movements of its own, just like sleep, just like his consciousness during the faint. More broadly, Montaigne insists again and again not on suppressing affect, but on catching it at that interval before it percolates into full consciousness and transforms consciousness in its image, on somehow arresting that movement whereby "at every minute methinks I make an escape." Spenser's "stound" refers to the "minute" in which that escape takes place, "the motion of an instant" in the full richness which, during and after Montaigne's swoon, that instant comes to have: not the absence of consciousness, but rather what Gilles Deleuze describes as "a qualitative duration of consciousness without a self."[8] For it is in such an instant—at once punctual and extended, the root of all our feeling even as it remains unfelt in itself—that, I have been arguing, consciousness apprehends its own activity, overcoming its inherent belatedness and perceiving its perception in a moment of total self-immanence. Spenser's "stound," conflating its Anglo-Saxon and Latin etymologies, is a unit of time which is also a unit of affect, a state of the soul in which life's immanent self-sensing comes to the fore.

It is my wager in this chapter, therefore, that by looking at Spenser's "stounds" we can unlock an account of Spenserian subjectivity which is neither anachronistic nor archaic—just as, in the previous chapter, analyzing Montaigne's "motion of an instant," a rhetorical construct initially imagined as empty, in fact opened the way to the wealth of self-sensing movements at the heart of *expérience*.[9] In two moments in particular—Red Crosse's "stound" in book 1, canto 7, and Guyon's "trance" in book 2, canto 7—the seeming paralysis of consciousness actually tells us something about consciousness itself. When we look through the microscope at the temporarily prone bodies of the heroes of books 1 and 2, what we discover is not dead matter but rather its opposite: a swirling, self-feeling vitality whose energy has been, if anything, intensified by the "stound." The "stound," we will then see, is naturally linked to a second concept which is equally important to Spenserian subjectivity: what Spenser calls "vital spright" or the "vital powers" and what the Renaissance knew as the "spirits." The notion of the spirits as Spenser understood them derives ultimately from Galen, and we have already seen Chaucer connect the spirits with a "stound" of astonishment: "And every spirit his vigour in knette, / So they astoned or oppressed were." In Spenser's hands, however, the spirits are transformed into a primary vehicle for restoring human consciousness to the self-sensing of a material body. The spirits, as Spenser presents them, are not merely the soul's material substratum, for they are capable of a sensory activity which is autonomous and at the same time more deeply rooted in the organism, in life, than the ostensibly higher functions of intellect or reason. Spenser's implicit account of these vital powers culminates in Guyon's visit to the House of Alma, where we learn how the body is truly "governed": not by the external mandates of consciousness, but rather by a self-regulating state of *eukrasia* premised on the body's capacity to sense its own feelings.

When we understand it in these terms, Spenserian subjectivity should not simply be opposed to consciousness or the Cartesian cogito. For while a dualistic account of Descartes remains dominant in Anglo-American literary criticism—and thus continues to inform historical accounts of the evolution of subjectivity and its representation in literature—a radically different reading of Descartes's work has now become available in the work of the French phenomenologists Michel Henry and Jean-Luc Marion. According to these thinkers, far from having opened an insurmountable split between thought and body, Descartes was the first Western philosopher to glimpse what Henry calls "thought's affectivity":[10] the immanent self-sensing of sensing which defines thought and transforms doubt into certainty. Henry argues that thought, when defined in such terms, is nothing other than life itself—a nonrepresentational and unrepresentable vitality whose capacity to feel its own workings is what Descartes really means, at least at this point in the development of his work, when he says "cogito." In Spenser's characters we may not find much in the way of detached monologue and reflection, but if we look closely, what we observe in their place is this reflexive form of feeling in which—precisely when such detachment is most compromised and consciousness seems to fail—the body experiences its own sentience. In this regard, Red Crosse and Guyon do not merely exemplify a widespread "pre-Cartesian" form of selfhood grounded in humors and passions. Rather—just like Henry's Descartes—they uncover a notion of subjective life that has rarely been glimpsed either before or since. At once unveiled and transformed by its "stounds," consciousness in *The Faerie Queene* becomes indistinguishable from the self-sensing life that is immanent to matter itself. It is this invisible vitality which Spenser characterizes in the paradoxical terms of a "Selfe, whom though we do not see, / Yet each doth in him selfe it well perceiue to bee" (2.12.47). The famously dreamlike quality of the poem, in turn, speaks not to a Spenserian rejection of objective reality, but rather to the self-sufficiency of this phenomenological element in which, much as in Montaigne's "seeming" during his swoon, what Spenser will call "Life" experiences nothing but itself.

"His Changed Powers": Red Crosse's Moral Stound

Spenser uses the word "stound" some thirty-nine times in the course of *The Faerie Queene*. Its first instance comes at the climactic point of book 1, the Legend of Holiness, at the end of a brief but complex sequence in which the book's hero, Red Crosse, succumbs to the effects of a magical fountain. Having defeated the pagan knight Sans Loy in the House of Pride, as recounted in canto 5, and after an intervening canto describing the wanderings of his companion Una, from whom he was separated by the deceptions of Archimago in canto 2, Red Crosse lies down "foreby a fountaine side" to rest:

> Hee feedes vpon the cooling shade, and bayes
> His sweatie forehead in the breathing wind,
> Which through the trembling leaues full gently playes
> Wherein the cherefull birds of sundry kind
> Do chaunt sweet musick, to delight his mind: (1.7.3)[11]

But the fountain has magical powers of which Red Crosse is unaware—"And all that drunke thereof, did faint and feeble grow" (1.7.5)—and these soon begin to take disastrous effect:

> Hereof this gentle knight vnweeting was,
> And lying downe vpon the sandie graile,
> Drunke of the streame, as cleare as cristall glas,
> Eftsoones his manly forces gan to faile,
> And mightie strong was turnd to feeble fraile.

His chaunged powres at first themselues not felt,
Till crudled cold his corage gan assaile,
And chearefull bloud in faintnesse chill did melt,
Which like a feuer fit through all his body swelt. (1.7.6)

Since Red Crosse has already begun sinking into a state of lassitude when he chooses to drink, the fountain's effects are on some level merely an allegory of the moral condition in which the Knight of Holiness already finds himself—one of lowered vigilance and careless susceptibility to sin. That "mightie strong was turnd to feeble frayle" suggests clearly the limitations of physical prowess and prepares us for the moral lesson about Pride which the episode is holding in store.

Yet such a reading does not do justice to the subtlety with which Spenser then describes not only the fountain's physiological effects on Red Crosse, but also his own muddled subliminal awareness of them: "[h]is chaunged powres at first themselues not felt." With surprising precision, this formula (which, as we will see, applies to Othello and Leontes as well) pinpoints a moment which probably occurs in the course of any human disease, at which the inner upheaval caused by the disease has begun on a physiological level, but without any corresponding knowledge or even feeling on our part. But Spenser's phrase simultaneously implies something else: that these powers *do* have the ability to "feel themselves," even if they are not yet using it. The same powers which are changed by the fountain are also those which, at least in theory, feel the effects of those changes, and indeed "till" in the next line suggests that they soon begin to do so (just as with Diamond's head—"till feeling life to fayle, it fell, and deadly slept"). Initially, therefore, the changes are not perceived by an external faculty such as first-person consciousness or the sensitive soul; the body registers its transformation by virtue of the transformation itself, in a process in which what feels and what is felt are one and the same. More broadly, to extrapolate from this moment, it seems that for Spenser the body's powers—the same powers which sustain our vital functions and give us physical strength—also possess a biological awareness of their own activity which is immanent to it and perhaps indistinguishable from it. The passage identifies the workings of that neurobiological "proto-self" described by Antonio Damasio, an unconscious neural map which represents changes in our physiological state to itself moment by moment, and which is synonymous with what Henry calls "life that experiences itself."[12]

As we saw in the first chapter, however, that map can never be made conscious, and indeed the next stanza begins: "Yet goodly court he made still to his Dame, / Pourd out in loosnesse on the grassy grownd" (1.7.7). Red Crosse's changed powers themselves now feel, but either Red Crosse himself is still simply unaware of them—of the reflexive feeling that is immanent to his own sentient "powers"—and continues to make goodly court, or, at the very least, he is easily able to suppress them. This account is confirmed when Red Crosse's changing physiological condition is described, at the end of stanza 6, as a third-person state of the body rather than as a first-person experience. The simultaneous mingling of hot and cold may briefly evoke Petrarchan lyric—"et ardo et son un ghiaccio" ("I burn and am of ice")—but where Petrarch experiences the mingling of hot and cold in the full first person, in Spenser's description "crudled cold" and "fayntnes chil" act as objective entities, without any reference to the subject who feels them.[13] Such a description almost strains logic, since "hot" and "cold" are subjective judgments rather than objective properties. But the whole point is that Red Crosse himself still does not feel his own feelings here: by displacing a Petrarchan oxymoron to the third person, and treating hot and cold as independent forces rather than subjective feelings, Spenser depicts Red Crosse's physiological state as one which is endowed with sentience, capable of feeling hot and cold, and yet remains distinct from his awareness. One might think here of the four qualities—hot, cold, dry, moist—out of which the Galenic body is comprised, and on which its *eukrasia* or *dyskrasia* depends: Galenism too tends to treat subjective qualities as objective bodily states. Spenser's stanzas take this Galenic tension between body-as-subject and body-as-object to its limit. Red Crosse's powers feel their own changes, they feel themselves traversed by feverish fits of hot and cold, but Red Crosse himself remains at most peripherally aware of this feeling.

At least three different degrees of cognition are implied by this fine-grained sequence of stanzas in which Red Crosse succumbs to the effects of the fountain, and in particular by the careful staging of its pronouns: changed feelings that do not feel themselves, changed feelings that do but without our awareness of them, and consciousness *of* this capacity for self-feeling which is immanent to physiological change. For if, as Spenser's sequence implies, Red Crosse's "chaunged powres" gradually begin to "feel themselves," at least "at first," it is only as what Montaigne calls "light effects, that my senses produced of themselves" (II, 6; 187)—sensory transformations that are independent of full first-person awareness. Galen argues that "a small change in bodies brings about a discriminating perception of the power of the thing that produced it—when the part altered is sentient, of course—but does not yet cause pain," an account which applies well to Red Crosse's internal changes here, in which the altered parts are sensible to their own changes without "yet" implicating consciousness.[14] For Spenser as for Montaigne, this middle state is in many ways the most interesting of the three, a threshold between unconsciousness and consciousness which proves to be a richly textured sensory state unto itself rather than a one-dimensional line—"a feeling of faintness" which, as we saw with Sidney's "forsaken Knight," emerges in the syncope between personhood and unconsciousness. Like Galen, both authors treat the self-sensing of the body as a cognitive power unto itself: Montaigne's "senses" and Spenser's "powres" are the subjects of their own grammatical clauses, just as they are the principal subjects of the sentient states the two authors are attempting to describe. Such a power is neither strictly first-person nor third-person in nature—rather, it seems to occupy the margin between the impersonal processes of the body and the self-aware space of mental experience.

Along these lines, what Spenser calls Red Crosse's "carelessness" can also be seen as a phenomenological disposition—a failure to fully register his changing internal state and what it is telling him. This failure leaves him vulnerable not only to Duessa's seductions, but also to the assault of the giant Orgoglio, who now bursts on the scene and handily defeats his unprepared opponent. Only after the arrival of Orgoglio, when it is far too late, does Red Crosse seem to become fully conscious of what is happening to him; directly thereafter, however, he falls into his "stound":

> Yet goodly court he made still to his Dame,
> Pourd out in loosnesse on the grassy grownd,
> Both carelesse of his health, and of his fame:
> Till at the last he heard a dreadfull sownd,
> Which through the wood loud bellowing, did rebownd,
> That all the earth for terrour seemd to shake,
> And trees did tremble. Th'Elfe therewith astownd,
> Vpstarted lightly from his looser make,
> And his vnready weapons gan in hand to take.
>
> . . .
>
> That when the knight he spide, he gan aduance
> With huge force and insupportable mayne,
> And towardes him with dreadfull fury praunce;
> Who haplesse, and eke hopelesse, all in vaine
> Did to him pace, sad battaile to darrayne,
> Disarmd, disgrast, and inwardly dismayde,
> And eke so faint in every ioynt and vaine,

Through that fraile fountaine, which him feeble made
That scarsely could he weeld his bootlesse single blade.

The Geaunt strooke so maynly mercilesse,
That could have ouerthrowne a stony towre,
And were not heauenly grace, that him did blesse,
He had beene pouldred all, as thin as flowre:
But he was wary of that deadly stowre,
And lightly lept from vnderneath the blow:
Yet so exceeding was the villeins powre
That with the wind it did him ouerthrow,
And all his sences stound, that still he lay full low. (1.7.7–12)

Besieged by Orgoglio, Red Crosse at last spurs his dissipated sensorium into awareness, the third of the three states described above. "Wary of that deadly stowre," he is now in a state of full consciousness which marks the counterpoint to the moment in which "his chaunged powres at first themselues not felt." But what this sequential unfolding of phenomenological states means in Red Crosse's case is that the state of full consciousness or "wariness" comes *after* the onset of the event he is supposed to be wary of. Indeed, there is considerable irony in Spenser's choice of word here, and in the discrepancy between feeling and awareness that it so precisely delineates: what it serves to highlight is the fact that Red Crosse was *not* wary when he should have been, but rather continued to "make goodly court" even after his changed powers began to feel themselves. A. C. Hamilton glosses "stowre" as "assault" here, but in Spenser the word more usually means—like the word "stound"—a "time of turmoil and stress" (*OED n.*, 3a).[15] It thus suggests that Red Crosse is finally aware not merely of Orgoglio's attack, but also, more broadly, of the dangerous state, at once internal and external, into which he has been lapsing since the beginning of the canto. Red Crosse's consciousness, his "wariness" or "awareness," is thus separated from itself by a "stound" not only in its senses of pain and stupefaction, but also in its original sense of a unit of time—the unit of time which here intervenes before he can grasp what self-feeling has already perceived. In situations of danger and trial, it is our state of feeling—and of our feeling *of* feeling—which really determines our actions and our moral state; consciousness looks on, if at all, as a tardy and helpless spectator. Much as Montaigne cannot reconstruct his own "stound" until he remembers it the next day, so Red Crosse's "wariness" here is intrinsically belated with respect to his biological self-feeling—and is intrinsically belated, therefore, with regard to the possibility of meaningful intervention. As with the brother Diamond, by the time Red Crosse is fully "feeling life to fyle," it is too late—he "fell, and deadly slept."

In his essay "On Some Omissions of Introspective Psychology," William James argues that all conscious experience is characterized by a structure of temporal deferral: "A feeling, to be named, judged, or perceived, must already be past."[16] Feeling itself, meanwhile, is characterized by a "feltness" which is entirely independent of consciousness: "But the feltness which is its essence is its own immanent and intrinsic feltness at the moment of being experienced, and has nothing to do with the way in which future conscious acts may feel about it."[17] James's account implies that "feltness" can itself be "experienced" independently of consciousness—that we can feel our own feelings without knowing it until later on. This is exactly what happens to Red Crosse in this sequence: his "changed powers" at first feel themselves unconsciously, while his "wariness" only registers them later. Spenser provides a more condensed account of a similar state at the analogous moment in book 5 when Radegund lifts up her visor and reveals herself to Artegall, enabling her to defeat and then imprison him just as Orgoglio does to Red Crosse: "He saw his senses straunge astonishment" (5.5.12). In both these cases Spenser describes, with a phenomenological precision that criticism of *The Faerie Queene* has not yet recognized, a cognitive state that goes beyond mere stupefaction. As with Red Crosse's changed powers, it is Artegall's senses rather than his mind that are at the center of the action; it is they that are subject to an astonishment which has already set in when seeing becomes apprised of it. Consciousness, meanwhile, looks on helplessly from afterwards, so that what both characters become conscious of, paradoxically, is a caesura in consciousness itself. This caesura is characterized by that interval of time called a "stound," and it is first experienced by the senses feeling their own change rather than by the first person. The deferred naming that is characteristic of Spenserian allegory is closely attuned to this inherent belatedness of consciousness, as exposed by the "stound": to the fact that we tend not to be aware of what we experience until after the fact—and thus until it is, more often than not, too late to respond or react.

James's account of the belatedness of consciousness can help us, finally, to connect this phenomenological account of the scene to its moral significance, which so far we have overlooked. If Red Crosse had become fully aware of the physical changes induced by the fountain as soon as they started to happen, he might have been able to forestall them in some way; at the very least, he might have already been on the alert when Orgoglio arrived on the scene a few moments later. But if the deferral of Red

Crosse's "wariness"—and the whole sequence of physiological changes he undergoes in the meantime—were not simply accidents but rather, as James suggests, intrinsic to the structure of the mind itself, then there was perhaps little that Red Crosse could do. The "feltness" of his altered state could not be translated into full consciousness without an interval—an interval in which Orgoglio leaps in and catches him defenseless. Spenser's nuanced phenomenology in this scene thus tells us something theologically relevant as well: it tells us that sinful states can take hold of us on a level that lies beneath that conscious awareness itself, that sin is inside us, and is changing us, before we know it.[18] The belatedness of Red Crosse's consciousness goes hand in hand with the irresistibility of sin: it is not simply that sensations and passions threaten to destabilize us, it is that they take advantage of a destabilization which has always already taken place, a permanent tremor of corporeal vitality in the face of which conscious self-knowledge is always tardy and weak. If the "stound" is, as in Massumi's account of affective autonomy, the missing half-second of decision and volition in which we might opt to avoid sin, then for Spenser it is, by virtue of its very structure, a volition which is by and large out of our hands and in those of God's grace.

Near the beginning of his *Institutes*, John Calvin describes the recognition of sin not in terms of an awakening or epiphany, but rather as a dismaying and destruction:

> Hereof proceded that trembling and amasednesse [*horror ille et stupor*], wherewith the Scripture in many places reciteth that the holy men were striken and astonished so ofte as they perceiued the presence of God. For when we se that they whiche in his absence did stande assured and unmoved, so sone as he discloseth hys glorye, beginne so to quake and are so dismayed, that they fall downe, yea are swallowed vp and in manner as destroyed with feare of death: it is to be gathered thereby that manne is neuer sufficiently touched and inwardly moued wyth knowledge of his owne basenesse vntil he haue compared himselfe to the maiestie of God.[19]

Calvin is describing exactly what Red Crosse experiences in the "stound," a state of "trembling and amasednesse" (*horror ille et stupor*) in which he is "so dismayed"—Spenser perhaps picked up on this word—"that [he] fall[s] down." For Calvin, a sinner attains "knowledge of his own baseness" not through introspection, but rather through this shattering experience in which he is "striken and astonished" by the unfathomable majesty of God. In *The Sinne Unto Death*, the seventeenth-century

Puritan divine Thomas Bedford describes such an experience as, precisely, a "stound." He is discussing those same sins of presumption and pride to which Red Crosse succumbs in book 1:

> There is a sinne of Presumption proceeding from pride, and arrogancie, *wilfulnesse and haughtines of heart*: which both wilfully and contemptuously causeth a man to sinne against God. *Wilfully*, as presuming upon Gods mercy and his owne future repentance, *Contemptuously*, as despising and contemning the Law of God. These are great, grosse, and grieuous, especially if the particular sinne be either Idolatrie which is the forsaking of God, or witchcraft, which is a ioyning Couenant with Satan. In these, to sinne against knowledge, against the checke of conscience, presumptuously, wilfully, and contemptuously, is a sinne that may make the earth to tremble, and the heauens to sweat with amazednes, that *earth should thus transgresse against heauen, man against God.*[20]

Despite our knowledge of the good and the "checks of conscience" which proceed from it, we still commit sinful acts of all kinds. Conscience—the consciousness of what is good and bad—is insufficient to *make* us good, and it is this impotence of conscience which makes the stound, which totally overpowers our consciousness, so necessary: "Yea it may on a suddaine set a man into a stound, and driue his thoughts to a perplexitie to consider what further degree of sinne there can bee founde or thought of, into which the Sonne of *Adam* may slip or plunge himselfe."[21] Bedford's "stound" consists not merely in self-awareness and realization, but also in an experience of "perplexitie" which strikes us "on a suddaine" and without our premonition or consent. What Spenser shows us in *The Faerie Queene* is how such a "stound" might fit into the passage of time and the flow of subjective experience: how a proto-apocalyptic moment, in which time is arrested and the sinner comes face to face with the sinfulness built in to the very fabric of his living body, might play out on the level of the senses before the day on which time comes to a stop once and for all.

Stounds and Spirits

When Arthur rescues Red Crosse from Orgoglio's dungeon, where he has been imprisoned since his hapless defeat in canto 7, we are given a vivid picture of the stound's long-term effects on his body:

> His rawbone armes, whose mighty brawned bowrs
> Were wont to riue steele plates, and helmets hew,
> Were cleane consum'd, and all his vitall powres
> Decayd, and all his flesh shronk vp like withered flowres. (1.8.41)

It is Red Crosse's "vital powers," then—the "chaunged powres" of canto 7—that have been at the core of Red Crosse's experience throughout this central sequence of book 1. Though the phrase "vital powers" is not necessarily a technical one, it is ultimately Galenic in origin, part of the dissemination of Galenic ideas in the European Middle Ages and Renaissance which also gave wide currency to the notion of the four humors.[22] For Galen, the human body is divided into three distinct systems, each characterized by a different set of activities and each seated in a different primary organ: the liver governs digestion and nutrition, the heart governs the flow of vital fluids, and the brain governs sensation and motion. Galen characterizes each of these systems as an autonomous *dunamis*—a word usually translated as "capacity," "faculty," or "power"—and argues that each *dunamis*, in turn, acts by means of an ethereal substance he terms *pneuma* or spirit:

> Now I showed clearly that the brain is a fount, as it were, of the psychic pneuma which is refreshed and nourished by the inspiration of air and from what the netlike plexus arrangement (*rete mirabile*) provides. My exposition of the vital pneuma was not, however, similarly clear. It is certainly not implausible that it seems to be contained in the heart and arteries, this too being nourished particularly from respiration, but now from the blood as well. If there is a psychical pneuma, it too would be contained in the liver and the veins.[23]

It is not a coincidence that this passage appears in a section of the *Method of Medicine* dedicated to fainting or syncope, which Galen defines precisely as an "acute collapse of capacity [*dunamis*]."[24] Galen's account is echoed by early modern writers such as Helkiah Crooke, who defines "*Syncope*" as "a swounding where the vital spirits faile,"[25] as well as by Robert Burton: "The *Vitall Spirits* are made in the Heart of the *Naturall*, which by the Arteries are transported to all the other parts: if these *Spirits* cease, then life ceaseth, as in a *Syncope* or Swouning."[26]

Neither Galen nor his early modern acolytes would therefore have been surprised by the "decaying" of Red Crosse's vital powers following his swoon, nor would they have wondered greatly to see Sans Joy, defeated in a duel by Red Crosse, lying "in slombring swownd nigh voyd of vitall spright" (1.5.19). Swoons and spirits were so closely linked by Galen that one of the fullest expositions of the spirits in all of his work is actually nested within his account of swoons. And yet where for Galen the vital spirits constitute only one of the three equally important systems that underlie bodily processes, in these and other passages of *The Faerie Queene* Spenser presents them as a more central force. "Vital spright" seems to be responsible not merely for a subset of physiological functions, but for the vitality and for the sentience of Sans Joy and Red Crosse as a whole. In this regard, Spenser's account accords with medieval and early modern medicine, which, while usually Galenic in inspiration, often gives the vital spirits a more significant position than Galen himself did. In one of the two major medical textbooks for the Middle Ages, for example—Avicenna's *Canon Medicinae*—there appears to be only one dominant form of spirit: the vital spirit or *rooh*, translated into Latin as *spiritus*. Originating in the heart, that is, in the natural faculty, *rooh* or *spiritus* supports not only the vital faculty but the natural and psychic faculties as well: "when the vital force [*rooh*] is produced with an appropriate temperament, it acquires a faculty which enables all organs of the body to receive the other faculties such as the nervous faculty."[27] For the "vital faculty," Avicenna tells us, "conditions the vital force and sensation and movement and prepares it for sensory and motor activity of the brain";[28] it "is the power which enables organs to receive sensory and motor activity and perform the various functions of life."[29] Avicenna is in some ways returning here to Aristotle, with whom he claims, against Galen, that "all faculties originate from the heart."[30] But by combining this Aristotelian claim with a Galenic insistence on the importance of *pneuma* (to which Aristotle does not give as much significance), Avicenna develops a physiological system vitalized by a single predominant form of spirit.

It is not surprising, then, that in Spenser and other medieval and early modern authors we frequently find references to the "vital spirits," or to the "spirits" broadly, without the tripartite distinctions that usually accompany them in Galen, and as being responsible for all sorts of activities. The poet Guido Cavalcanti, an early European reader of Avicenna, describes vision as "quel sottile spirito che vede" ("that subtle spirit which sees"), making *spiritus* not merely the instrument of vision but actually capable of vision itself.[31] Meanwhile, in the earliest extant critical commentary on Spenser's *Faerie Queene*—Kenelm Digby's short treatise on the mysterious numerology in the 22nd stanza of book 2, canto 9—the vital spirits alone are mentioned, not as part of a specific bodily system, but as responsible for keeping soul and body together:

> By which Quadrate, I conceive, that he meaneth the foure principall humors in mans Bodie, *viz. Choler, Blood, Phleme*, and *Melancholy*: which if they be distempered and unfitly mingled, dissolution of the whole doth immediately ensue: like to a building which falls to ruine, if the foundation and Base of it be unsound or disordered. And in some of these, the vitall spirits are contained and preserved, which the other keep in convenient temper; and as long as they do so, the soul and bodie dwell together like good friends.[32]

Digby here echoes John Donne, who in his poem "The Extasie" also connects the spirits to the relationship of body and soul:

> As our blood labours to beget
> Spirits, as like souls as it can,
> Because such fingers need, to knit
> That subtle knot, which makes us man.[33]

For both Donne and Digby, the spirits are not tied to specific functions; rather, the vital spirits—or simply the spirits in general—serve to keep the soul tied to the body during life; thus it is they which, in closest proximity to the soul itself, seem to be most intimately tied to the state of the organism as a whole. Digby's account also hints at what happens when the spirits no longer function properly—"as long as they do, the soul and bodie dwell together like good friends," he says, but presumably when the spirits fail to operate properly—in a moment such as Red Crosse's stound or Guyon's swoon—that friendship is threatened. For Avicenna, in fact, the vital spirits are also what bring us back when we swoon: "the faculty of life continues to exist in a paralysed organ so that when the morbid process disappears it is able to recover its sensation and movement"; "it is because of the vital faculty being there that the organ is able to regain its sensation and movement."[34] Because the spirits underlie all of our other functions and tie soul and body together, they are both particularly vulnerable to attack and are particularly important in our defense.

For medieval and early modern medicine, it is the vital spirits—whether alone or as the most significant of three different forms of spirit—that embody the soul, giving it life in the context of a material world; when they are threatened, the link between body and soul itself threatens to dissolve, and only they can keep it together. Yet while several critics have commented on the significance of these notions for Renaissance literature—and in particular for the more fully embodied subjectivity that it implies—to my knowledge none have seen just how far they extend in the imagination of a writer such as Spenser.[35] For most if not all of the authors I have cited here, the spirits are merely the seat or "instrument" (Galen's term is *organon*) of the soul.[36] But Spenser does not feel obliged to qualify their role in this way. For Spenser, the spirits do not merely sustain feeling; just as Cavalcanti's *spirito* is itself capable of seeing, so Spenser's spirits are themselves capable of feeling, and indeed of feeling their own activity and state. In this regard, Spenser echoes the ideas of Bernardino Telesio and anticipates those of Francis Bacon, who believes, as D. P. Walker shows, that "spirits can themselves feel and perceive"; for Bacon it follows that all matter, insofar as it is animated by *spiritus*, is endowed with perception.[37] As we will see, Spenser too imagines a cosmos innervated by sentient *spiritus*, and whether or not Spenser actually identifies the spirits with the soul (as did Melanchthon and Servetus), in his descriptions the spirits are treated as responsible for many of the states which today would be understood in terms of consciousness.[38] Michael Schoenfeldt has argued that humoral language speaks in a palpable way to what the body feels like—"these accounts describe not so much the actual workings of the body as the experience of the body"[39]—and surely his account can be applied to the spirits as well. If they do not seem to correspond to "a particular description of bodily process,"[40] this is because what the spirits feel like is simply the feeling of vitality itself—the feeling of being alive, being "there," that intensity of "sensible warm motion" experienced in the strange temporal rupture known as a "stound." The spirits, in other words, are the material expression of the feeling of feeling generally, rather than of a particular sensation or object, and to think about how they feel, we should try think about what it feels like simply to exist, to be alive, to partake of that faculty whose operations are at once heightened and compromised when we faint. If for Guido Cavalcanti, visual *pneuma* is not merely what enables vision but itself that which sees, then for Spenser what the spirits in general feel is simply the fact of consciousness itself. Since the vital spirits are, in Avicenna's account, what sustains sentience in general, it stands to reason that they too (at least in principle) should be palpable, for without the feeling *of* feeling which they enable, the five senses themselves are not operative.

Thus Spenser's idea that Red Crosse is in possession of powers that can feel their own activity takes what was originally a Galenic-Avicennian idea to its extreme, Baconian conclusion. He imagines that those spirits are in fact capable of a kind of proprioreception—a capacity to feel their own state which we might understand as a kind of consciousness without selfhood, as the self-experience of biological life itself. Insofar as vitality and sentience are inseparable, then the vital spirits must have a power of feeling that is virtually indistinguishable from their operations more broadly, which we can discern to the extent that we can feel our own body's workings. The spirits must be able to feel themselves, and the moment they stop doing so, we die, for their sentience and their life-supporting function are inseparable. To live is to sense and vice versa, and it is in the vital spirits, for Avicenna, that these two interchangeable functions are seated. Regarding Henry's concept of life's auto-affection in terms of the activity of the spirits makes it easier to grasp intuitively: if sensory action is embodied in a mobile, fluid substance—if consciousness itself is comprised by the movement of a rarefied fluid—then for sensation to sense itself means for it simply to feel that substance's movements. What Henry understands as the self-affection of thought is, in this account, the self-awareness built in to the sensitive spirits themselves—thought conceived, quite literally, as a current of self-sensing life that flows through us at all times.

Yet since it is what underlies the activities of the external senses, self-sensing is not often palpable as such; indeed, in its very orientation toward itself, it remains elusive to *us*, comprising a layer of unfelt affect which is almost always invisible, the substance of that "self, whom . . . we do not see." As Drew Daniel has argued, insofar as Baconian *spiritus* has the capacity to putrefy and die of its own accord, it "instantiates the fundamental ontological disparity between plural spirits and singular Persons,"[41] and a similar disparity is evident in Spenser as well. But although the affective life of the spirits may be, as Daniel suggests, distinct from our first-person emotional life, it *can* be felt when our outer senses break down and the self-feeling of our sensorium becomes apparent, just as we see in Red Crosse's "stound." When the external orientation of our powers of awareness and sense is threatened, the underlying operations of the spirits themselves come into view, as though we had to lose consciousness in order to feel them fully. In the House of Alma, Spenser will take this paradox to its fullest limit: Guyon's trance will take him deep into "the original dimension of life's phenomenality in which life experiences itself in the invisible," and make it briefly but brilliantly visible.[42]

Guyon's Vital Trance

Guyon's trance at the end of book 2, canto 7—a long-standing crux in interpretations of the book—bears many analogies to Red Crosse's "stound" in book 1. Broadly speaking, the two books are similar: both heroes must encounter a range of allegorical figures who embody the opposite of the books' titular virtues before they can fulfill their tasks: the rescue of Una's parents from the dragon in Red Crosse's case, and the destruction of the Bower of Bliss in Guyon's. In canto 7 of each book, at the midpoint of their journeys, both heroes descend underground for about a canto, Red Crosse into the dungeon of Orgoglio's castle and Guyon into Mammon's Cave. Both subsequently have to be rescued by Arthur, and then spend a canto in a healing house before fulfilling their quests. At the center of each sequence is a faint: Red Crosse's "stound" at the hands of Orgoglio, and Guyon's "trance" on exiting Mammon's Cave.

Given the broader similarities between books 1 and 2, it is hardly surprising that critics should have interpreted the two faints along similar lines. Red Crosse's "stound," we saw, has a phenomenological dimension which has hitherto gone unnoticed, but it has a fairly clear moral meaning as well: it represents Red Crosse's continuing entrapment by sin, and in particular by pride. Hugh MacLachlan applies a similar lens to Guyon's trance, seeing it too as a spiritual metaphor: "There is, I think, no way to explain satisfactorily this curious episode except to understand Guyon's faint, not as a physical collapse, but as a metaphor for his spiritual state after (and before) his stay in the Cave of Mammon."[43] Yet while we do not have to look far to find the moral and theological explanation for Red Crosse's "stound," Spenser himself explicitly declares that the causes of Guyon's faint have less to do with "foolish pride" (1.8.1) than with "want of food, and sleepe":

> And now he has so long remained there,
> That vitall powres gan wexe both weake and wan,
> For want of food, and sleepe, which two vpbeare,
> Like mightie pillours, this fraile life of man,
> That none without the same enduren can.
> For now three dayes of men were full outwrought,
> Since he this hardie enterprize began:
> For thy great *Mammon* fairely he besought,
> Into the world to guide him backe, as he him brought.
>
> The God, though loth, yet was constraind t'obay,
> For lenger time, then that, no liuing wight
> Below the earth, might suffred be to stay:
> So backe againe, him brought to liuing light.
> But all so soone as his enfeebled spright
> Gan sucke this vitall aire into his brest,

> As ouercome with too exceeding might,
> The life did flit away out of her nest,
> And all his senses were with deadly fit opprest. (2.7.65–66)

There is something very Montaignean about this matter-of-fact account of the swoon. Where we might have expected moral or metaphysical commentary—an excursus on human frailty or a divine vision—Spenser instead presents us with a mundane bodily ailment. To supply our own moral or theological allegory here is, therefore, to ignore the striking fact that for once it is absent—absent, moreover, where a series of parallels to book 1 might well have led us to expect one, and where Spenser must therefore have been very aware of what he was doing.

What Spenser does call our attention to are Guyon's "vitall powres," which are weakened by "want of food, and sleepe." These "vital powers," I have argued, are identical to Galenic *pneuma*, and indeed in the *Method of Medicine* Galen himself lists both lack of nourishment and sleeplessness as possible causes of the weakened *pneuma* which leads to *syncope*.[44] Again, the vital powers are described in terms which render them almost independent of the character himself, part of that "Selfe . . . whom we do not see": Spenser's language in stanza 63 suggests that it is not Guyon but rather his powers themselves that need the sustenance. Guyon himself, after all, has somehow managed to ignore that need for three days, and it is for this reason that they assert themselves with such intractable urgency now, bypassing his agency altogether. Throughout his time in the cave, after all, Guyon's attention was intently absorbed by a range of tempting spectacles; not merely refusing to satisfy bodily needs, he was failing to feel them altogether. The hunger itself must have been present physiologically, of course, growing far beyond its customary levels in order to strike him with such force now. In his case, too, we can therefore say that "his changed powers at first themselves not felt," that at first they were merely unfelt affects—and that it is still they, rather than he, that do finally feel themselves as he comes up toward the mouth of Mammon's Cave. In the form of hunger, and "want of sleep" as well, the vital powers are thus not simply sources of energy and movement subordinate to consciousness; they are also sentient and subjective powers unto themselves, and are deeper and more foundational than it.

While hunger and thirst are the ultimate causes of Guyon's swoon, its proximate cause is his intake of vital air on exiting the cave; here too Spenser's account suggests a highly Galenic conception of fainting. In his discussion of *syncope*, Galen warns us to "take heed of the substance of [the air] being inspired in order that it may be most *eukratic* and extremely pure without anything defiling, not taking on any admixture from mines, kilns, or pits";[45] *pneuma* itself, after all, is formed by the inhalation of air in the first place, so it is not surprising that the quality of the air should affect it. Guyon's case might seem to be the opposite: he has just *left* a cave which was presumably full of stifling and toxic air, and he is now breathing *eukratic* air for the first time in three days. Why should it be this "vital air" that causes him to swoon? Presumably the influx is simply too sudden and too great. His internal *krasis* has been shifted by his three days in the cave, and it is therefore ill-adjusted to this sudden flood of fresh air. As Galen frequently reminds us, cures must always be tempered to the internal constitution of the patient, and thus there is something almost inadvertently intemperate about the sudden intake of "vital air" here. As James Nohrnberg puts it, Guyon faints because of "an adverse reaction to a too violent application of a contrary."[46]

Guyon's faint is thus less an allegory of his spiritual condition, or a lesson in the vicissitudes of self-regulation, than it is a moment in which, at the edges of total unconsciousness, embodied subjectivity experiences itself—the immersion in physical life that it is—with heightened intensity.[47] This experience necessitates a passage through insentience, in which unfelt affect makes itself felt so suddenly, and with a power so great that, paradoxically, it temporarily neutralizes feeling altogether. When Guyon emerges from the cave, his insentience serves to silhouette, as it were, not only his neglected inner feelings, but a whole world of feeling "outside" him as well. While first-person consciousness is now absent, everything surrounding Guyon—from the "living light" to the "vital air"—is very much alive, and indeed now seems to come alive with new intensity. If Guyon's attitude in the cave exhibited an excessive confidence in his own self-sufficiency, therefore, that self-sufficiency in part reflected a belief that he could withdraw himself from this system of vital circulation that transcends the bounds between subject and object—a system in which his "vital Powers" are interconnected with "vital air" and "living light" and with what Spenser earlier called, in a characteristic hypallage, "liuing aire" (2.proem.1). Spread out across this external world of living substance (like Bacon's), Guyon's impersonal, "vital powers" have in a sense become more visible than ever before.[48] But by temporarily displacing them to the world outside him, the swoon also speaks to a mode of sentience which ultimately does not respect boundaries between inner and outer at all. It makes explicit the third-personness which is always characteristic of self-sensing, and which, before Guyon's descent into the cave, was as much a matter of what was inside Guyon as of what was without.

Initially, Guyon does appear to have been emptied out of all life by his swoon. He lies on the ground unconscious for almost all of the subsequent canto—with, as the Palmer puts it, "all his senses drowned in deepe senselesse waue" (2.8.24). Yet this line is something of a paradox, for while telling us that Guyon is drowned in insentience, it also offers a powerful evocation of what this insentience *feels like*—a feeling of going under, of being pulled into an element in which our ordinary awareness will no longer be functional. The wave that carries Guyon along unconsciously and involuntarily is, in a way, a characterization of the world of third-person vitality into which Guyon's life has been temporarily dispersed. But just as in Montaigne's description of his swoon, this yielding has a felt quality of its own: like Montaigne, Spenser compares it to being pulled into an encompassing tactile element, to swimming or to floating in a cloud. To be "sencelesse" here is, therefore, not to be lacking in feeling altogether, but to transcend, as it were, those external and internal senses by means of which we perceive intentional objects, and to interact with an encompassing material element in a different, more immediate way—by means of that "cerebral auto-affection" which Catherine Malabou attributes to patients with brain damage. When Spenser describes Guyon as "slumbring fast / In senselesse dreame" (2.8.4), his phrasing again paradoxically associates "senselessness" with a form of felt experience: a "dream." Guyon's dream is "senselesse" in that it lacks the rich sensory and pictorial content which is usually associated with dreams, and which is characteristic of Spenser's own dream poetry; yet it is still a dream. Montaigne too had described his swoon as a dream: "Whatsoever the soule did assist it with was but a dreame, being lightly touched, and only sprinkled by the soft impression of the sense" (II, 6; 187). As we saw, it is the sheer feeling—the "soft impression"—of sensation as such rather than any particular object of sensation that Montaigne experiences in his dream, and Guyon, I would submit, is "dreaming" in the same way. That is, he is experiencing nothing other than the self-feeling and self-manifestation of the body's vital powers themselves, humming away while outer and inner sentience are dormant—or rather, since Guyon himself is absent, we should say that they are experiencing themselves, that life is experiencing itself. In the next canto we will get a closer view of what that impersonal "humming" looks like. For now, we can see that where Spenser's early poetry, like medieval dream poetry, offers a form of transfigured objective experience, dreaming in *The Faerie Queene* (like *The Faerie Queene* itself as dream) is so deeply subjective, so immanent to the rhythms of affective life, that it experiences no object at all—only itself.

The faint thus opens a portal in the direction of that physical and physiological vitality which the following cantos will describe for us in so much detail: away from first-person consciousness and towards everything that takes place in its absence, what Montaigne calls our "internall progress." Spenser is stripping consciousness away and finding not blind mechanism, but rather a living welter whose self-experience radiates out into the physical world itself. The attempt to contain that welter only causes it to surge out more violently, so that prompted by the explosion of suppressed feeling which occasions Guyon's swoon, we are now plunged into a world of affects to which we are normally blind. Hunger, sleep, and breath are just some of its constituent elements, and as we move into canto 8, Spenser focuses more on the affective dimension of nonconscious life. (As opposed to the unconscious in the Freudian sense, which is dominated by repressed desires, for Spenser, *non*-conscious life consists in the range of processes which keep us alive on a biological level—this life, I have been arguing, is itself a form of consciousness, disclosed by the faint.) The brothers Pyrochles and Cymochles—representing Rage and Concupiscence respectively—did battle with Guyon throughout cantos 4 to 6; he managed to defeat but not destroy them. Now, as the Palmer watches over Guyon's "slumbering corpse," the two brothers return with renewed vehemence (much like Adam and Eve's conscious dreams):

> At last he spide, where towards him did pace
> Two Paynim knights, all armd as bright as skie,
> And them beside an aged Sire did trace,
> And farre before a light-foot Page did flie,
> That breathed strife and troublous enmitie;
> Those were the two sonnes of *Acrates* old,
> Who meeting earst with *Archimago* slie,
> Foreby that idle strond, of him were told,
> That he, which earst them combatted, was *Guyon* bold.
>
> Which to auenge on him they dearely vowd,
> Where euer that on ground they mote him find;
> False *Archimage* prouokt their corage prowd,
> And stryfull *Atin* in their stubborne mynd
> Coles of contention and whot vengeance tynd.
> Now bene they come, whereas the Palmer sate,
> Keeping that slombred corse to him assynd;
> Well knew they both his person, sith of late
> With him in bloodie armes they rashly did debate. (2.8.10–11)

It is as if Guyon's temperance, having exhausted itself in Mammon's Cave, now unravels, leaving him more vulnerable to the depredations of intemperate drives than before (just as, after resisting the lures of the maidens in the Bower of Bliss, he will unleash a "tempest of wrathfulness"). Thus, as we saw with Red Crosse's "stound," Guyon's faint bears witness to those unconscious corporeal stirrings which limit our capacity to transform ourselves without external aid. Here, however, it is a matter less of sensory and sensual attractions than of invisible exigencies buried deep within the unfelt layers of the self. The pressures of passion and desire will in fact become temporarily visible in the second part of the House of Alma, but insofar as Guyon's swoon is needed to unlock that vision, Spenser forcefully reminds us that such feelings ordinarily lie, as Gordon Teskey puts it, on a "level deeper than the senses themselves," where sensation abuts on the "senselesse":

> We realize now that the point of putting Guyon on the brink of death, keeping him unconscious throughout, is to isolate and emphasize these somatic consequences—the unconscious power of rage and concupiscence as habits—which take hold on the body at a level deeper than the senses themselves: "By this Sir *Guyon* from his traunce awakt, / Life having maistered her sencelesse foe" (2.8.53). The "sencelesse foe" is death, which is beaten back when Guyon returns to his senses; but it is also, as Hamilton remarks, the morbid effects represented by Cymocles and Pyrocles. While manifesting themselves in the senses, rage and concupiscence fasten on the body addictively, on a level deeper than the senses themselves.[49]

Self-control is impotent to rescue us from forces that operate within an "addictive" somatic system that is largely independent of the conscious mind. There is no way to escape the consequences of that system without outside intervention, which in fact is abundantly present in canto 8—in the form of the angel, the Palmer, and finally Arthur. Without such assistance, the effort to oppose them is not only fruitless but counterproductive, enabling them to bounce back with a force that is redoubled inasmuch as it is now unanticipated.

These sources of intervention are all, so to speak, "vertical": they come to Guyon's aid not only from without but also, as it were, from above, from a place of higher moral perfection and purity. Their heavenly provenance may seem to reinforce the idea that Guyon's swoon is a spiritual condition which, like Red Crosse's in book 1, requires transcendental intervention—grace—for it to be remedied. And yet in a little-noticed but crucial line, Spenser names a different source of power as that which, finally, saves Guyon from his swoon, in other words from the unconscious processes, figured by the characters of Cymochles and Pyrochles, which have been victimizing him throughout canto 8: "By this Sir *Guyon* from his traunce awakt, / Life hauing maistered her sencelesse foe:" (2.8.53). The discreet and yet all-important past participle in the second line suggests that, besides the battle between Arthur and Cymochles and Pyrochles, a second and perhaps more significant battle has been going on, this one inside Guyon, between "Life," the vital powers, and a "sencelesse foe" to which that "Life" is in close proximity. If life's enemy is described as "her sencelesse foe," then as in Galen and Avicenna, "Life" itself must simply be "sense" at the most basic and broadest level—not the activity of any one particular sense, whether inner or outer, but rather the power that governs them all, enabling them to operate in general and enabling us to feel their activity; in other words, those vital spirits which Avicenna simply called *rooh* or *spiritus*. As in Avicenna's account in the *Canon Medicinae*, these vital spirits do not simply fail when the body faints; on the contrary, it is they which fight against insentience in order to restore our sensorium to itself. If the vital spirits are not directly responsible for the activity of the five external senses, it is nevertheless they which govern sensation as such, the sheer fact of feeling; it is they which we feel when we feel merely that we are alive and are sentient; and thus it is they which—sensible to sensation's abeyance and the workings of its "sencelesse foe"—step in here to rescue it. Although the angel descends from above and charges the Palmer with Guyon's protection, he accomplishes little else on Guyon's behalf; it is this "life," hovering around him horizontally in the "vital air" and "living light," which ultimately intervenes to save the Knight of Temperance here.

Spenser's personification is perfectly poised. His grammar creates a distinction between Sir Guyon himself, subject of the main verb, and "Life," subject of the participle—allowing us to see that this Life has been covertly active while Guyon has been absent. As the feminine gender also suggests, Life (the vital spirits) is being personified here as an allegorical force that is independent of Guyon's conscious agency, just as the life which is shared by Priamond, Diamond, and Triamond transcends any one of them. At the same time, Spenser does not turn that Life into a full-blown human character, and in this way he allows his personification to work as more than a vehicle or mere artifice. What the Galenic theory of the spirits (and its medieval version in Avicenna) help us see is that to describe such "life," as Spenser does, as having sense and agency of her own is not merely to indulge in poetic fancy; rather, it is to hint at a system in which the senses and vitality are actually properties of a matter to which first-person consciousness is subordinate. Such personification is thus not defined by the attribution of human consciousness to something inanimate, but rather by the effort to think consciousness itself differently, as an impersonal self-sensing inherent in living matter rather than as the abstract space of first-personness and representation. For although Spenser does not say here, as he did with Red Crosse, that Guyon's powers "feel themselves," from their hunger and thirst to their rearguard action against his "sencelesse foe" it is clear that they do, somehow, sense Guyon's plight, and respond to it—without ever representing it to themselves or being "aware" in our post-Enlightenment sense of that word. Instead, we should think of the activity of these powers as a "phenomenon of life, welling up in the radical interiority of its self-affection" to come to Guyon's rescue.[50] As Walter Charleton points out, if in "syncopes" and "swooning fits" "the *Heart* doth variously move, and agitate it self; as being offended with something preternatural and noxious to it, and irritated to resist and repell the same," it can do so "in respect only of some sense or feeling, by which it discerneth what is incommodious and harmfull"—though this sense is not, Charleton claims, available to consciousness.[51] Thus far from demonstrating either a descent from above or the "indistinction of life and death," Guyon's swoon and his subsequent awakening testify to the self-engendering of a vital spirit which, mobilizing itself out of nothing more than its own power of feeling, separates life from death at every instant and not only here.[52] Inasmuch as that spirit is invisible to the senses and to thought, Guyon's death serves to bring it to the fore—and, as we will shortly see, to plunge him into its depths.

Spenser's personification of Guyon's powers as Life is thus closer to the way Montaigne talks about the impersonal activities of his body than to the other allegorical characters in Spenser's own poetry. What Guyon, like Montaigne, discovers in his swoon is not the alternate objectivity of a dream-world, but rather the alternate *subjectivity* constituted by the autonomous life of the environmentally embedded human body—in other words, of what the Middle Ages and the Renaissance knew as the spirits. Far from being an image of spiritual death, the trance instead proves to be an essentially vital moment, one which corrects an excess of self-restraint by permitting Guyon's biological powers—"a life that is prior to and deeper than his capacity for conscious articulation"—to come into their own.[53] For those powers go beyond a sustaining role here: at bottom, what Montaigne and Spenser's near-personification of "Life" suggests is a vision of the human in which the line between the self-experience of bodily processes and subjective personhood no longer exists.

Spenserian personification returns in full force, of course, in the House of Alma, in which the body's anatomy and inner workings are all expressed by the extended allegory of a castle and its human garrison; Guyon is given a tour of the House by Alma (or the soul) herself. Criticism of Guyon's faint has tended to look backward to his descent into the Mammon's Cave rather than forward to this tour of the House of Alma, presumably because a canto-and-a-half intervene. Yet for Guyon, who was unconscious for almost all of canto 8, the two episodes directly follow one another, artfully syncopated by his syncope. And he faints, as we know, from inadequate attention to the ordinary processes of his body, of which he is now granted a much more intimate view than is normally feasible. Those "vital powers" first glimpsed in Guyon's swoon, and that sustain us just below the surface of first-person consciousness, are now explored in much greater depth and detail. And yet rather than giving Guyon a lesson in early modern anatomy or instructing him in the ways of self-discipline, what the House of Alma ultimately shows him is just how much of his own life transpires *beyond* what he can know or direct, as an element of vitality in which he is permanently immersed and which he is therefore unable to hold at the distance required for first-person consciousness—a distance which only the swoon allows him to overcome. If in the House of Alma that law is temporarily broken—if Guyon is briefly permitted to "see" processes which are normally invisible—it only serves to underscore how alien, precisely in their intimacy, those processes are. Inasmuch as Guyon's self-experience here is visual, it is itself a profoundly alienating one; the body's own self-experience, as the House of Alma itself will show us, happens independently of all conscious representation.

The order of the temperate body, after all—as opposed to that of the continent body—is independent of external control and repression; it is not so much a body whose drives are disciplined as it is a body whose drives regulate themselves.[54] Unveiled by Guyon's swoon, their autonomous activity resembles the motions Montaigne too describes as taking place during his faint: "our members have certaine offices, which they lend one to another" (II, 6; 187). Arthur and Guyon must fight off Alma's external enemies—Maleger and his troops—and yet provided that they do so, her inner workings require no supervision or intervention whatsoever in order to keep fulfilling their "certaine offices." Thus, Guyon and the Palmer visit the human body as tourists rather than as overlords, perceiving the "selfe, whom . . . we do not see" in a state of sustained wonder rather than of growing enlightenment: "[With] gazing wonder they their minds did fill; / For neuer had they seene so straunge a sight" (2.9.33).[55] The insistent personification of bodily anatomy and function serves to render the body's operations autonomous and strange rather than malleable and familiar; from the steward "Diet" (2.9.27) through "the maister Cooke . . . *Concoction*" (2.9.31) to that "old oldman" Memory (2.9.55), these figures are clearly the "mouvemens incogneus" described by Montaigne rather than the objects or instruments of conscious self-discipline. Harry Berger Jr. argues that Alma herself is "the rational power of consciousness," seated (as per Aristotle) in the heart, and yet this argument underestimates the originality and sincerity of Spenser's personifications, the way in which they detach consciousness from self-awareness and instead distribute it throughout the body—throughout which, after all, Alma herself seems to circulate.[56]

Indeed, the house's inner order is preserved not merely by a kind of unconscious mechanism, but rather by a sensory activity which is intrinsic to it and which lies deeper than the senses proper. For inasmuch as the *eukrasia* of the Galenic body depends on a "goodly ordinaunce" of qualities which are fundamentally subjective in nature, the self-regulating body is an inherently self-sensing one:

> It was a vaut ybuilt for great dispence,
> With many raunges reard along the wall;
> And one great chimney, whose long tonnell thence,
> The smoke forth threw. And in the midst of all
> There placed was a caudron wide and tall,
> Vpon a mighty furnace, burning whot,
> More whot, then *Aetn'*, or flaming *Mongiball*:
> For day and night it brent, ne ceased not,
> So long as any thing it in the caudron got.
>
> But to delay the heat, least by mischaunce
> It might breake out, and set the whole on fire,
> There added was by goodly ordinaunce,
> An huge great paire of bellowes, which did styre
> Continually, and cooling breath inspyre.
> About the Caudron many Cookes accoyld,
> With hookes and ladles, as need did require;
> The whiles the viandes in the vessell boyld
> They did about their businesse sweat, and sorely toyld. (2.9.29–30)

The well-ordered Galenic body is characterized by a balance of the four fundamental qualities: hot, cold, dry, and moist. In order to correct and adjust its own internal state, that body must therefore be able to sense itself and to sense its own sensations at any given time, and qualities which today would be understood as purely subjective are instead described—as in Red Crosse's "stound"—as intrinsic to a sensory life which is, if not quite objective, then independent of first-person consciousness. Spenser's personification serves less to embellish or teach than to acknowledge that bodily states can be subjective in and of themselves, and that vitality and sentience are therefore one and the same. How else, after all, can we speak of the body as maintaining a balance of cool and hot, for example, or dry and moist: qualities which must necessarily be experienced? Guyon and Arthur fight off enemies coming from without, through the five senses, so that the House of Alma's inhabitants can continue to sense their own *inner* state in peace—an essential prerequisite of self-regulation. Sensory organs serve more to keep out than to let in—the nose, for example, is described as a "portcullis" (2.9.24), while the eyes are "Two goodly Beacons" (2.9.46) which give rather than receive light—and it is no coincidence that the flesh or "Castle wall" is not, as some early editions had it, "sensible" but "fensible" (2.9.21). External sensation must be strictly regulated precisely so that internal self-sensing, on which the order of the whole body depends, can occur without interference.

It is hard to say what lesson there is for Guyon in all of this, and indeed, it is hard to know whether Guyon ever realizes that he is touring an extended representation of his own body in the first place: as Suzanne Wofford has observed, Spenser's characters tend to remain unaware that they are participating in an allegory.[57] But that is precisely the point, for in the case of the body, the unawareness that Wofford identifies is itself a distinct and distinctly productive state—not simply the privation of awareness, but rather the condition in which the body's inner processes are constantly at work. Guyon must, it is true, protect the house from its outer enemies, but once he has done that he is better off, in Montaigne's words, allowing the body to "[keep] his play apart, and [let] me keep mine own" (III, 13; 563) than trying to control it. Inasmuch as the self-sensing of the well-ordered body seems to exclude Guyon's consciousness, his wonder in the House of Alma is a kind of "conscious dream" which simply prolongs his trance from canto 7, the event which first allowed him to enter his own body and to experience the autonomous workings of its "Life" in the first place. For if "auto-affection is subjectively invisible," if "our life is not and can never be seen," then the suspension of Guyon's first-person consciousness is the necessary precondition for his wondrous perception of life's self-experiencing as he encounters it in the House of Alma. On the one hand, Guyon's tour of the house is the counterpoint to the intrinsic intemperance that is revealed in his swoon, but on the other hand, the two experiences are profoundly complementary: both serve to shift our point of view to the self-sensing of a bodily life that transpires outside first-person consciousness.[58]

Michel Henry's account of material phenomenology allows us to see Guyon's adventures from canto 7 to canto 9 as an experience of his own bodily workings grounded in feeling rather than knowledge, in self-immanence rather than in self-control:

> Things differ entirely depending on whether they are immersed in the pathos of life in which they never see themselves, or whether they are held in front of a regard. These are not, it seems, the same thing. To the former category would belong drives, forces, affects—everything that we are deep within ourselves, everything that matters. They do not belong in immanence simply because they are put there by change but because they are only possible there. The same, however, goes for the regard, for seeing, which never sees itself, and consequently for knowledge and science itself. Everything falls back into life and only has its being in it; everything is alive.[59]

The swoon, in my reading, is what allows Guyon (literally) to "fall back into life" so that, in the House of Alma, he can encounter "everything that we are deep within ourselves, everything that matters"—just as Montaigne, thanks to his swoon, gradually discovers the auto-affective life of the body, what in his final essay he calls *expérience*. And if Guyon never *learns* that "drives, forces, affects" are what he really is—if he can lapse again, in canto 12, into a "tempest of . . . wrathfulnesse"—it is because the kind of knowledge incarnated in the House of Alma is by its nature impervious to learning, and can be known, if at all, only through experience. For both Montaigne and Spenser, the swoon represents an experience so absolute that it forecloses the knowledge which would otherwise inevitably follow in its wake. Where the structure of ordinary consciousness, as we have seen, at least allows us to make sense of sensory experience retrospectively, in the swoon even that possibility is strictly cut off. Beyond the line where *connaissance* in all of its senses ends, Montaigne and Spenser must therefore imagine a form of experience that is utterly different from any that we might truly know—one in which, beneath the limited perceptions of self and mind, the perfectly ordered body senses nothing but its own workings. What Galen calls *eukrasia* is for Spenser the highest kind of temperance, a purely natural state of harmony so rare and imperceptible that, strangely enough, it is almost like a divine gift.

Guyon's Humanity

The most obvious framework for thinking about trance-states as well as about problems of consciousness more broadly in the Renaissance may well still seem to be that provided by Florentine Neoplatonism. Certainly this has been the case in Spenser scholarship, and indeed, a whole issue of *Spenser Studies* (2009) was recently dedicated to questions of "Spenser and Platonism."[60] And yet without denying the extent of Spenser's debts, in *The Faerie Queene* and elsewhere, to Marsilio Ficino, Pico della Mirandola, and other Neoplatonists, I hope to have shown here that the transcendence achieved in the Spenserian "stound" is one which, again and again, takes us not "up" into a world of disembodied forms but rather "down" into the material, mobile, and sensory processes that comprise embodied experience, and that are best defined in terms of the classical notion of spirits. The vision of human consciousness that emerges from such a journey finds its clearest early modern analogue not in the work of Marsilio Ficino but rather in that of Michel de Montaigne, who near the end of "Of Experience" criticizes all those who want to "escape man" (III, 13; 575). He declares that "such transcending humours affright me as much as steepy, high, and inaccessible places; and I finde nothing so hard to be digested [*à digerer*] in Socrates his life as his extasies and communication with Daemones" (III, 13; 575). *À digerer*: the metaphor is not an accident, since it is the denial of the body and bodily needs which, for Montaigne, is the clearest example of the folly which he attributes to Socrates here:

> Which the better to see let such a man one day tell you the ammusements and imaginations which he puts into his owne head, and for which he diverteth his thoughts for [i.e., from] a good repast, and bewaileth the houre he imployeth in feeding himselfe; you shall find there is nothing so wallowish in all the messes of your table as is that goodly entertainment of the mind (it were often better for us to bee sound asleepe, than awake unto that we doe), and you shall find his discourses and intentions are not worth your meanest dish. (III, 13; 574)

As Harry Berger Jr. and many others after him have suggested, Guyon's faint results from his denying his body in just the way that Montaigne repudiates here.[61] When it is seen in this way, Guyon's faint thus entails not a transcendence of the body but its opposite: an affirmation of that immanent and embodied vitality which, under the heading of *expérience*, Montaigne's final essay champions.

It is not, however, because the body is somehow more familiar to us or more ordinary that Montaigne exhorts us to know it and pay more attention to it in that essay, and if Montaigne repudiates here the *raptus* of Neoplatonic and Christian mysticism, the wisdom he wishes us to acquire in its stead is nevertheless better approached when "sound asleepe, than awake." The body is at the heart of Montaignean *expérience* because it is actually stranger and *more* mysterious than anything we might encounter outside ourselves: "Seeing the doubt and ignorance of those who will and do meddle with expounding the drifts and shifts of nature, with her internall progress; and so many false prognostications of their arte should make us understand her meanes infinitly unknowne" (III, 13; 563). Montaigne encourages us to accept this "internall progress" and "meanes infinitly unknown" almost as we might learn to accept the inalterable behavior of another human being. This is exactly what Guyon discovers during his trance and in the House of Alma—the self-sensing of a body that "keeps its play apart"—and if there is a lesson for him in these episodes, it is to foster the conditions which best allow his body to continue doing so. Socrates's trances, as described by Montaigne, and Guyon's trance thus serve opposite ends: while the former is about escaping from what is human, the latter is about returning to it and reaffirming it; while the former is about self-knowledge, the latter is about self-sensing. And yet both require a passage through the same state. If, in the final canto of book 2, "gins this goodly frame of Temperance / Fairely to rise" (2.12.1), it is not because Guyon has learned to master his body, but on the contrary, because he has learned from his trance to let it play its game by itself.

CHAPTER 4

Shakings: Epileptic Cognition in Shakespeare's *Othello*

Othello's trance in act 4 of *Othello* happens so quickly that it has been easy to overlook: it tends to be forgotten by readers, ignored by critics, and cut from performance.[1] As the stage direction in the Folio has it, Othello "[f]alls in a traunce" (4.1.40), and when Cassio appears on stage, Iago tells him that "[m]y lord is fallen into an epilepsy" (4.1.46).[2] Cassio wants to "rub him about the temples" (4.1.47) but Iago warns him to "forbear," explaining that "[t]he lethargy must have his quiet course" (4.1.48) and assuring him that Othello "will recover straight" (4.1.52)—indeed, Othello comes back to consciousness just as Cassio exits. The whole scene transpires in a matter of about fifteen lines, probably less than a minute of time on stage. Where Montaigne and Guyon both lie unconscious for a relatively extended period—Montaigne, he tells us, for about two hours, and Guyon long enough for Pyrochles and Cymochles to fight with Arthur—Othello lapses into and out of awareness in the space of a few moments, a mere tremor in consciousness rather than a deep swoon. He seems to have no memory of what has happened to him when he revives, for when Iago asks, "Have you not hurt your head?" (4.1.55), he does not understand: "Dost thou mock me?" (4.1.56) he answers.

And yet short-lived though it is, Othello's trance is considerably more unnerving than Montaigne's and Guyon's faints, for it foregrounds an element that was absent from Guyon's swoon and less pronounced in Montaigne's: motion. Where Guyon simply falls into a swoon and lies motionless on the ground, Othello—as he himself tells us—is physically convulsed by what is happening to him: he "tremble[s]" and "shakes" right before falling into his trance, and he may well continue trembling while lying unconscious on the stage. If convincingly performed, such writhing would be frightening to behold, suggesting a breakdown of our voluntary motor functions and the usurpation of consciousness by an uncontrollable and volatile force. The causes and patterns of epileptic fits are still only partially understood today; one can therefore imagine how much more acutely terrifying the sight of such a fit would have been in the early seventeenth century, when so much less was known about the workings of the body and of the brain in particular. The actor may well have seemed as though he was unleashing, for the first time in the play, a powerful demonic force, whose impersonal workings culminate in Othello's murder of Desdemona in act 5 and only restore him to himself after the deed is done.

At the edges of first-person experience, Montaigne and Guyon discover an impersonal vitality that buoys them up even as their ordinary cognitive powers break down. Montaigne calls it *expérience*, and Spenser calls it "Life," and its self-sensing is, I have argued, at the core of the reconception of consciousness beyond the first person which these episodes permit. Othello, too, feels the workings of such a vital principle in and around his swoon, and yet for him its effects are not so benign. For in the Moor's shakings and tremblings—and indeed in the shakings which, we will see, pervade the whole island—the body appears not simply to shut down, but rather to act of its own accord, with only a minimal element of consciousness. Not only, it turns out, does consciousness depend so fully on the body that it can close down at a moment's notice (as Lucretius suggests in the passage quoted in part by Montaigne); it now also seems to share its powers of control *with* the body, so that our actions and behaviors are only partially subject to first-person awareness and will. Thus, Stanley Cavell has argued that Othello's swoon in act 4 is merely his "explicit trance," for his words and actions in act 5, when he strangles Desdemona, still seem to be only partially willed, "those of a man in a trance, in a dream state, fighting not to awaken."[3]

In the face of such a spectacle, Iago's diagnosis of epilepsy appears icily matter-of-fact, almost nonchalant. It may well be a ruse, designed, as Michael Neill puts it, to "cover his tracks" (4.1.47n.). And yet whether or not it is medically accurate, Iago's description of what befalls Othello as "an epilepsy" is uncannily appropriate: Othello's broken speech, his shaking and trembling, his falling to the ground in a trance, and his failure to remember anything of what happened to him on returning to consciousness are all highly characteristic of that disease which the Renaissance knew as "the falling sickness" and which at times had been associated with genius and greatness (Hercules, for example, was said to suffer from epilepsy). Indeed, Iago's diagnosis taps into one of the most controversial medical questions of his day, for at the beginning of the sixteenth century, the Swiss-German physician Paracelsus had aggressively rejected the humoral explanations of epilepsy handed down from antiquity and still quite widely accepted in his day. Instead, Paracelsus argued, the causes of epileptic convulsions are ingrained in the macrocosmic nature of human beings themselves, reflecting not the state of our internal humors but rather our immersion in an external world made up of vital, volatile matter. Othello's fit accords with this account, for his shakings resonate across the island of Cyprus as a whole, from the storm which accompanies Othello's arrival on Cyprus to Cassio's drunkenness and the brawling it arouses. Paracelsus's theory thus allows us to develop a notion that we began to explore in the scene of Guyon's emergence from Mammon's Cave: a sense of how consciousness is distributed not only across the human body, but also across the epileptic body of the material world itself. What has been characterized as Othello's discovery of interiority is, in turn, better understood as a manifestation of the "epileptic aura"—analyzed in depth by Paracelsus—in which changes wrought on the body by its environment are experienced by the epileptic himself as a series of changes in consciousness preceding the fit.[4] Paracelsus's account of the epileptic aura supplies a powerful illustration of how, in Gail Kern Paster's words, "emotional change *resides* in internal bodily alteration," while also demonstrating how such change might plausibly extend to include conscious experience itself.[5]

Othello's epistemological agony is not, in this reading, the tormented skepticism of a mind turned in on itself and cut off from the physical world. Rather, his agony is itself a physical condition, as his shaking and trembling so powerfully remind us. At the height of his fit, his mind no longer represents the outside world at all, whether accurately or not—not because it has shut down but because it has become fully part of that world itself, a third person rather than a first. Seen in this light, *Othello* anticipates contemporary externalist accounts of mind, which, in François Tonneau's words, "identify consciousness with the part of the environment that evokes specific changes in someone's brain. A person's conscious experience at any time will be a set of properties present in the environment and acting on this person from the outside. This bundle of properties will be a cross-section of the public environment lawfully related to (but located outside) the person's brain."[6] Iago's ability to insinuate his own consciousness into Othello's is itself best seen in the context of this externalist account of mind. Othello's fit, however, represents the culmination not only of Iago's sway over him, but also of the play's more general metamorphosis of consciousness into something at once affective and environmental, a violent, self-sensing and self-producing shaking that resonates throughout the material and social fabric of Cyprus, the play's island, world, and stage.

From Sacred Disease to Falling Sickness

Where the earliest traditions saw epilepsy as a "sacred disease" directly inspired by the gods, classical accounts centered squarely on the four humors.[7] In the first major text we have on the subject, *The Sacred Disease* (ca. 400 B.C.), Hippocrates argues that epilepsy is "not any more divine or sacred than other diseases, but has a natural cause."[8] It is, he explains, a hereditary disease arising when an excess of phlegm in the womb remains unpurged. "If while [phlegmatics] are children," he says, "sores break out on head, ears and skin . . . the phlegm is discharged and purged away which should have been purged away in the womb."[9] But if it is not released by this process, the excess phlegm eventually descends into the veins connecting the brain with the rest of the body, where it blocks the flow of air and blood and causes each of the symptoms associated with the "sacred disease." When Desdemona says of Othello "I think the sun where he was born / Drew all such humours from him" (3.4.28–29), she seems to echo Hippocrates's account: enough unpurged humors remain to "puddle his clear spirit" (3.4.139). For Galen in *De Locis Affectis* (*On the Affected Parts*, second century A.D.), meanwhile, epilepsy is the result of "a thick humor obstructing the outlets of the *pneuma* in the cerebral cavities";[10] since the *pneuma* is "the primary instrument of the soul for all sensory and voluntary [motor] activities,"[11] this blockage explains the failure of mental functioning. But at the same time the brain is naturally impelled to rid itself of the excessive humor, and thus the nerves attempt to shake it off—"the origin of the nerves is agitated during extrusion of this noxious substance."[12] This shaking in turn transmits itself to the limbs, explaining the convulsions which are the most visible symptoms of epilepsy.

In a series of treatises published between 1520 and 1530, the Swiss-German physician, theologian, and alchemist Theophrastus Bombast von Hohenheim—who styled himself Paracelsus—decisively rejected these humoral explanations of epilepsy. Man and nature, he argued, are more deeply and fully connected than the theory of the humors suggests, and every attempt to account for human disease must begin with this fact. The Hippocratic and Galenic humors are *derived* from the four qualities that make up the macrocosm—hot, cold, moist, and dry—and yet they remain distinctively human features; they do not occur in other beings or in the world at large. For Paracelsus, by contrast, man and nature are made up of exactly the same substances, and there is nothing distinctive about matter in human form. When we understand the processes to which matter is subject in the world at large, we understand what happens to human beings in the throes of a disease as well. The identity of microcosm and macrocosm is, therefore, the key to understanding not only Paracelsus's explanation of epilepsy, but also his striking account of the epileptic aura and its transformative effects on consciousness.

In "Von den Krankheiten die der Vernunft berauben" ("The Diseases That Deprive Man of His Reason," 1525), Paracelsus attributes epilepsy to the "boiling of vapors in the *spiritus vitae*," favoring it over the humors as an explanation because it is shared by other living creatures as well as by the earth itself:

> The boiling of vapors in the *spiritus vitae* (but not in other humors and qualities which are also in the body) is another cause. If the *spiritus vitae* is shifted from its right disposition, it boils and effervesces, and this happens so quickly that memory and reason are destroyed. This boiling may be compared with the approach of an earthquake, which makes the whole earth tremble. Earthquakes and falling sickness have the same causes. Falling sickness is not a disease coming from nature in its regular course, or from ill health of the organism or destruction of the humors, but solely from the same causes as earthquakes, for the motion of the earth is also the motion of man, and is experienced by all which grows on earth.[13]

What differentiates the *spiritus vitae* from Galenic *pneuma* is that *spiritus vitae* can be found in the macrocosm as well, and indeed pervades it: in his *De Spiritu Vitae* Paracelsus writes that "from all the stars and influences of the entire heavens as far as the firmament extends lies the force of the spiritus vitae, and it is like an invisible celestial vapor and is united with [the heavens] as cold and warmth in order to make a temperature."[14] Because the *spiritus vitae* has this universal quality, and is shared by other living creatures as well as by the earth itself, the shaking of an earthquake and of an epileptic are not merely analogous, as is usually the case when man and universe are treated as a microcosm and macrocosm; rather they come, as Paracelsus says, "from the same causes . . . for the motion of the earth is also the motion of man." They are effects of the same process "experienced" in the same way by the same kind of substance. The shaking of an earthquake, after all, closely mimics the symptoms of an epileptic fit and vice versa: "trembling, falling, foaming, and spasms of the limbs are caused because the living spirits of the patients are ill, and therefore the patients too are suffering."[15] Paracelsus grounds reason itself in this cosmic substance: "Reason resides in the living spirit and is in the process of being destroyed until its destruction is complete, when vapor and brewing are no longer possible."[16] It is not the case, then, that an alien substance somehow invades and corrodes the *spiritus*; the same substance is responsible both for reason and for reason's breakdown. Reason, as Shakespeare might put it, is consumed with that which it was nourished by.

Paracelsus again insists on the importance of banishing the humors—from which, he tells us, "all the errors and falsehood of medicine have arisen"[17]—in his 1530 study of epilepsy, "Von den hinfallenden siechtagen" ("On the Sick-Days of Epileptics"). As he announces at the beginning of the second section, we must look to man's macrocosmic nature for an explanation of epilepsy: "The outer world," he says, "is mirror of man's nature as well as its anatomy and theory; thus through the outer world man can be understood in all of his aspects."[18] The principle here is the same as in the earlier text, but it is laid out more explicitly; in this treatise, moreover, Paracelsus looks not to earthquakes but to storms as the macrocosmic expression of epilepsy. Storms and epileptic fits, he argues, are not merely analogous, since human beings and atmospheric formations consist of the same kind of matter: "The birth of thunder comes from three things—from mercury, sulphur, and salt; these three things are the 'corpora' of thunder. Now these things are also present in man, for man is formed from mercury, sulphur, and salt, and that is his body."[19] Whether they are located in the microcosm or the macrocosm, mercury, sulphur, and salt are subject to the same kinds of processes and transformations. They all "bear an impetus" which is "in a body, in the same way as if it were surrounded and enclosed with a shell or structure."[20] But the impetus has a natural tendency to break out of its shell, at which point "the paroxysm of thunder begins and violently shakes itself [*erschüt er sich*] and breaks the shell in which it lies."[21] And this process is characteristic of epilepsy as well: "You should know that as thunder shakes itself, so (should you also know) is it with this falling sickness, in all ways, with the matter and body of mercury, sulphur, and salt."[22] Here and throughout the treatise, Paracelsus emphasizes the "shaking" which an epileptic fit and a thunderstorm have in common: "As you see, when the violent type of thunder begins, that it moves both heaven and earth, so also in man, when the breaking of bubbles begins and shakes the entire body, then everything inside him is shaken [*erbidmet*], as thunder shakes the earth, for as long as the material is burning."[23] The relationship between the "shaking" in an earthquake and that in an epileptic fit is, therefore, not merely an analogy, but rather a manifestation of the same process transpiring in the same kind of substance.

John Donne closely echoes Paracelsus when he describes the onset of his illness in the first of his *Devotions*:

> Is this the honour which Man hath by being a *litle world*, That he hath these *earthquakes* in him selfe, sodaine shakings; these *lightnings*, sodaine flashes; these *thunders*, sodaine noises; these *Eclypses*, sodain offuscations, & darknings of his senses; these *blazing stars*, sodaine fiery exhalations; these *rivers of blood*, sodaine red waters? Is he a *world* to himselfe onely therefore, that he hath inough in himself, not only to destroy, and execute himselfe, but to presage that execution upon himselfe; to assist the sicknes, to antidate the sicknes, to make the sicknes the more irremediable, by sad apprehensions . . . ?[24]

Like Paracelsus, Donne sees the premonitions of disease as "earthquakes in him selfe, sodaine shakings." But Donne's description of these earthquakes as forms of perception unto themselves, "sad apprehensions," also draws attention to what is perhaps the most significant consequence of Paracelsus's monism, namely, that this epileptic "shaking" of the world extends its effects to the epileptic's perceptions themselves. Already in the 1525 discussion, Paracelsus had stressed the "great difference between those patients who feel the attack before the fall and then faint, and those who do not feel it before the fall and the fainting-spell."[25] In 1530, Paracelsus elaborates on the former experience at some length, and goes into more detail about the "sad apprehensions" that allow epileptics to feel the coming of a fit beforehand—what Montaigne would call its "certaine forethreatnings and degrees as forerunners" (III, 13; 551):

> As you see in thunder, when it wants to come, the weather changes and becomes warmer and more sultry, thus the birds in the air and flying recognize and understand this change by themselves: that another kind of weather is arriving, one that is not good for them. Thus in the body when such a beginning of the paroxysm occurs, premonitions come to the sick, *a change of their reason; for any kind of weather modifies the animal understanding and weakens it*; that very weakening is communicated by the birds and the animals with screams and madness and wild behavior, as in the case of chickens and roosters when they fly and furiously bite human

> beings and the like. In the same way the human being feels that kind of a beginning too and is himself frightened and even changed in his proper innate way, whatever that might be. This then is a beginning and a heralding of the epileptic paroxysm in days of sickness since it is much the same as for the birth of thunder.[26]

Birds know that bad weather is coming because "any kind of weather modifies the animal understanding and weakens it," and a similar process explains an epileptic's premonitions of a fit. It is not the case, for either birds or epileptics, that they understand the change coming over them by virtue of a power within them—reason—which remains unchanged; rather, it is the change itself which enables them to understand it. They feel what is about to happen because its effects have already started to take place, and these effects are themselves a form of feeling. Paradoxically, therefore, for both birds and epileptics it is a *weakening* of the intellectual powers which alone enables them to "understand" what is about to happen. The change explains how animals understand what is about to happen even as it represents in itself the very event whose coming they fear. The weakening of our cognitive powers during an epileptic fit is a form of cognition unto itself: a state of auto-affection in which, as Spenser would put it, one's changed powers themselves do feel.

Where Galen writes that the epileptic does not "understand what happens, since his reasoning power is damaged together with the power of memory," for Paracelsus the fit alters our sentient powers in a way that actually heightens their self-awareness.[27] Paracelsus argues for a transformation in our powers as the fit is coming on, a transformation which weakens them but simultaneously endows them with an uncanny premonition of what they are undergoing. This self-apprehending change in our perceptions, Paracelsus explains, is due to the fact that we ourselves are sites of macrocosmic processes: "As you also see, that after such a beginning clouds arrive . . . therefore also in man clouds come before the eyes, as well as muteness, a weakness of sight, and sleep descending. These things are all of the cloud's kind, making one sleepy and heavy. Therefore as both names are *one* thing, so are they *one* material and *one* reason."[28] This passage rests on the clear but striking assumption emphasized in the last sentence: that our perceptions are not something over and above physical nature, but rather are integral parts of it; they are physical fluctuations occurring in the same underlying material substance as the movements of clouds, and are ultimately indistinguishable from them. Paracelsus describes our perceptions in the meteorological terms that Montaigne applies to his thoughts just after awakening from his swoon. Again, Paracelsus's explanatory principle is identity, not analogy, and here its ultimate consequence is that perception itself occurs as a vibration of atmospheric substance that is at once material and sensory in nature. As with Montaigne's "vaine conceits, as in a cloud" (II, 6; 187), the atmospheric fluctuation is inseparable from the altered state which perceives it. The word "aura" itself, which may mean breeze, smell, or felt atmosphere, captures well the way this perceptual state is inscribed in the workings of a larger ecosystem.

Paracelsus's theory of epilepsy offers a model for understanding consciousness more broadly as an ongoing series of changes shared by body and world, apprehended not in the mind but at the site of their occurrence. For to argue that microcosm and macrocosm are fundamentally identical is to argue, at the limit, that consciousness itself takes place in the world—a series of material "shakings" which continually alter our constitution such that events in the external world and our perceptions of those events are always one and the same. Thus, if for Montaigne and Spenser it is the body that becomes conscious when the mind feels faint, for Paracelsus this consciousness extends to include matter more broadly. The self-consciousness of Paracelsus's epileptic is not that of an "I" separated from the flux of matter by a firm boundary, but on the contrary a self-experience which is enabled only when that boundary begins to weaken, and our organs and sinews begin to register their own changes. Although Paracelsus, too, resists explicitly supernatural explanations of epilepsy, there remains something mystical about the epileptic fit in his description of it. His epileptic is still, in a sense, possessed—not by a god or demon, but by the third-person, sentient vitality that is inherent to material processes themselves, whether they are inside or outside of the human.

Paracelsus represents an extreme and controversial pole of early modern medicine, whose rejection of Galenic humoralism was by no means universally accepted. Writing around the same time as Paracelsus, the more moderate Andreas Vesalius broadly concurs with Hippocrates and Galen in attributing epileptic fits to an "oppilation" of spirits due to the buildup of "gross and viscous superfluous humours" in the sinews.[29] And yet interestingly enough, in his account of epileptic consciousness Vesalius does depart from Hippocrates and Galen, neither of whom doubts that during a fit an epileptic is completely devoid of awareness. Paracelsus, we saw, offers a more nuanced picture, and Vesalius, too, denies that consciousness is completely absent. "They that fall," his English translator writes, "be not utterly private of sense and motion, for we see them beating their heads and body; and that beating of their head, no doubt, is done by the instinct of nature."[30] For Vesalius, the epileptic's writhing and beating indicates not the obstruction of blood in the limbs or the nerves trying to shake off the humors, but rather the continued presence of sensation. And it is precisely this persistence of sensation which eventually enables the victim to recover:

> By reason that whereas the passage of the sprites of Motion, is not quite stopped up, but only that by the access of such corrupt humor, their course is interrupted, and they thereby as it were strangled, nature which always is industrious to save herself in her due being, moveth the patient to bestir himself: but especially to steer the part offended or grieved; thereby the better and sooner to deliver it self from encumbrance of the wicked humor, occasion of such disturbance.[31]

Vesalius's account of an epileptic fit thus looks back in some respects to Galen's theory, but it also anticipates both Montaigne's accounts of his swoon in "Of Exercise or Practice" and Spenser's description of Guyon's faint in book 2 of *The Faerie Queene*. In both of these cases, as we saw, nature is "industrious to save itself": Montaigne compares his stirrings during the swoon to the way "those that fall, doe commonly by a naturall impulsion cast their armes abroad before their falling, which sheweth that our members have certaine offices, which they lend one to another, and possesse certaine agitations, apart from our discourse" (II, 6; 187), while in Guyon's case biological "Life" intervenes to "conquer her senseless foe." Just as Montaigne's "parts . . . which often without any consent of ours doe stirre, stand, and lye down againe" (II, 6; 187) and gradually bring him round, so Vesalius's epileptic is restored by the persistence of "sense and motion" beyond the boundary of first-person consciousness. For all three authors, it is this persistent cognitive core of sensation and motion, which Spenser simply calls "Life," that enables us to regain our normal sense of self and cross the threshold from the third back to the first person. Consciousness is not completely absent inasmuch as sensation is still present, but for Montaigne and Vesalius it is clear that, in Montaigne's words, "*I* was not there": what saves and restores us to ourselves during a fit is the activity of a third-person sensory vitality, of that consciousness-without-self which intervenes on Guyon's behalf too. This principle, which Spenser also calls the "spirits," is perhaps what modern neuroscience refers to as "core consciousness": "a simple, biological phenomenon" which "provides the organism with a sense of self about one moment—now—and about one place—here" but lacks the presence of a temporally extended self or identity.[32] It is just such consciousness, somewhere between first-person self-awareness and mere biological process, which, for Vesalius as for Paracelsus, an epileptic fit lays bare.

Shakespeare certainly knew of Paracelsus by the time he was working on *Othello* in the early years of the seventeenth century. When the King of France is cured by Helena in *All's Well That Ends Well*, his courtiers hail it as a miracle that one who had been "relinquished of the artists" (2.2.10) and "both of Galen and Paracelsus" (2.2.11) should be cured by a young lady. Galen and Paracelsus are presumably among those who "say miracles are past," "philosophical persons [who] make modern and familiar things supernatural and causeless" (2.2.1–3), but whose rationalism is now controverted by Helena's success.[33] For Shakespeare, it would seem, Paracelsus was famous enough to rank with Galen as one of the two major medical authorities of his day. The differences between the two schools are also clear, for to be "relinquished" of both Galen and Paracelsus is for both of the two major competing medical theories of the day to fail.[34] The passage thus speaks to the wide reach of Paracelsus's theories in early seventeenth-century England as well as to Shakespeare's knowledge of it, and indeed in the only sustained analysis of the swoon in *Othello*, Stephanie Moss has read it, too, as reflecting the dispute between Galenic and Paracelsian medicine. But whether by chance or design, Shakespeare's depiction of the fit's gradual onset reflects Paracelsus's discussion much more than it does Galen's, exemplifying in particular the "subjective" approach which Moss herself highlights in Paracelsus's work, distinguishing it from Galen's objectivity.[35] For the Paracelsian "change in our reason" affecting birds before a thunderstorm and epileptics before their fit provides a strikingly accurate account of Othello's condition before and during his swoon. Fatally, Othello's consciousness recognizes how it is changing only by virtue of the change itself, so that his self-recognition is inseparable from his self-loss—from a form of self-feeling which comes to the surface only inasmuch as it undermines the first-person consciousness which could translate that feeling into true self-knowledge. Before turning to Othello's fit itself, however, I want to consider two earlier moments in the play which also reflect the form of cognition described by Paracelsus in his work on epilepsy: a knowledge of altered physiological states inseparable from the alteration itself, a knowledge which is in other words inseparable from a form of affect in that word's double sense of feeling and change. All three cases are characterized by an epileptic "shaking" which blurs the boundary between microcosm and macrocosm, but which is also what enables the characters to feel and to know.

Shaking the Island in *Othello*

The first use of the word "shake" in the play comes at the beginning of act 2. Montano and two Venetian gentlemen are looking out from Cyprus at a raging storm which threatens to sink the boats from Venice. Like so many things in *Othello*, the storm and its effects defy accurate perception and enforce reliance on opinion and conjecture: Montano and the gentlemen point above all to the difficulty of apprehending what is happening. Yet where in other accounts of the play (Cavell, Maus, and Neill) such moments might be seen in terms of their proto-Cartesian skepticism, or in the related terms of the epistemological cruxes surrounding an emergent discourse of interiority, with Paracelsus in mind we can understand them differently: they are scenes in which cognition takes place not by virtue of detached observation, but rather as the *action* of an event on those who undergo it, as a "change of inner state knowable *as* and also *by means of* changes, defined as broadly as possible, in the outer world."[36] These are events which we experience not because we stand outside and above them and can observe them taking place from a safe distance, but rather because we are immanent to their happening, feeling their effects by virtue of immediate contact and whether or not we are aware of them as objects of representation. What is seen here is, in a sense, nothing, and yet seeing nothing turns out to be a powerful mode of vision in its own right:

> MONTANO: What from the cape can you discern at sea?
> FIRST GENTLEMAN: Nothing at all: it is a high-wrought flood;
> I cannot 'twixt the heaven and the main
> Descry a sail.
> MONTANO: Methinks the wind hath spoke aloud at land—
> A fuller blast ne'er shook our battlements;
> If it hath ruffianed so upon the sea,
> What ribs of oak, when mountains melt on them,
> Can hold the mortise? What shall we hear of this?
> SECOND GENTLEMAN: A segregation of the Turkish fleet;
> For do but stand upon the foaming shore,
> The chidden billow seems to pelt the clouds,
> The wind-shaked surge, with high and monstrous mane
> Seems to cast water on the burning Bear
> And quench the guards of th'ever-fixèd Pole:
> I never did like molestation view
> On the enchafèd flood. (2.1.1–17)

The language of this exchange is a classic example of *enargeia* or *evidentia*, the rhetorical trope which, as the classical names suggest, creates the illusion that the reader or listener is actually seeing a vivid scene. The Second Gentleman invites us to share his point of vantage and, through his description, to participate in his perceptions. And yet this almost self-consciously virtuosic exercise in a rhetorical trope is ironically undercut by the initial reminder that, in fact, "nothing at all" is visible—not entirely unlike the way in which, in a similar scene in *King Lear*, Edgar's powerful evocation of the Dover cliffs almost makes us forget that the characters are nowhere near them. In this scene, however, the visual "nothingness" is precisely what we are supposed to see. For it is, paradoxically, the very impossibility of seeing the storm as a conventional object—of discerning its component parts or distinguishing it from its surroundings—that makes it such a uniquely vivid experience. Shore mixes with sea and sea with sky in a way that makes vision itself one big, blind blur, but which is also what makes the storm a perceptually thrilling spectacle worthy of *enargeia*. Like Guyon, each gentleman has "all his sences drowned in deep sencelesse wave" (2.8.24).

The blur of the storm reduces everything to an indistinct but all-encompassing macrocosm, absorbing even the vantage point proffered to us by the gentleman: the "foaming shore," which has become indistinguishable from the sea. Hardly distinct from what we are supposed to see, "the foaming shore" seems almost to symbolize the way in which a detached place of observation can be overwhelmed by the phenomenon it should permit us to observe. It is, in fact, this very condition of immersion which suggests the shore to the Second Gentleman as the best place to behold the storm—not from a safe remove, but in the midst of its foaming action. No longer sufficiently distant from our object to make it out clearly, we experience the storm from the shore in a way which is nevertheless more truthful, for there we can *feel* the storm's energy more acutely than we could ever merely see it. We are invited to experience the storm not by the mediation of the five senses but as a feeling of immersion, not through the distance of sensory representation but through the proximity of affect and unmediated contact. To experience it in this way is not to represent it in our minds but, first and foremost, to feel its action on us almost as we feel the inner workings of our own body. This is how, Paracelsus tells us, birds feel the coming of a storm and epileptics feel the coming of a fit—not through detached observation, but because they work changes on our cognitive powers before we are even capable of seeing them, because "any kind of weather modifies the animal understanding and weakens it." Indeed, with its "wind-shak'd surge" and "foaming shore," this scene itself seems almost like a premonition of Othello's fit, inscribing it within an order of macrocosmic changes that are felt before they are seen or fully understood.

Before the storm reaches Othello, however, it strikes Cassio, whom Iago makes drunk in act 2, scene 3 in the hopes of causing him to incur Othello's disfavor. But beyond its function in the plot, the scene also allows Shakespeare to extend his exploration of what it means, and how far it is possible, to be conscious of the world not through detached representation of its constituent objects, but rather through the alterations which its physical action produces in us—through what Montaigne would call our "natural drunkenness." When we have ingested too much alcohol, our body feels, moves, and works differently than it normally does, and yet we may or may not be fully conscious of that difference. First-person consciousness abuts on a more primal and immanent mode of feeling, which is one and the same as changes taking place in the body itself.

> CASSIO: Ay; but, by your leave, not before me: the lieutenant is to be saved before the ensign. Let's have no more of this: let's to our affairs. God forgive us our sins! Gentlemen, let's look to our business. Do not think, gentlemen, I am drunk: this is my ensign; this is my right hand, and this is my left. I am not drunk now: I can stand well enough, and speak well enough.
>
> GENTLEMEN: Excellent well.
>
> CASSIO: Why, very well, then—you must not think, then, that I am drunk. (2.3.101–7)

Cassio denies his drunkenness just as the gentlemen, at least initially, deny that they see the storm—both are, as it were, too intoxicated by the experience to describe it in a detached and accurate way. There is, of course, a difference between the lofty *enargeia* of the storm scene and Cassio's humorously repetitive and disjointed effort to sound serious, but in a sense the marked discrepancy in style only serves to emphasize the underlying similarities. In both cases, the condition in question is one which, by affecting the very processes which make perception of it possible, renders verbal report unreliable. And thus again, in both cases, the negation of the experience—the negation that it is observed through the ordinary means of apprehension, whether seeing or thinking—serves as the best way of demonstrating its effects. Cassio's repetitions of "I am not drunk," "Do not think . . . I am drunk"—aided presumably by the actor's performance—only serve to make his drunkenness obvious.

Cassio, however, is not merely attempting here to prove his sobriety to others, and demonstrating his intoxication in doing so. The speech also registers his effort to prove to *himself* that he is sober and, if he is not, to get back to normal and "look to our business" as soon as possible by reestablishing an ordinary state of consciousness. As he says "this is my right hand, and this is my left," he looks at his own hands and attempts to confirm that he still feels them—for we know that a hand is ours not because we look to confirm that it is connected via our arm to the rest of our body, but because we feel its presence and can control its movements whether or not we see it (hence the phenomenon of phantom limbs, in which patients with missing limbs still feel pain in them). And as he says, "I can stand well enough, and speak well enough," he is similarly paying attention to his own motor state and to the quality of his own voice. Throughout the passage, then, Cassio is both addressing others and at the same time assessing his own internal state, feeling within himself in the attempt to make sure of sensations which we usually take for granted. Those sensations are not objective perceptions, but rather that tissue of ongoing feelings which Montaigne understands as the true form of self-knowledge, which neuroscience now refers to as the "body schema," and which Malabou and others call "auto-affection": the self-awareness of the body in its biological rhythms and routines. As in Malabou's account of neural damage, precisely inasmuch as drunkenness threatens to destabilize our detached, first-person self-consciousness, it brings a different mode of self-consciousness to the fore—that auto-affection we have just seen dramatized in the House of Alma, in which the body constantly registers and regulates its own feelings and movements with or without our awareness. We normally take such self-knowledge for granted: we do not need to make ourselves aware of our body's position or energy levels, for example, in order to stand up. We may become aware of those aspects of the body after the fact, but only if our effort to stand up has failed or met with unexpected resistance.[37] Thus, even though Cassio avers that nothing has changed, that he can "stand well enough" and that he knows his own hands, these very assertions testify to the change they deny, since we would only become attuned to our self-sensing bodily state, and feel the need to affirm or deny that it has changed, if such a change had already begun to take place (and "well enough" itself is a half-concession that it might have). As a similarly intoxicated Red Crosse's "chaunged powres at first themselues not felt," so the insentience registered by Cassio's "I am not drunk" actually marks a stage in his transformation. His insistent unwillingness to fully recognize his internal change reflects the felt onset of the very state it denies—a condition to which Othello himself will soon be subject.

Cassio's hands may well shake and tremble as he says, "this is my right, and this my left hand," and certainly the actor would feel licensed to stumble about the stage as he performs this speech. Cassio's drunkenness thus anticipates the way in which Iago's suggestions will change Othello's bodily state as well, culminating in the shaking and the disjointed language of his fit. Indeed for Iago, the careful induction of Cassio's drunkenness works almost as a trial run for his manipulation of Othello in acts 3 and 4. He hovers over Cassio's and Othello's bodies in a similar way, tracking his effects on them with a chilling clinical acuity: he pronounces of Cassio's drunkenness that "'[t]is evermore the prologue to his sleep" (2.3.120) much as he will tell Cassio himself that Othello's "lethargy must have his quiet course; / If not, he foams at mouth, and by and by / Breaks out to savage madness. . . . He will recover straight" (4.1.49–53). In both cases, Iago describes a body that he has skillfully turned inside-out, enveloping consciousness in impersonal biological process and thereby setting in motion a chain of effects outside its owner's control but under his own. At the same time, Shakespeare shows us the character's own helpless awareness of these effects, which are experienced as a series of changes taking place in the body and in consciousness simultaneously—as a bodily self-sensing that is analogous to what, in Paracelsus's account, birds experience in the coming of a storm.

"It Is Not Words That Shakes Me Thus": Epileptic Cognition

Thus, where the atmosphere in *Hamlet* is characterized by a contagion which seems to contaminate the air itself, the world of *Othello* is brooded over by a storm which catches up more and more characters in its turbulence. The "real" storm ends within act 2, scene 1, but the shaking and foaming it unleashes on the island have only just begun:

> I fear the trust Othello puts in him
> On some odd time of his infirmity
> Will shake this island. (2.3.117–19)

Each "shaking" is at once a change in the fabric of the macrocosm and a change in the makeup of the body, perceived not by virtue of our detachment from it but, on the contrary, because we are unreservedly immanent to its action. In such moments, subjectivity is rewritten as what Fredric

Jameson calls "a registering apparatus for transformed states of being"; we might think of a thermometer or barometer whose measurements of nature are originally changes *in* nature, parts of a process before they are descriptions of it.[38] In a tragic key, *Othello* is exploring what it means for consciousness to be spread across an environment whose changes are one with the feelings whereby we perceive them. Nowhere is this clearer than in Othello's fit.

For Othello's fit is itself embedded in a larger process, as is suggested first of all by the series of increasingly intense symptoms and signs which precede it: a headache, a weakened voice, and a visibly altered manner. When we read them with Paracelsus in mind, we can see these symptoms as evidence of an extended epileptic aura: Othello feels his body changing by virtue of the changes themselves, so that the symptoms and Othello's response to them are one and the same, while his consciousness of the change lags behind. His language itself becomes strained and curt, as if the effort of keeping those changes in check were rapidly vitiating his great rhetorical powers:

> IAGO: I see this hath a little dashed your spirits.
> OTHELLO: Not a jot, not a jot. (3.3.217–18)

> IAGO: My lord, I see you're moved.
> OTHELLO: No, not much moved. (3.3.228)

> DESDEMONA: Why do you speak so faintly?
> Are you not well?
> OTHELLO: I have a pain upon my forehead, here. (3.3.285–86)

> DESDEMONA: Something sure of state—
> Either from Venice, or some unhatched practice
> Made demonstrable here in Cyprus to him—
> Hath puddled his clear spirit. (3.4.136–39)

Readers and viewers of the play naturally understand these symptoms as signs of mounting anger, slowly engendered by Iago's insinuations: a process flowing from language to mind to body. To describe them, instead, as signs of an "epileptic aura" is not to deny their emotional nature, nor is it to dispute the influence of Iago's suggestions. Rather, it is to argue that those suggestions are, from the beginning, experienced as feelings and as physiological changes rather than as abstract possibilities contemplated by the mind. For it is precisely Iago's genius not only to have made his own thoughts inseparable from Othello's, but also to have insinuated those thoughts on a bodily level as a kind of slowly unfolding epileptic aura, which is itself the first phase of the attack—on the level of a nagging feeling which itself then raises more and more troubling questions in Othello's mind. Indeed, although our understanding of these passages depends in part on the actors' interpretations, we need not assume that Iago is responding to a visible alteration which has already affected Othello's manner. Rather, it is precisely by forcing Othello to deny that he is "moved" that Iago nudges Othello closer to such a state. Much like Cassio's denial of his drunkenness, Othello's denial here actually serves to confirm his altered state both to himself and to us. We should think here of how difficult it can be to deny that we are angry or upset without investing that denial with some of the force of the condition that we are denying—of how the very denial can risk implicating us in a condition we did not think we felt. This double bind is a consequence of the social and distributed nature of cognition: to the degree that emotions are shared, and are as much created through socially mediated forms of gesture and expression as they are merely expressed thereby, another's report on our feelings will always be hard to forswear completely.

In the next chapter I will explore the social nature of feelings in more depth. Here I want to focus on the particular feeling which Iago engenders, or rather on the feeling *of* that feeling. Othello crosses a threshold between a state in which he does not feel his changing feeling to one in which he does, from "not a jot" to "not much moved" to "I have a pain." In his tenth *Devotion*, John Donne describes the early stages of his disease as changes which he only feels "insensibly": "My forces are not enfeebled, I find no decay in my strength; my provisions are not cut off, I find no abhorring in mine appetite; my counsels are not corrupted or infatuated, I find no false apprehensions, to work upon mine understanding; and yet they see, that invisibly, and I feele, that insensibly the *disease* prevails."[39] Like Donne, Othello occupies a threshold where, paradoxically, he feels only by virtue of feeling his own insentience—the result of an inner and yet alien upheaval, of internal changes that feel themselves ("*they* see," Donne writes) without being registered fully in consciousness. Such changes can be apprehended only by what Charleton calls "a certain sense of *Feeling*, which is not referrible to the Common sense, nor communicated to the Brain, and of which we take no cognisance, but by the various effects and commotions that it causeth in our bodyes."[40] From the start it is, at least from Othello's point of view, these seemingly uncaused "effects and commotions" within himself, and not Iago's insinuations, that he is attempting to feel more fully and thereby to understand; those feelings are then further contributed to by the cognitive strain of attempting to understand them. At once the subject and object of itself, Othello's unease continually engenders itself in a never-ending cycle—in Emilia's words, it is "[b]egot upon itself, born on itself" (3.4.157). What we often think of as Othello's skepticism and solipsism might better be described in terms of this bodily self-sensing and the way in which—as it gradually percolates into Othello's consciousness—its self-engendering engulfs the "Othello music" of the first three acts.[41] In such a reading, Othello's skepticism, his mounting questions about whether his representations of Desdemona correspond to her reality, are not the causes of a bodily change which results in a breakdown intentionally misdiagnosed by Iago as epilepsy—Othello's trance is not a "psychogenic" fit. On the contrary, his epistemological crisis is itself the result of these unsettling changes whose origins are mysterious to him. Since he only begins to feel them after they have already begun to set in, and since they do not correspond clearly either to a disease within him or to anything in his external world, he is forced to seek out a source for them.

It is right before falling into a trance that Othello's feelings at last feel themselves fully, traversing that threshold crossed by Red Crosse in book 1 of the *Faerie Queene* and glimpsed in act 2 of *Othello* by Cassio's drunkenness. Othello's symptoms—what Paracelsus would describe as the "bubbling" of the fit—come to a boil in a speech in which Othello seems almost to see the nature of his delusion even as he is about to succumb to it fully: like Red Crosse, he moves from unfelt changes, to changes that feel themselves, to a dim "wariness" of those changes and what he takes their self-feeling to be telling him, to an unconscious "stound." Self-feeling usurps the place of self-knowledge, but for a moment, right before his trance, they almost converge:

> Lie with her? Lie on her? We say 'lie on her' when they belie her. Lie with her? 'Swounds, that's fulsome! Handkerchief—confessions—handkerchief? To confess, and be hanged for his labour? First to be hanged and then to confess! I tremble at it. Nature would not invest herself in such shadowing passion without some instruction. It is not words that shakes me thus. Pish! Noses, ears, and lips! Is't possible? Confess? Handkerchief? O, devil! (4.1.33–40)

This speech has been described as representing a "decline into incoherence," "incoherent ravings," and a "kaleidoscopic volatility of reference,"[42] but something more subtle is indicated by Othello's language. When he says "I tremble at it" he is not merely reporting his physical state, or simply reinforcing or underscoring the extent of his rage. His shaking and trembling would presumably be visible already, and so he describes them not in order to alert his audience to them, but rather to register his own bewildered awareness of the indescribable changes coming over him. Those changes are themselves a form of feeling, for Othello trembles *at* something obscure which he cannot quite pin down. At the same time, Othello describes that trembling as if from outside, as if his body were autonomously feeling and responding to things which Othello himself, who senses only this obscure displacement of his own experience, cannot discern. Michael Witmore describes Othello here as "both the object and the organ of sense, a site or trembling pressure that makes him both the subject who senses certain 'shadowing passions' and the object of that sensed fact," but insofar as the trembling body is its *own* subject, itself a site of feeling, Othello's subjectivity here is relegated to the margins of his own experience.[43] The exclamation "I tremble at it" captures consciousness in the moment of this displacement from the first person to the third, a displacement registered by an "I" which has a curiously impersonal force. Just as the epileptic feels the fit coming on only by virtue of the epilepsy itself, so Othello's trembling is a physical change which is also a state of self-feeling, in which embodied consciousness registers changes in its own condition independently of the first person. In his trembling Othello undergoes a physical change which, like the mercury in a thermometer, constitutes its own measure.

Iago succeeds, therefore, not because of his compelling logic or evidence but because of his ability to induce a bodily change which senses itself not through detached awareness but through its own aura. Something Othello feels with his whole body must have a reality which "words" alone do not possess, and must therefore have some external though unnamable "cause" (5.2.1)—as Othello insists right before killing Desdemona. Yet Othello's denials here are so contorted, and so closely tethered to what they deny, that they almost read like confessions. As in Cassio's denials of his drunkenness, there is a striking overlay of denial on admission; indeed, the speech is particularly acute in diagnosing, in reverse, that which is precisely Othello's predicament. Behind Othello's statements we can hear silent questions, epistemological possibilities which Othello must banish before he can proceed, doubts which, despite his seeming certainty at the end of act 3, have not yet been fully addressed: *could* nature invest herself in such passion without any instruction? *Could* words alone shake me thus? More pointedly still, Othello seems to acknowledge the possibility that Desdemona might be "belied" even as he confronts the possibility that Cassio might "lie with her"—and is it the possibility of "belying" or lying with her that he calls "fulsome"? He envisions confession and punishment—"To confess, and be hanged for his labour?"—only to insist that, in this case which is so extreme, the punishment should precede the crime: "First to be hanged, and then to confess!" Again, however, he now reacts to his own statement, saying, "I tremble at it," leaving it hard for us to say whether he is trembling at Cassio's villainy or at the magnitude of the injustice he has just contemplated—of a punishment meted out before the judgment itself. The glimmers of self-awareness which appear to emerge in this speech—momentary flashes of recognition that his own belief may have no basis in actuality, that his feeling may feel nothing beyond itself—become, paradoxically, more and more difficult to disentangle from Othello's rising conviction and his mounting rage.[44] For the speech is pervaded by a tension between the contrasting pulls of possession and recognition which comes to a head when Othello shouts, just before falling into his fit, "O devil!" Does this refer to Desdemona, of whose guilt he is now convinced? Or to Iago, the "demi-devil" (5.2.299) who has caused him to be so possessed by that conviction that he cannot shake it off even though he wishes to? Or does Othello truly believe that he has been possessed by a devil? All of these possibilities are implicit in Othello's exclamation. It is impossible to decide whether any of his statements stem from a momentary flash of residual awareness or from the demonic encroachment of an utterly impersonal affect, for in this richly liminal moment these two powers temporarily and unbearably overlap. The two are impossible to disentangle, so that Othello must now fall into an unconscious state in order to get the better of his own irrepressible misgivings.

The scene thus raises an inverse form of the version of the question we have been tracing from the start: can someone who is possessed, whose feelings have been displaced to a kind of inner third person, be aware of that fact? If there is no clear answer in this scene—to this question or to any of the others I have posed above—it is perhaps because possession and awareness, affect and consciousness, have become almost indistinguishable, because like the epileptic, Othello knows what is happening to him only by virtue of that which empties out his knowledge. It is because, as I argued in chapter 1, consciousness perceives its own state only in a moment which borders on total insentience—because auto-affection only becomes palpable when the detachment of first-person consciousness breaks down in a state that temporarily resembles brain damage. Othello's feelings feel themselves only by virtue of an influence which is vitiating them, and a similar predicament characterizes his knowledge as well: he momentarily recognizes what is happening to him (a classical anagnorisis), but only in reverse, as a kind of photographic negative of the truth. For he is aware of the changes coming over him in the way that Paracelsus describes, and his self-knowledge, likewise, is a knowledge that comes from the destructive process itself rather than from a capacity to observe it, and it can therefore only be expressed as a kind of not-seeing, only by the negation of what is in fact so obviously the case. As in the storm scene, when the normal perceptual faculties are suspended, not-seeing itself becomes a form of insight, as a physical state of shaking and trembling which usurps, without simply effacing, the roles of consciousness and cognition. In a much more complex form, Othello is saying: "Now I am not drunk": it is the closest he can come to an acknowledgment of drunkenness.

Since Othello's powers, like Red Crosse's, feel themselves only by virtue of that which is rapidly vitiating them, it stands to reason that his moment of anagnorisis—perfectly poised between self-awareness and passionate oblivion—would last only as long as "the motion of an instant," a "stound" of blurry self-apprehension followed immediately by an insentient swoon. Syncopating speech and trance, knowledge and oblivion, Othello's stound marks not so much the nadir of his cognitive descent as the vanishing point at which self-awareness meets a horizon at once interior and exterior: the line at which the first person fades into the third, at which self-consciousness and anagnorisis can no longer be distinguished from an impersonal vibration in the material world. When Othello says, "I tremble at it," he speaks to us from that horizon at which the first and third persons cannot be told apart, but once he has fallen to the ground, their syncope—the cutting of both which joins them together—is already over: his consciousness has fully merged into his physical trembling and with the storm system that has been brewing over the island since the beginning of act 2. Thus, his statement does not come from the assured perspective of a self-present first person; rather, it emanates from the self-feeling of a feeling from which—as in Montaigne's swoon—the self is in precipitous retreat.

To understand this condition as epileptic is not to make a medical diagnosis. It is to see it, with Paracelsus and François Tonneau, as a cosmic "shaking," like the storm in act 2 and like Cassio's drunkenness. These are all events in which, as in Tonneau's description, consciousness is fully identified with "the part of the environment that evokes specific changes in someone's brain." We perceive these events not by means of a higher-order cognition which is immune to their effects, but by the self-feeling of a feeling that is intrinsic to the shaking itself, and which Othello's syncope has unveiled. In the next chapter we will explore some of the ways in which such a redefinition of knowledge might be redemptive. For

Othello, however, it remains a tragic form of limitation, one which he only exacerbates by trying to resist it.[45]

Coda: Performing the Trance

The keynote of the central sequence in *Othello*, then, is not passion, rage, or even jealousy, but rather an epileptic aura in which Othello's feelings feel their own transformation, and its climax comes not in Othello's vow at the end of act 3, scene 3, but when Othello falls down in a trance at the beginning of act 4. Cutting this scene from performance—as was standard from the early eighteenth to the late nineteenth century—not only undermines the careful development of the epileptic sequence, but it also deprives the play's many references to "shaking" of their obvious epicenter.[46] For when Lodovico asks, "Is this the nature / Whom passion could not shake?" (4.1.257–58), and when Desdemona says, "Some bloody passion shakes your very frame" (5.2.45), their phrases, coming after Othello's fit, are not merely metaphorical. Othello's shaking is a genuine physical condition, one which ripples throughout his "frame" as well as throughout the island as a whole. In order to make this clear, the fit itself cannot be omitted or minimized, and the actor playing Othello must shake and tremble as he performs it.

The choice to write a scene including an on-stage epileptic fit, with all of the demands it would inevitably place on the actor playing Othello, can hardly have been a casual one. Shakespeare had already written an epileptic fit in *Julius Caesar*, in which Caesar suffers from one when he is offered the crown by the people in act 1. But where Caesar's fit takes place offstage and is described to us at secondhand by Casca, in *Othello* it is performed before the audience's eyes, as if Shakespeare now wanted us to behold "an epilepsy" in its full-throttled action, and to contemplate to the full its frightening effects on human consciousness, starting with the uncanny experience of its aura. In order to achieve this, the actor must shake physically and at the same time convey, with words and gesture, the feeling that this shaking is overcoming him almost against his will; he must speak disjointedly, fall to the ground, continue trembling, and then resume speaking as if nothing at all had happened to him. He must, in other words, enact a breakdown of our voluntary physiological functions—a highly challenging mandate for any actor, but one which would be thrilling for the audience if successfully performed.

Othello's decline in acts 3 and 4 thus requires a style of acting which uses the whole body, and it puts such a style to its highest test. It requires, in other words, the kind of acting which so horrifies and impresses Hamlet in the Player's speech on the death of Priam:

> Is it not monstrous that this player here,
> But in a fiction, in a dream of passion,
> Could force his soul so to his whole conceit
> That from her working all his visage wanned,
> Tears in his eyes, distraction in's aspect,
> A broken voice, and his whole function suiting
> With forms to his conceit? And all for nothing.
> For Hecuba! (2.2.539–46)[47]

What amazes Hamlet is the way in which a mere "fiction" elicits emotions with a palpable effect on the whole body, so that, as we see in the shift of pronouns, it slips from a voluntary into an involuntary state. In the first four lines, the player is still the subject of the action, "forcing" his soul to express the "conceit" that he has chosen. But after he has done so, it is not from his forcing but from *her* (i.e., his soul's) working that "all his visage wanned," and so on. The soul sets in motion a whole chain of physiological reactions seemingly without the actor's intervention, for he has summoned a feeling so genuine that he no longer fully controls its manifestations. The shift in pronoun and gender suggests a shift from first-person awareness and control to a third-person, involuntary "working"—to a soul which, much like Spenser's "Life" and much like the third-person soul of the dying Julius Canius, stands in an essentially impersonal relationship to its bearer even as it governs and sustains him. An actor acting in accordance with Hamlet's description would not merely express Othello's condition during his fit. He would be in the same sort of condition himself, for this slippage from first to third person is precisely what happens to Othello as well: "the lethargy," as Iago puts it, "must have *his* quiet course." Hamlet's speech has been seen as a description of Richard Burbage, who was the first actor to play Othello, and thus it seems plausible that the swoon was written with Burbage's particular abilities, as described here, in mind. Burbage was celebrated for his ability to die "so livly, that Spectators, and the rest / Of his sad Crew, whilst he but seem'd to bleed, /Amazed, thought even then hee dyed in deed," and he would presumably have excelled at Othello's trance as well.[48]

Far from forcing the actor to distort the text, therefore, reading Othello's swoon as the culmination of an epileptic breakdown would allow the actor to fulfill the unique vision of theater articulated by Hamlet and exemplified by actors such as Burbage: theater understood not as a world of sophisticated make-believe but rather, in Michael Witmore's words, as "a substance made up of embodied processes."[49] Although Hamlet's monologue has sometimes been taken as an implicit description of "personation" acting, in which the actor appears "to become an entirely different person according to the demands of every separate role," nowhere does Hamlet suggest that the player *becomes* Hecuba or Priam.[50] Notions of personation or method acting are inapplicable here because they involve a presumption of first-person consciousness which it is precisely the role of the actor, in Hamlet's description, to put aside. He describes the actor's transformation not into another person, but into a conduit for a feeling so powerful that it seems to empty out personhood and recast its attributes as the workings of impersonal substance. "His whole function suiting / With forms to his conceit," the actor enters not the psychology of a given character, but rather a state of intensely embodied consciousness which no distinct person, whether actor or character, can be said to inhabit at all. The discrepancy between reality and appearance in an actor's performance—so troubling to Hamlet in act 1 of the play—would not arise in such moments, for the actor's true being has faded altogether, replaced by a third-person emotion in which performance and reality blur.

The kind of intense affect praised by Hamlet in his speech and exemplified in scenes such as Othello's breakdown may well have transgressed emerging theatrical norms. In his *Apology for Actors* (1612), Thomas Heywood singles out for censure a series of excessive, melodramatic gestures including standing "in his place like a liveless Image." The actor should be careful, he says, "neither to frown when he should smile, nor to make unseemely and disguised faces in the delivery of his words, not to stare with his eies, draw awry his mouth, confound his voice in the hollow of his throat, or teare his words hastily betwixt his teeth, neither to buffet his deske like a mad-man, nor stand in his place like a liuelesse Image, demurely plodding, & without any smooth & normal motion."[51] Heywood is probably thinking of gestures more exaggerated than Othello's faint, and yet it is hard to imagine this faint being performed in the style that Heywood endorses: with a "comely and elegant gesture, a gratious and a bewitching kinde of action, a naturall and a familiar motion of the head, the hand, the body, and a moderate and fit countenance sutable to all the rest."[52] Perhaps, then, Iago's diagnosis of epilepsy served in part to justify the shaking and writhing which, for an audience beginning to value self-restraint, might otherwise have come too close to an old-fashioned "histrionic bluster . . . with no necessary connection to passion."[53] In naturalizing Othello's swoon by giving a medical explanation for it, Iago's diagnosis tells us that in its own terms, a passionate swoon might have appeared excessively histrionic. By incorporating a scene which is "epileptic" above all in the sense that it is both cognitive and corporeal at once, Shakespeare thus enabled the actor to transcend mere rage, avoiding the sorts of excesses censured by Heywood even while capturing the nuances of Othello's predicament. As Hamlet suggests, in order to do so the actor would straddle the border between the voluntary and the involuntary, drawing on a distinctive style of acting that is reducible neither to crude bluster nor to Neoclassical elegance. It was at just such a style—somewhere between Heywood's extremes—that actors such as Burbage and Edward Alleyn excelled. In the cognitive and corporeal strain of scenes such as Othello's trance, Shakespearean theater thus enabled the emergence of a whole new phenomenology, in which the distinction between interior and exterior, and thus between reality and performance, was replaced by a bodily self-sensing and self-moving that was both inner and outer at once, and which was the joint creation of the dramatist and actor working in symbiosis.

Despite strictures such as Heywood's, the trance remained a popular moment in the play until the early eighteenth century, when nascent Neoclassical norms called for its omission. This letter written to *The Tatler* in 1725—just as it was starting to be cut from performance—gives us a glimpse into how earlier audiences saw the trance: "I have likewise a notion that Othello's trance being a thing not strain'd, but very natural, and which did once give great satisfaction, how that comes to be omitted I know not, except the players are resolved not to humour us in good sense and reason."[54] If later audiences came to view the scene as superfluous or uncomfortable, the writer of the letter to *The Tatler* suggests that for earlier generations the scene was a familiar favorite: it "did once give great satisfaction." His language captures both sides of the change in sensibilities: he acknowledges the Neoclassical decorum according to which such a scene might appear "strained" even as he looks back to a taste for which it was perfectly "natural." The description of the trance as "natural" accords with Hamlet's description of the Player's passion, which is natural inasmuch as it is real, activating all of the same vital channels as grief itself. The Neoclassical rejection of such passions was probably a question not only of their degree, but also of an emerging Enlightenment vision of consciousness as purely logical and representational in nature, and thus uncontaminated by the emotive and sensory workings of the body.[55]

In contrast, the affective, material concept of consciousness I have been tracing in scenes such as Othello's swoon called for an embodied style of acting which reached its heyday in Shakespeare's tragedies. Or we might conclude, more provocatively still, that the unique demands that Shakespeare's tragedies made on his actors themselves shed a new light on the physiological processes underlying human consciousness—as seems to happen for Hamlet in act 2. However that may be, if life as such is encountered not as an object of first-person cognition, but rather by and as the self-sensing of an affect experienced throughout the body as a whole, then at least in theater the actor's body becomes the central site of its depiction. And if in Montaigne and Spenser's trances we found evidence that consciousness itself might be reimagined in such terms, we can now see how, in *Othello*, Shakespeare draws on all the resources of his art to depict it in a similar light, as a palpable current of blind yet ineluctable vitality which feels its own activity even when we are not aware of it. From the storm in act 2 through Cassio's drunkenness to Othello's swoon, *Othello* develops a form of theater which does not merely represent life from a safe distance, but rather plunges us into the midst of its stream, much as Montano and the two gentlemen are almost overwhelmed by the storm they try to describe. In *Othello* this plunge is a tragic one, perhaps because of everything that still wishes to resist such life, and to convert its swirling vitality into the fixity of vision and judgment, "ocular proof" (3.3.362). In the next chapter, *The Winter's Tale* will take us to the very same brink only to pull back right before it, converting judgment back into affect and cold stone back into living warmth.

Chapter 5

Sympathies: Sharing Feeling in *The Winter's Tale*

Othello's fit, we have just seen, is not merely psychosomatic—a bodily state engendered by a mental anxiety which could somehow be distinguished from it. Rather, it is by infiltrating the body's own mechanisms of self-feeling that Iago is able to goad Othello into a state of suspicion. The nature of this process entails, however, that the fit is not only bodily but also intersubjective: Iago is able to induce feeling in Othello simply by ascribing it to him, and thus the reality of that feeling is as much social as it is personal—it is there as soon as Iago says it is. Iago takes advantage of that interpersonal dimension of feeling described by Montaigne: "[m]y visage and eyes do presently discover me. Thence begin all my changes, and somewhat sharper than they are in effect. I often moved my friends to pitty ere I feel the cause of it" (III, 13; 564). As we saw in chapter 2, a temporal gap persistently separates these "changes"—the invisible movements we today understand as "affects"—from Montaigne's consciousness of them, a gap whose attempted traversal he names *expérience*. Yet as Montaigne recognizes here, this gap also provides a space into which others may intrude before he himself can cross it. It is not merely that they can see his feelings, but rather that they too are moved by those feelings before they enter his awareness, in a process which Teresa Brennan names the "transmission of affect": a process whereby "the emotions or affects of one person, and the enhancing or depressing energies that these affects entail, can enter into another."[1] Such a process, in which feeling is shared across bodies before it is known in consciousness, is how sympathy arises, but in Iago's case it is also what makes manipulation of that feeling possible.

If the motions and energies of the sentient body are not immediately available to first-person consciousness—if they are, as Catherine Malabou puts it, "subjectively invisible"—this is not simply because they are somehow even more private and even more deeply buried within the self than consciousness. On the contrary: Montaigne's observation suggests that the place where consciousness falls short of our own inner motions is the place where feeling "begins," and that this, in turn, is the place where such feeling is potentially shared, communicated with others before it is shared with ourselves in interior communion. In his *Passions of the Mind in General* (1601), Thomas Wright suggests, like Montaigne, that we may not know our own feelings until we see them mirrored in another:

> Another remedy to know thyself, more palpable to be perceived and most profitable to be practiced, I think to be a certain reflection that thou mayest make of thyself after this manner: mark in other men their words, gestures, and actions when as they seem to thee to proceed from some inordinate Passion . . . . . After thou hast well noted the fruits of these Passions, make then a reflection upon thyself, and weigh whether thou hast not done heretofore and daily dost such like.[2]

Our passions, in other words, are by no means coextensive with our self-awareness, and the space that separates them is an essentially intersubjective one, in which another's feelings are more visible to me than my own and vice versa. Insofar as I am aware of them, the contents of my own consciousness may be private until I choose to make them public. But the presence within us of a feeling felt only by itself, prior to the intervention of first-person consciousness, makes the public-private distinction secondary to a publicness which is deeper and more fundamental than privacy itself—a sharing of affect which precedes the closing off of feelings from other people, and which is simultaneously physical, impersonal, and *inter*personal. Such sharing was arguably more familiar in the Renaissance than it is today: "The sight of others anguishes," Montaigne writes in an early essay, "doth sensibly drive me into anguish; and my sense hath often usurped the sense of a third man" (I, 20; 35), while for Agrippa von Nettesheim "pitty, which is a kind of sadness, doth often ill affect the body of him that takes pitty, that it seems to be the body of another man affected."[3] Mary Floyd-Wilson has recently demonstrated the pervasiveness in early modern culture of "sympathetic contagion, a concept in the period that explains not only the contraction of certain diseases but also the invisible penetration—from one body to another—of poisonous vapors, material spirits, and strong emotions,"[4] while Allison Hobgood has shown just how central such contagion was to early modern theatrical experience.[5]

In the last chapter, I focused on the ways in which feeling can be spread across a material environment before it is consciously articulated by and for the self. Here, in this final chapter, I will be thinking about how that feeling—however private and isolated it may seem—might also be shared across an intersubjective space, and thus experienced in ways that are fundamentally social, among which fainting will be a prime example. The notion of consciousness today almost invariably denotes an inner sphere of feeling and thought which is privately available to the self before it is shared with those around one; when it is defined in this way, consciousness and the transmission of affect will seem incompatible (as they are for Brennan and most affect theorists).[6] But in its original, etymological sense of "knowing-with," con-sciousness is shared by definition—as knowledge that necessarily occurs *with* others, it precedes consciousness as a private experience. Consciousness in this sense of private awareness may be secondary to its sharing, just as the word "consciousness" in the sense of first-person self-awareness is derivative. *The Winter's Tale*, as we will see in this final chapter, moves "backwards" in this regard: away from consciousness as an individual phenomenon and towards, in its final scene, an experience of consciousness in its original etymological sense of a knowledge that is primordially shared. Swooning in *The Winter's Tale*, therefore, does not undo consciousness but rather restores it to its original shared dimension.

As Montaigne's observation of his observers suggests, such sharing is not necessarily symmetrical or equitable. Montaigne's friends experience his feelings before he does so himself—almost as if it were impossible for all parties to partake of the same feeling simultaneously. Thus he describes this exchange of pathos not as a sharing but rather as a "usurping." To the extent that sympathy itself (deriving from the Greek *sym-pathos*, "same-feeling") refers not to a multiplication of feelings but to a "catching" of pathos in the singular, we can see why this asymmetry might be inevitable. In that blind spot where consciousness intersects with biology and our own affective energies are inaccessible to us—where we fail to feel our own feeling—others may grasp it, and even "usurp" it, in our stead. As a result, if consciousness is, as per its original sense, extended across multiple subjectivities, it is only extended in a kind of economy: the sharing of feeling means not that we both feel the same thing, but that at any given moment you may feel what I do not or vice versa, while I (or you) feel feeling's sudden lack. In *The Winter's Tale*, the transmission of affect will obey the law of this economy: feeling will be distributed or circulated, but only in a kind of zero-sum game where we each feel the other's feeling at the expense of feeling our own.[7] As we will see, fainting and stupefaction in *The Winter's Tale* are markers of the surpluses, imbalances, and asymmetries that are always built in to affective transmission, and to consciousness itself when it is understood as intrinsically shared.

This chapter will argue that the play is driven not by the theological and epistemological questions which have dominated recent discussions of it, but rather by a circulation of affect which is framed by Hermione's exit from and reentrance into "life," and resisted by Leontes's efforts to convert that circulation into knowledge.[8] Hermione's swoon, I will argue, evokes Mary's swoon at the foot of the cross, only to treat that swoon as a fully biological phenomenon, from which Hermione is eventually redeemed by organismal "life" itself. In this regard her swoon recalls Guyon's swoon; when "dear life redeems her," we will see, it is life in a literal, biological sense—Derrida's "auto-motricity and auto-affection," and the same life which rescues Guyon from his swoon.[9] Hermione's death and resurrection, I will suggest, are best understood in biological rather than theological terms: as extreme fluctuations in the economic distributions of a single, monistic substance which the play calls "life," and with which consciousness is deeply entangled (tragedy is the result of our failure to accept this entanglement). But that life is simultaneously social in nature, challenging the distinction between biological and political forms of life, *zoe* and *bios*, by showing that they are mutually constitutive: as Brennan puts it, "the traffic between the biological and the social is two-way; the social or psychosocial actually gets into the flesh and is apparent in our affective and hormonal dispositions."[10] If, as Michel Henry has suggested, "the subjectivity of life is precisely a community, not only of life but also of a potential group of the living," then the social swoons of *The Winter's Tale* provide a powerful example of how such a community might be enacted out of the very forces that threaten it.[11]

"Too Hot": Infectious Sentience at the Court of Sicily

The Winter's Tale begins in the royal court of Sicily, where the Sicilian king Leontes has been hosting his boyhood friend, the Bohemian king Polixenes, for nine months. Leontes has been trying in vain to convince him to stay longer, and when he asks his wife to try and she immediately succeeds, he is quickly overwhelmed by painful feelings of suspicion. Thus the play begins not with loss of sentience but rather with its overpowering excess, described in a tortured aside which Leontes delivers as Hermione and Polixenes give each other their hands in a warm sign of their agreement. It is hard not to wonder what in their seemingly innocuous exchange provokes this sudden, agonized outburst:

> Too hot, too hot!
> To mingle friendship far is mingling bloods.
> I have *tremor cordis* on me; my heart dances,
> But not for joy, not joy. This entertainment
> May a free face put on, derive a liberty
> From heartiness, from bounty, fertile bosom,
> And well become the agent—'t may, I grant.
> But to be paddling palms and pinching fingers,
> As now they are, and making practised smiles
> As in a looking-glass, and then to sigh, as 'twere
> The mort o'th'deer—O, that is entertainment
> My bosom likes not, nor my brows. (1.2.107–18)[12]

What is "too hot" here? Leontes's phrase at first seems to apply to the warmth exchanged between Hermione and Polixenes, and felt by each in the handshake—a feeling which is felt, then, outside Leontes himself, and which vexes him all the more inasmuch as he registers its transmission but cannot make it part of his own sensory world. But "too hot" also tells us how *he* feels about the warmth which is exchanged between *them* and from which he is excluded, so that paradoxically Leontes too is quickly overwhelmed by that warmth in a manner which might almost be erotic in itself. "The social . . . actually gets into the flesh" here, since in its very ambiguity "Too hot, too hot!" registers quite precisely this displacement from the warmth exchanged between Hermione and Polixenes to an incomprehensible surge of emotion within Leontes himself. He is afflicted by a *tremor cordis* whose sudden "thisness," as with Claudio's sensible warm motion, brings consciousness to felt awareness of itself only inasmuch as it erupts into it from without. Nothing Leontes *sees* can justify his reaction, but that is part of the scene's point, for (as Brennan argues) it is as unconscious feeling rather than visual stimulus or rational analysis that affect "gets under our skin," in a process for which tactility and olfaction are better sensory analogues than vision (Leontes resorts again and again to the sense of smell).[13] It can be no more easily explained than the contagious circulation of a disease.

That to which Leontes responds so negatively, I want to suggest, is simply this undue influx of warmth from without, instantly registered by him as a surge of physical discomfort in the body. But if Leontes's tendency to recoil from the physical and social world has often been noticed, and associated with his subsequent skepticism, it has less often been pointed out that this condition, as we are seeing, does not begin in separation from that world, but rather in a state of unsettling vulnerability to it.[14] We presume that the emotion giving rise to Leontes's sudden torment is jealousy, but his feelings initially lack jealousy's intelligibility; they are closer to a physical disease than to an emotion clearly related to something in the outside world.[15] Leontes's cognitive process thus allows us to see jealousy as an interpretation of a somatic disturbance which precedes it and is less clear-cut than it—a disturbance which, I have suggested, is at once social and biological in nature. It is Leontes himself, in his next monologue, who offers a surprisingly perspicacious description of the process whereby emotion turns such affect into belief:

> Sweet villain,
> Most dear'st, my collop—can thy dam, may't be
> Affection!—thy intention stabs the centre.
> Thou dost make possible things not so held,
> Communicat'st with dreams—how can this be?
> With what's unreal thou coactive art,
> And fellow'st nothing. Then 'tis very credent
> Thou mayst co-join with something, and thou dost,
> And that beyond commission, and I find it,
> And that to the infection of my brains
> And hard'ning of my brows. (1.2.135–44)

Again, Leontes's notoriously tangled and ambiguous syntax in fact reads quite clearly when we understand that it refers to a phenomenon which is equal parts social and physiological: "affection" is at once a reference to Polixenes and Hermione's putative romance, and an apostrophe to his own surge of "affection," which then becomes the antecedent of "thy."[16] Leontes's mind works by means of a kind of syncopation here, leaping forward to a new line (or musical "bar") of verse and thought before the old one has fully concluded, and thus slurring the two together. Again, the ambiguity that results from this powerfully conveys the unconscious process whereby the social is converted into the biological. Here, however, Leontes also begins to rationalize that process, converting feeling in turn into belief. Just as Othello insists that his "shadowing passion" must contain some "instruction," so Leontes tells us that his affection "stabs the centre": the metaphor captures the highly physical nature of that "affection" while also giving it epistemological validity by imagining its physical impact in terms of correspondence to a particular object in the outside world, a "centre" which evokes the target struck by an arrow. This self-description could still be ironizing or self-critical, for if we translate it into the modern philosophical terms of which it is already so suggestive, it spells out clearly the nature of Leontes's error: to the non-intentional affect which has seemingly overwhelmed him out of nowhere, he now attributes the intentionality (the "about-ness") of representational consciousness.[17] Half-knowingly, he is converting feeling into vision, seeming into seeing, *videor* into *videre*—the very same procedure adopted by Descartes in the *Meditations*. Like Othello, Leontes briefly lingers on the border between self-conscious recognition of that process and helpless acquiescence in it before succumbing fully to the latter. Between the onset of Leontes's feeling and his translation of that feeling into conviction, there transpires "the motion of an instant," a stound, a missing half-second: a syncope in which affect has not yet been fully converted into belief, so that self-feeling and self-awareness, as in Othello's speech, are still precariously tethered.

In Leontes's case, the instant's motion unfolds in a physical, bodily location—his "brows"—where those around him can read it and where it is capable of moving and being moved by them; they are also the site where he imagines—and perhaps feels—his cuckold's horns growing. Just as Montaigne's "visage and eyes do presently discover me. Thence *begin* all my changes," making them more readily available to his friends than to Montaigne himself, so Leontes's initial reaction to Hermione and Polixenes's gesture appears to originate from his brows, which are treated as equivalent to his heart: "My bosom likes not, nor my brows."[18] Only in Leontes's second speech do the brows occupy the position we might expect of them, in which they are secondary to a cognitive process leading "*to* the infection of my brains / And hard'ning of my brows." Between these speeches Leontes retrospectively "smooths over" the relationship between affect and cognition "to fit conscious requirements of continuity and linear casuality," and while the *result* of this process may well be the congealing of an interior mental space defined by corrosive skepticism towards an outside world in withdrawal, the process itself is by no means a purely interior one—it "begins," as in Montaigne's description, in the visage, and it ends there as well in a state of infection which is readily sharable with others.[19] Perhaps, therefore, we can understand Leontes's asides less as inner monologues, "the dreadful solitude of a soliloquy voiced at the heart of a social and domestic scene," than as versions of the cinematographic close-up as described by Gilles Deleuze in *Cinema 1*, which centers on the face.[20] Since the face, Deleuze argues, "expresses in a free way all kinds of tiny local movements which the rest of the body usually keeps hidden," the face itself is already a close-up. The double meaning of the early modern notion of "complexion"—both face and humoral constitution, for "the humours sometyme to resort vnto the skynne & vtter parts"—anticipates Deleuze's reading of the face as a site of affect in itself, and not merely its outward sign:[21]

> Sometimes the face thinks about something, is fixed on to an object, and this is the sense of admiration or astonishment that the English word *wonder* has preserved. In so far as it thinks about something, the face has value above all through its surrounding outlines, its reflecting unity which raises all the parts to itself. Sometimes, on the contrary, it experiences or feels something, and has value through the intensive series that its parts successively traverse as far as paroxysm, each part taking on a kind of momentary independence.[22]

It is the second mode of close-up, in which the face is traversed by an "intensive series" of what Deleuze calls "micromovements" culminating in paroxysm, which most closely captures Leontes's state in these passages—the way in which a sequence of ineluctable feelings successively ripples across his "brows," seeming to cast him finally into the paroxysm of an "infection." His brows are furrowed by a series of micromovements, "vitality effects" that are at once linguistic and affective: the fragmented syntactical units in which Leontes speaks are simultaneously spasms of affect successively contracting his brows, so that each movement of Leontes's thought is just that—a movement rather than a logical step. The notorious obscurity of Leontes's early speeches represents a carefully calibrated artistic effort to bring thought, feeling, and body as close together as possible, so that—as in Hamlet's speech—the player's distraction is "*in*'s aspect" and not simply conveyed by it. As complexion in both of its senses, the "brows" here are simultaneously the sign and site of an indistinct yet overwhelming humoral turmoil.

All of this means that Leontes's affect is a fundamentally social phenomenon, not only generated by an influx of shared feeling, but itself creating an atmosphere which alters that feeling in turn, changing how it is experienced by others. Insofar as Leontes's brow itself is what "experiences or feels something," it does not disclose, to the acute observer, a hidden inner core (as so often in *Hamlet*) where it is fully felt only by a private subject; rather, it is the locus of an "infection" transmitted by means of unconscious bodily contact across open material surfaces and felt impersonally in social space before it is internalized by the particular constituents of that space. Just as the origins of that infection are social, so its effects are felt socially as well: right after his second monologue, Leontes's unease begins to transmit itself back to those surrounding him:

> POLIXENES: What means Sicilia?
> HERMIONE: He something seems unsettled.
> POLIXENES: How, my lord?
> LEONTES: What cheer? How is't with you, best brother?
> HERMIONE: You look
> As if you held a brow of much distraction.
> Are you moved, my lord? (1.2.145–49)

Hermione does not, of course, quite know what Leontes is thinking—but as we have just seen, at least initially he does not either, nor is it the *content* of his thoughts after which Hermione asks. His "brow" serves not as an index to an occulted interiority, but rather as the shared site of an inexplicable transition in mood which is momentarily "held" by Leontes and yet quickly circulates among the group in a movement whose precise origin remains mysterious. Leontes's question to Polixenes—often reassigned to Polixenes himself, for whom it might seem more natural[23]—suggests either that Polixenes too is "infected," or that Leontes is trying to deflect attention from his own changed mood. Either way, a few moments later, after the subject has been changed to their children, Polixenes's thoughts do seem to have taken a more brooding turn: his son, he says, "with his varying childness cures in me / Thoughts that would thick my blood" (1.2.168–69). The precise nature of these thoughts is left unspecified—as yet Polixenes is only thinking *of* them—but perhaps that is because like Leontes's feelings they are experienced, in the first place, physically rather than intelligibly: thickness here, as for Leontes twice later on in the scene (1.2.184, 1.2.266), denotes the materiality of an experience which resists being made fully perspicuous. And that physicality, in turn, extends beyond individuals to form an affective atmosphere, encompassing each character but transparent to none. Certainly, the challenges that textual critics have faced in attributing some of these lines speaks to the difficulty of discerning not merely who is saying what, but who is feeling what in the context of a mood whose changes are experienced collectively rather than in isolation.

To Leontes himself, however, this idea of a feeling that is fundamentally shared, part of "a multiplicity, an expressive array of materials and postures and cases distributed across the social surround" before being private, quickly becomes intolerable.[24] Either his feelings are his own, or they are entirely the property of others—there is no room, in his descriptions, for a feeling that is shared, blurring the boundary between mine and yours. "Boundaries, paradoxically, are an issue . . . where the transmission of affect is denied," and indeed we soon find Leontes concerned to stabilize and settle the boundaries between what he feels and what those around him feel.[25] "[M]any thousand on's," he says to Camillo, "have the disease and feel't not" (1.2.203–4): for Leontes the fear of cuckoldry is the fear that, as in Montaigne's description of his own changes, what should be a private condition will be more palpable to others than to the self. As we saw, Leontes is initially surprised by the strength of his passion, but he was surprised because that strength came from without, from an exchange of feeling between others. Thus, as he broods, that surprise at his own feeling is gradually converted into its opposite—a fear that he can never be sentient enough, that others will always feel more than he does. The very strength of his feeling, and the sudden way in which it takes hold of him, apprise Leontes of a gap between that feeling and his awareness of it, so that he realizes, with Montaigne, how the same space that makes feeling available to others makes it invisible to the self: "How sometimes nature will betray its folly, / Its tenderness, and make itself a pastime / To harder bosoms!" (1.2.150–52). Leontes's fear of cuckoldry thus boils down, again and again, to an anxiety about being insensible to something taking place right under his own nose, about not sensing something that all others sense, and this anxiety is reflected in an increasingly shrill insistence on the prowess of his own sensorium:

> You smell this business with a sense as cold
> As is a dead man's nose; but I do see't and feel't,
> As you feel doing thus, and see withal
> The instruments that feel. (2.1.151–54)

It is as if Leontes, in order to compensate for that initial experience of imbalance in which feeling lay outside him, wishes that all sentience in the world could now belong to him. He apparently strikes himself in the breast here, equating his certainty about a fact in the external world with the certainty that accompanies feeling which is self-induced and self-felt; along the same lines, he is as certain about Hermione's unfaithfulness as he is certain that he has sense to begin with.[26] Once again, the sense *of* sensing—the awareness of the instruments that feel—becomes the guarantor for the certainty of Leontes's other perceptions as well, removing them from the unsettling play of social cognition which consistently threatens to leave him out of the picture, and giving them priority over the feelings of all others. Leontes's fantasy of seeing the instruments that feel is the fantasy of bridging the gap between first-person consciousness and the affect which underlies it—a fantasy whose fulfillment, as we have seen, requires us to relinquish our grasp on the first person. Indeed, there is a way in which Leontes's final, emphatic flourish here inadvertently opens onto a bottomless uncertainty, an aporia that we confront as soon as we try to get outside our own senses to confirm their soundness and bring the sources of our own feeling into the purview of the first person. For I actually cannot see the instruments that feel, just as I cannot see my own face and its myriad micromovements, where my changes begin. Only another is able to see them, and confirm for me that they exist: a generalized "you," perhaps, or a you with whom I am in conversation—but not I. Leontes's "you" names a necessary other which the social play of affect cannot do without, even—or especially—when such affect attempts to feel itself in an experience of "auto-affection." But since this "you" is something Leontes repudiates, he is forced by the frustrating evanescence of his own self-feeling to follow the Cartesian path in reverse, arguing, in a fallacious reductio ad absurdum, from the presumed reality of the external world to the reliability of his own self-sensing: "Is this nothing? / Why then the world and all that's in't is nothing, / The covering sky is nothing, Bohemia nothing, / My wife is nothing, nor nothing have these nothings / If this be nothing" (1.2.289–93).

Other characters in the play, as we have seen, are also attuned to the shared and mutable nature of feeling, but they do not respond to it in the same paranoid manner. In a brief speech at the end of act 1, Polixenes describes the infectious transmission of feeling which Leontes has apparently set in motion. But Polixenes is much more capable than his childhood friend of accepting the vagaries of feeling's circulation, which again take place in and through the face:

> Your changed complexions are to me a mirror,
> Which shows me mine changed too; for I must be
> A party in this alteration, finding
> Myself thus alter'd with't. (1.2.376–79)

In the "mirror" of Camillo's face, Polixenes finds an image of his own "changed complexions"—of a "brow" which, just like Leontes's, has been inexplicably infected. His "complexions" have already been changed when he sees himself, but only now does he realize this consciously, and thus the image of the mirror serves only to underscore its own inadequacy as a means of capturing feeling; it offers a "certain reflection" which, as in Thomas Wright, is necessarily belated with regard to our own passions and the behaviors they have caused. "Complexion" refers both to facial appearance and humoral constitution; like Leontes's "brow" and Deleuze's "affect-face," therefore, it is a site of feeling which blurs the boundaries between inner and outer. It is not merely, then, that Polixenes lacks a mirror in which to see his changed face, but also that the affective changes of his complexion in its full humoral sense are inaccessible to seeing and to consciousness in the first place, just as the instruments that feel are in fact invisible. The impossibility of seeing our own face becomes in this way a metonymy for the impossibility of pinning down our own affective life, the workings of our inner humoral "complexion," more broadly—the impossibility of making, in brief, consciousness coincide with complexion in all of its senses. Since the changes "begin," as Montaigne would have it, in one's brows or complexion, they are shared and intersubjective before they become available to private consciousness. One last time, then, we can say that "his chaunged powrs at first themselues not felt"—here because those changes are first articulated and those feelings are first felt in a "complexion" that is humoral, facial, and social before it is self-aware. Like Montaigne, Polixenes "finds" his changed complexions only when they become visible by being transmitted to another, echoing Leontes's own cognitive belatedeness from earlier ("and I find it"). But where Leontes quickly converts this tardy "finding" into a truth about the objective world with which he in turns makes claims on the knowledge of those around him, Polixenes is far more willing to be "party" to the social give-and-take of feeling, and more tolerant of the ways in which its changes, embedded in a shared world of sentience, persistently elude our knowledge. When it comes to the relationship between feeling and knowledge, Polixenes, we might say, is the Montaigne to Leontes's Descartes, accepting the fact that feeling, though inaccessible to representation, is fundamentally shared. Leontes had insisted that he could feel his own feelings, and indeed that he could see the very instruments that feel. In a perfect counterpoint to this delusion, Polixenes acknowledges that the changes in one's own complexion are invisible to the self until they are displaced to another, to that "you" which is inadvertently interpolated but never consciously acknowledged by Leontes.

Feeling Too Much: Hermione's *Spasimo*

Leontes imagines feeling as a zero-sum game: either he is blind to what all others feel, or his own sentience is endowed with an acuity of which all others fall short. Our sensoria, in other words, are deeply intertwined, and yet they are never shared in a balanced way: one person's feeling, for Leontes, must always usurp that of another. Paranoid though this vision may be, act 3 initially bears it out: Mamilius's sickness and death, and Hermione's swoon, are both tied to the hyperactivity of Leontes's senses and passions in acts 1 and 2, for which they compensate by depriving these characters of any sentience whatsoever. If feelings in *The Winter's Tale* all belong to that communal sentient substance which Spenser calls "vitall sap" (4.2.43), the play's pangs and swoons speak to the perpetual imbalances that are intrinsic to the processes of its transmission. At the same time, by evoking the controversial *spasimo* of the Virgin Mary, Hermione's swoon for the first time opens up a different vision of the sharing of affect: one that is grounded in the shared pathos of compassion rather than in the zero-sum distribution envisioned by Leontes.

In act 3, scene 2, Leontes puts Paulina on trial for her ostensible adultery with Polixenes (who in the meantime has fled back to Bohemia, suspected by Leontes of conspiring with Camillo to murder him). In the midst of Hermione's trial, Cleomenes and Dion return from Delphi with an unusually clear message from the oracle: "'Hermione is chaste, Polixenes blameless, Camillo a true subject, Leontes a jealous tyrant'" (3.2.130–31). In Shakespeare's source, Robert Greene's novella *Pandosto*, the oracle suffices to convince the king Pandosto (on whom Shakespeare bases Leontes) of his wife Bellaria's innocence. Pandosto immediately repents, and begins to explain his suspicions and subsequent actions. But he is interrupted by the news of his son Gartiner's death, which sets in motion a highly compressed series of faints:

> As he was thus relating the whole matter, there was word brought him that his young son Gartiner was suddenly dead, which news so soon as Bellaria heard, surcharged before with extreme joy and now suppressed with heavy sorrow, her vital spirits were so stopped that she fell down presently dead, and could be never revived. This sudden sight so appalled the king's senses, that he sank from his seat in a swound, so as he was fain to be carried by his nobles to his palace, where he lay by the space of three days without speech.[27]

The news of Gartiner's death upsets Bellaria so much that she swoons and dies, and this in turn "appalls" the king himself, causing him to fall into a "swound" for three days. Shakespeare follows the basic outlines of this sequence, but in his version it is only on the news of his son's death that the Sicilian king accepts the oracle's message, whereupon he falls into silence and repentance but not a "swound."

The Winter's Tale certainly leavens the melodrama of Greene, but this scene from the heart of *Pandosto* nevertheless serve to expose, in compressed and clearly visible form, that circulation of feeling with which Shakespeare's play is also suffused. Indeed, in Shakespeare's version the fundamental dynamic of the scene in *Pandosto*—the exchange of affective energy—is, if anything, even more clearly present by virtue of acting across greater distances. In the first place, Shakespeare gives us more background to the death of the king's son, who first becomes sick, at least according to Leontes, when he hears about his mother's "dishonour":

> To see his nobleness
> Conceiving the dishonour of his mother!
> He straight declined, drooped, took it deeply,
> Fastened and fixed the shame on't in himself,
> Threw off his spirit, his appetite, his sleep,
> And downright languished. Leave me solely; go,
> See how he fares. (2.3.12–18)

Leontes's account of his son's sickness no doubt reflects his solipsism, and when he immediately turns back to thinking of Polixenes—"Fie, fie, no thought of him" (2.3.18)—his line is oddly also applicable to the way in which, in his failed efforts *not* to think of Polixenes, Leontes simultaneously bars any kind of sympathetic response to the illness of his own son. At the same time, his description attributes to his son just what he himself lacks: an uncanny capacity to share another's feelings, to experience sympathy in the etymological sense of the word: he "fastened and fixed the shame on't in himself" even while "throwing off" his own self, "his spirit, his appetite, his sleep." It is, presumably, his mother's distress and not her shame which Mamilius has "straight . . . fastened and fixed . . . . in himself," but Leontes's phrase nevertheless captures well the underlying affective dynamic, in which Mamilius takes the causes of another's pain and instinctively inflicts them on himself, experiencing them fully in his own person.

This moment is one of a sequence of interpersonal affective reverberations in the play, all of which express the workings of sympathy not as pity but in its stronger, etymological sense of same-feeling. Just after Leontes has rejected the message from the oracle, a messenger arrives to tell him and Hermione that their son has died: "The prince, your son, with mere conceit and fear / Of the Queen's speed, is gone" (3.2.142–43). The messenger's account suggests that Leontes was not entirely off the mark when he described the causes of his son's illness, but that it was Paulina's "speed," her condition, rather than her "shame" which he "fixed and fastened upon himself." On hearing this news, Hermione swoons, just as in *Pandosto*; she is taken offstage, and shortly thereafter Paulina returns to tell Leontes that she too has died. One can truly speak of a circulation of affect here: Hermione's "speed" solicits strong emotion and then death in Mamilius, reciprocally sparking the same sequence in Hermione herself. When Paulina recounts all these events at the end of the scene, she lays out a causal chain in which what Leontes termed his "affection" and what she names his "fancies" are responsible for everything that follows:

> Thy tyranny,
> Together working with thy jealousies—
> Fancies too weak for boys, too green and idle
> For girls of nine—O think what they have done,
> And then run mad indeed, stark mad; for all
> Thy bygone fooleries were but spices of it. (3.2.177–82)

For Paulina, it is Leontes's own delusion which has set this whole chain of events in motion, the circle of affect that lays low his wife and son: his surfeit of sentience has, as it were, successively negated that of everyone around him, bearing out in tragically ironic form that inequitable distribution of feeling in which all except him are "stupefied" (2.1.165), and upon which Leontes himself had initially insisted. If it was Leontes's "conceit" which set this cycle in motion, then justly enough Paulina envisions that it will finally circulate back to him: "And then run mad indeed, stark mad."

If on the one hand, Shakespeare spaces out the highly compressed transmission of affect that we see in *Pandosto*, on the other hand his version, by dwelling more on the causes of Mamilius's swoon and relying more on messengers and offstage action, makes even clearer the workings of that interpersonal affective substance in which all of the characters are caught up. All of these features of the play serve to emphasize the presence of an affective network in which each individual's emotional state has consequences for those around him—in a proximity that is, however, only visible indirectly and secondhand. Indeed, that network, established in a series of actions-at-a-distance operating through the invisible arteries of human affect, has an almost magical quality to it, a mysterious oracular power which the oracle itself had lacked: "Apollo's angry, and the heavens themselves / Do strike at my injustice" (3.2.144–45), Leontes says, right as Hermione swoons. In Shakespeare's version of *Pandosto*, then, it is not the oracle but rather the operation of obscure interpersonal dependencies which, in the oracle's place, brings Leontes to his senses. Perhaps this is not so surprising: we have witnessed throughout the first two acts Leontes's obsession with the power of affection, his fixation on "the instruments that feel," and the hypersensitivity he comes to feel that he possesses. If earlier in the play Leontes had falsely attributed to those instruments the power of judgment, here those same instruments, almost in rebuke, lay claim to a very different power: a fatal, physiological effectiveness enacted in what is almost an allegorical tableau displaying mortality's absolute and arbitrary power. Affection's "intention stabs the centre" in a way that is very different from what Leontes had imagined; it is as if Leontes is being punished for having believed that he could translate its operations into certain judgments. Mamilius's and Hermione's deaths bear out, in a cruelly ironic way, Leontes's own insistence on the sheer power of feeling, in whose circulation Paulina, too, gets caught: "Woe the while! / O cut my lace, lest my heart, cracking it, / Break too!" (3.2.170–72). The middle acts of *The Winter's Tale* overwrite the idea of judgment and truth with a concept of an affective event—a feeling of feeling so strong that it negates feeling altogether—which plays out on the border between consciousness and loss of consciousness, between knowledge and blindness, between self and other.

Hermione's swoon, a climax of emotion followed by a long interim of wintery numbness, is at the center of these transfers of sentience. Unlike Mamilius's death, and Hermione's reported death a few moments later, her swoon takes place onstage, though it is still presented in a surprisingly oblique way. Paulina must direct Leontes's attention to this event which, despite his insistence on the power of his own senses, he needs guidance in order to see:

> PAULINA: This news is mortal to the Queen—look down
> And see what death is doing.
> LEONTES: Take her hence.
> Her heart is but o'ercharged; she will recover. (3.2.146–48)

Leontes's response evokes the way he had spoken of himself in the first two acts, in which his own heart had been "o'ercharged," implying, once more, a continuity between his own "*tremor cordis*" and Hermione's faint here.[28] But this almost breezy "diagnosis" also suggests that Leontes is still incapable of perceiving those around him as participating in a feeling which is independent of his own. While Leontes can only imagine Hermione's condition as an extension of his own condition, her swoon is in fact entirely one of sympathy: she does not merely feel pity for her son, but rather "usurps" (to borrow Montaigne's word for this process) his fatally powerful sorrow, expressing this identification by undergoing the same sequence of physiological symptoms as he does, a swooning followed by death. That Leontes does not swoon in Shakespeare's version heightens the contrast between him and Hermione: she is emptying out her own subjectivity in order to make space for feeling, not merely feeling for another but the feeling *of* another.

In this regard, Hermione's swoon subtly but powerfully evokes the iconographic tradition in which the Virgin Mary swoons at the foot of the cross on which her son has been crucified. Known as *lo spasimo*, Mary's swoon was a popular motif in early modern painting; it was influentially depicted by the Flemish painter Rogier van der Weyden in his mid-fifteenth-century altarpiece *The Descent from the Cross*, and was taken up in Italy by Filippino Lippi in an altarpiece for the church of Santissima Annunziata in Florence, completed in 1506 by Pietro Perugino.[29] Shakespeare would probably not have seen these paintings, but he certainly could have encountered *lo spasimo* at the end of the Catholic convert Thomas Lodge's *Prosopopeia Containing the Teares of the Holy, Blessed, and Sanctified Marie, the Mother of God*, published in 1596: "thus plagued in bodie and distressed in soule, sate poore Marie (a holy and happie virgin) enacting her griefe with her armes. . . . The image of her griefe before her, and the domage of her losse within her, she sownded on the senselesse earth."[30] In this description, Christ's suffering has become so completely her own that Mary sees it as a reflection of hers, "the image of her grief," rather than the other way around. And in *Salve Deus Rex Iudaeorum*, published in the year of the first recorded performances of *The Winter's Tale*, Aemilia Lanyer explicitly depicts *lo spasimo* in a section dedicated to "the sorrow of the Virgin Marie":

> His woefull Mother wayting on her Sonne,
> All comfortlesse in depth of sorow drowned;
> Her griefes extreame, although but new begun,
> To see his bleeding body oft shee swooned.[31]

The motif was a highly controversial one: in 1506 Cardinal Thomas Cajetan, whom Pope Julius II had charged to investigate the matter, issued an epistle arguing that there was no scriptural authority for it whatsoever, and that moreover, as a purely physical condition swooning was inappropriate to the Virgin "because it would have impeded this plenitude and perfection of grace."[32] Despite Cajetan's strictures, however, Italian painters continued to depict *lo spasimo*; as Harvey Hamburgh has argued, moreover, they did so not merely out of nostalgia for a vanishing cult of affective piety. Rather, by creating close visual parallels between Mary's swooning body and Christ's dead body above it (as can be seen in both van der Weyden and Lippi/Perugino), they drew implicitly on the notion, developed by medieval theologians including Saint Bernard of Clairvaux and Saint Bonaventure, that Mary's state at the foot of the cross "was no ordinary pathos" but rather full participation in the passion of Christ: "the imagery of the Virgin fallen beneath the cross that developed in art and literature could be excused because Mary experienced this *compassio* with the same spirit . . . with which Christ experienced his passion."[33] Her *compassio* for Christ, leading to her swoon, was to be understood not merely as pity, but rather as a deep sharing of Christ's own pain and suffering. And this sharing in turn could be understood as part of her role as *co-redemptrix*, for by sharing in Mary's passion, human sinners might, in turn, participate in Christ's suffering as well, and therefore in the grace obtained by his sacrifice on their behalf.

Thus, if the figure of Hermione can be seen "as evidence for not the disappearance but the traces and transformation of the Virgin into early modern culture," it is not only, as Gary Waller and others have suggested, in the resurrection scene in act 5, but also in her sympathetic *spasimo* in act 3.[34] The iconography of *lo spasimo* speaks not merely to the affective nature of medieval piety, but also to the ability of Mary and other saints to intercede with God on the behalf of a sinful humanity through the power of shared feeling. The result is a chain of affective sympathy in which the faithful are all invited to participate: human *compassio* with Mary enables *compassio* with Christ, and this in turn allows us to be redeemed by his suffering. This cascade of sympathetic feeling is just what Hermione's swoon is designed to evoke. Where her husband repudiates the sharing of affect, insisting that his share must be larger than everyone else's in order to counter the threat of its being usurped, Hermione's sympathetic swoon embraces that participatory experience of *compassio* underlying Mary's swoon as well—the mutual changing of complexion to which Polixenes too, in his own words, is "party." Where Cajetan and others had seen the notion of Mary's swoon as ascribing too much physicality to the mother of God, Shakespeare's play reverses this judgment, showing how it is precisely the physical immediacy of Hermione's response which distinguishes it from Leontes's persistent denial that feeling can or should be shared.

In acts 1 and 2 Leontes had reduced everything to sensation—insisting again and again that the truth was something he could see or even "smell." What turns out to elude the senses, however, is not a transcendent truth or idea, but rather the shared power of sensation itself—a self-sensing which, as we have seen in previous chapters, is incommensurable with the sense of self or identity, and which is invisible to first-person representation. As we are now beginning to realize, it becomes available to consciousness only in the measure that it also becomes available to others—not as other selves, but rather as other members of a community of affect grounded on experiences of transmission and sentient exchange that precede our distinction into discrete subjects. Leontes cannot "see" Hermione's swoon because he imagines it as an extension of his own feeling rather than as an instance of the shared feeling whose existence he has so consistently denied, and whose workings are, in fact, invisible. Paulina suggests that Hermione is suffering in a way that is immanent to her own body, that "death is doing" something to it—we might imagine here a shaking or trembling—which, since it is a thoroughly bodily condition, experienced in intimate contact with the material earth, Leontes will not perceive unless his attention is directed towards it. Under the aegis of Paulina, the sheer power of life, of physiology, takes on a truth-value unto itself, but it is not something that can be grasped through the operation of the ordinary senses or through consciousness itself as long as we conceive of it as tied to a self—it requires that kind of sympathy which Mamilius and his mother possess and which Leontes lacks, that capacity to enter into and to be entered by the feeling of another. As Leontes will say in the final act, "I saw her, / As I thought, dead" (5.3.139–40); to see her alive, as we will discover, will not be to *see* her at all. Hermione's swoon thus points up the way that Leontes's hypersensitivity has become a kind of numbness to the intersubjective sources of his very own feeling (just as part of Montaigne's *expérience* involves accepting how difficult it is to feel his own bodily workings). Though he will eventually learn to find himself in a feeling he shares with others, he must first pass through numbness himself; indeed, even after recognizing the oracle's authority, he seems strangely insensitive and dull. It is as if the wellsprings of his own feeling have been dried up by his long bout of jealous passion, and he lacks the emotional resources to respond adequately to what has happened, even as all those around him succumb, one by one, to the overmastering passion he has unleashed. The numbing of Leontes represents, at least for now, the final disposition of that shifting system of interpersonal sentience in which he too is caught up, and on whose persistently asymmetric, economic terms, although they leave him senseless now, he himself had insisted.

Hermione's swoon is notably different from all of the other examples that we have considered so far. It lacks any overt phenomenology: we do not get a verbal report from the brink of unconsciousness (as in

Montaigne and *Othello*), nor do we have a detailed description of her entrance into that state or what it reveals (as in Spenser). If the moments we have considered so far have served to disclose the phenomenology of those moments in which the first person becomes third person—in which feeling is not felt by a subject over against an object, but rather by its own immanent powers—Hermione's faint has little in common with them. But if this is the case, it is because in Hermione's case that transition from first to third person is both more sudden and more complete: unlike Montaigne, Guyon, Othello, and Leontes, she does not struggle to hold on to first-personness, but rather yields herself fully to a state of third-person feeling which is, in the moment of the swoon, fully identified—just as in Mary's *spasimo*—with the feeling of her son.

"Admiring the Nothing of It": Hypnotic Communities

For Leontes and Hermione, feeling is only shared in gendered extremes: Leontes insists that his feeling has usurped that of all of those around him, while Hermione proves willing to relinquish it altogether in joining her son. Extending this meditation on the asymmetrical partition of sentience, the final two acts of the play at the same time seek out ways of distributing feeling which are, if not more equitable, then at the very least more sustainable. From Autolycus's ballads through the song and dance of the sheep-shearing to the unveiling of the statue in the final scene, the last two acts of the play are centered on the question of aesthetic experience, and it is in the domain of the aesthetic, we discover, that feeling can be shared without being subordinated to either knowledge or death. Where Leontes attempted to transform his feeling of feeling into certainty about the world outside him—repressing, in the process, that feeling's fundamentally social origin—aesthetic experience in the conclusion of the play allows us to tarry acquiescently in the "nothing" of a feeling which refuses distinction into subject and object, and therefore refuses apportionment to discrete selves. Hypnotized into a sixteen-year-long swoon of its own by Time—"give my scene such growing / As you had slept between" (4.1.16–17)—the audience too is ready to participate in a process which restores them to the biological vitality of "growing" by means of a passage through insentience.

We saw in the first half of the play how Leontes's paroxysm of sensation, his sense of himself as endowed with a kind of hyper-sensibility, seemed to usurp everyone else's power of sensing altogether, causing them to lapse into a swoon and die. Act 4 also features a character whose sensory powers are heightened at the expense of everyone around him: the rogue Autolycus, that "snapper-up of unconsidered trifles" (4.3.25–26). Here too, in the pastoral world of Bohemia, sentience initially appears as a zero-sum game, a two-way affair in which one figure's surplus of sentience is always registered in another's deficit. Autolycus describes his heightened sensory attunement in terms which closely echo Leontes's assertion to Antigonus that "You smell this business with a sense as cold / As is a dead man's nose; but I do see't and feel't / As you feel doing thus": "I understand the business, I hear it. To have an open ear, a quick eye and a nimble hand is necessary for a cutpurse; a good nose is requisite also, to smell out work for th'other senses. I see this is the time that the unjust man doth thrive" (4.4.666–70). As in Leontes's speech, the nose is a metonymy for the senses as a whole, and indeed for a kind of master-sense, a sense of sensing, which governs and seeks out work for all the others. Autolycus always uses this power in a context which is social, performing deceptive scenes and singing ballads which cast his victims into a "stound" while he picks their pockets. He then draws on his own intensified sensorium in order to take advantage of them:

> My clown, who wants but something to be a reasonable man, grew so in love with the wenches' song that he would not stir his pettitoes till he had both tune and words, which so drew the rest of the herd to me that all their other senses stuck in ears—you might have pinched a placket, it was senseless; 'twas nothing to geld a codpiece of a purse; I would have filed keys off that hung in chains. No hearing, no feeling, but my sir's song, and admiring the nothing of it. (4.4.601–9)

It is as if Autolycus usurps from his victims not only their money but their senses as well, amassing sentience for the enhancement of his own excessively endowed faculties.

Yet if Autolycus's description of himself recalls Leontes's insistence on the prowess of his own sensorium and the numbness of all others, in Autolycus this stance is essentially benign: inasmuch as he regards the sharing of sentience as a purely economic opportunity, in which both feeling and capital may be freely redistributed, he accepts such sharing much more fully than Leontes. In this way his thievery, though it is grounded on our vulnerability to exchanges of feeling, acts as a corrective to the extreme imbalances to which such exchanges gave rise in the first three acts, and which still threaten to leave Hermione permanently numb. Rerouting feeling from the court to the country, Autolycus's "distribution of the sensible" also takes on that sociological significance which is essential to Jacques Rancière's concept of it: in him pastoral is figured not as a lost or idealized Arcadia, but as a rearrangement of affective economies which, when monopolized by the court, had proved deadly.[35] Where Leontes was determined to convert his heightened power of sensing—his sense *of* sensing, centered in the nose—into knowledge about the outside world, Autolycus is satisfied by the mere activity of sentient exchange as such, figured now in terms that are purely economic and nonhierarchical.

Such a vision may be Arcadian in its own right. For Michel Henry, it is in intersubjective exchanges of feeling such as Autolycus's hypnosis of his victims that the possibility of a community grounded in life's self-sensing can be found. Although it is profoundly intimate, the relationship between hypnotist and hypnotic does not involve mutual representation of one to the other—they do not, Henry argues, exist "for" one another, and their relationship, therefore, is not dependent on the preexistence of discrete subjects. It is not "based on sensory forms of communication that present individuals to one another as separate self-contained entities," an exchange in which "the response is imitated; it is precisely *not* transmitted."[36] Rather, the hypnotist and the hypnotic both participate "in life": "Neither the hypnotist nor the hypnotic exists for the hypnotic. This is because neither one of them appears in a world or is a phenomenon in the Greek sense. To put it in another way, the hypnotic does not represent either the other or him or herself, because the hypnotic is in life and in life there are no representations."[37] Hypnosis allows two subjects to relate in a way which is nonrepresentational, sidestepping the problem of other minds by restoring mind to the stream of felt vitality—an immersion which is only possible, however, in a trance-like state, and which remains asymmetrical in its distribution. Henry's description of the miniature sentient community involved in hypnosis is perfectly applicable to Autolycus's effect on his victims, and it shows how his sensory form of theft might be compatible with the pastoral, Arcadian world of the last two acts of the play. In his exchange of sentience with those he thieves from, Autolycus establishes a hypnotic community grounded not in their mutual representation of one another, but in their participation in a sensory life which is fundamentally shared—shared, however, before it pertains to parallel subjects, and therefore resisting division into "equal" portions, existing instead only in the transient asymmetries of sentient exchange. Indeed, although Autolycus's language echoes Leontes's description of himself, it also embodies what Leontes fears most: having "no hearing, no feeling" while, so to speak, his pockets are robbed—a deprivation in which sentience and property become practically synonymous. In contrast to

Leontes, Autolycus conditions us to accept the pleasures of a circulation which may always extend beyond our reach—to accept that feeling ourselves feel may also mean encountering a place where our feeling eludes us entirely, in moments of what Massumi calls "affective escape." Both Autolycus and his audience participate in the hypnotic admiration of an aesthetic "nothing" which is the counterpart to the nonsubjective state into which they have been cast; this "nothing" is not, as it was for Leontes, the opposite of a concrete reality, but rather a depersonalized sensory state unto itself.

The intersection of stupor, sentience, and life in communal aesthetic experience comes to a head in the scene of Hermione's resurrection. Although this scene has been the subject of much critical analysis in the last two decades, it has not always been noticed how closely Hermione's revival parallels Autolycus's relationship with his audience—and thus how stupefaction in this play always acts so as to beget more of itself. In enjoining dumbfounded contemplation from those around her, Hermione herself is able, as it were, to return to life by rerouting their relinquished sentience towards herself. As he takes in the statue, Leontes describes Hermione and the reaction she induces in her onlookers in terms of transferred sentience:

> O, thus she stood,
> Even with such life of majesty—warm life
> As now it coldly stands—when first I wooed her.
> I am ashamed. Does not the stone rebuke me
> For being more stone than it? O royal piece!
> There's magic in thy majesty, which has
> My evils conjured to remembrance, and
> From thy admiring daughter took the spirits,
> Standing like stone with thee. (5.3.34–42)

If Hermione's swoon evoked Mary's *spasimo* at the foot of the cross, her appearance here as a statue speaks to a later stage in her Mariological evolution: her transformation into an icon, an object of veneration that stands in for a divine being. But as we saw in that earlier scene, it is not on the confessional dimension of the swoon that Shakespeare draws so much as on its capacity to trigger an intersubjective chain of affective response, a "ripple effect of vitality across bodies."[38] When we see this scene as framed by the hypnotic effects of the roguish Autolycus, it appears resolutely secular, grounded in the transmissions of feeling that are immanent to a vital and physical cosmos rather than in a higher moral order. Replaying her swoon in reverse, Hermione's reawakening completes the social circle of affect which was so crucial to its iconographic function.[39] The swooning Hermione entered her own stony state in response to her son's condition, and Leontes and Perdita now both take on the stony state of the statue even as the statue enters life once more. Hermione, Leontes says, "took the spirits" from Perdita—the spirits here are, as in Spenser, the intersubjective stuff of feeling, distributed between two seemingly separate subjects. Aesthetic experience becomes the vehicle for a circulation of feeling which finally allows Leontes—like Polixenes and Montaigne—to find his "changed complexion" mirrored in another. As this final scene suggests, losing and regaining consciousness are more related than they are distinct: both bring us closer than is normally possible to the palpable yet invisible texture of life itself. As we saw with Othello's swoon, moreover, such moments are characteristic of theater when we understand it as, in Witmore's phrase, a "substance made of embodied processes," or, in Wojciehowski's phrase, of "vitality effects."

"Dear life redeems" (5.3.103) Hermione from her coma, therefore, just as "Life having conquered her sencelesse foe" awakens Guyon from his trance: if the weakening of the spirits is what causes the trance, it is those same spirits which, as Avicenna argues, restore it. As Leontes recognizes when he declares that "if this be magic, let it be an art / As lawful as eating" (5.3.110–11), his wife's reawakening is a phenomenon no less mysterious for being fully biological and sentient in nature. Like Guyon, Hermione has been restored to life by nothing other than that life, by the miracle of a feeling that engenders and feels itself at the same time. The emphasis throughout the scene is not on a transcendent power, but rather on the miracle of a vitality that is both sentient and sensible: "The very life seems warm upon her lip" (5.3.66), Polixenes says. It was Leontes who had been overwhelmed by the sheer warmth of vitality in the opening act: "Too hot! Too hot!" but in his struggles to make that vitality *his*—to sense his self-sensing and see the instruments that feel—he negated the vitality of all those around him.[40] Now, he sees that such vitality is intrinsically shared—that it is only truly palpable when we touch each other. "O, she's warm" (5.3.109), he says as his wife comes back to life: perceiving another's warmth as opposed to his own, Leontes does not simply acknowledge the existence of a separate other—or if he does so, it is only after participating in the shared current of life which precedes distinction into self and other entirely.[41]

That current can never be seen, it can never be represented as the object of a discrete subject standing outside of it.[42] It can only be felt in an immanence which is intractable to all representation—it is this condition which makes it so difficult for consciousness to perceive itself. But here, in the final scene of *The Winter's Tale*, we reach a resolution to that impasse, and we find it in a feeling that is at once communal and physical, at once aesthetic and natural. Feeling feeling, it turns out, means accepting the fact that *this* feeling will always be other than *our own* feeling, that it will always be better embodied in another even as our own feeling may in turn be more palpable to those around us. In feeling another's feeling—Hermione's "warmth"—Leontes is finally restored to his own, but first that feeling must pass through the medium of insentience embodied here in works of art, from Autolycus's hypnotic "nothings" to the astonishing statue unveiled by Paulina. Fainting, in our final example, means confronting the limits of our own capacity to feel, which in turn means being capable of inhabiting the place where feeling is something we share with others. That is the place where consciousness reverts to the collective form of sentience which Henry terms "pathos-with"—or, to return consciousness to its original meaning, a knowledge that is shared *with* the other before it is *of* the other.[43] As the stony state of Hermione's onlookers reminds us, such knowledge is only made available by passing first through a "stound" in which we are willing to relinquish our hold on consciousness altogether, making way for that of another.

NOTES

Chapter 1

1. For useful discussions of the history of the terms "consciousness" and "conscience," see C. S. Lewis's chapter on "Conscience and Conscious" in *Studies in Words* (Cambridge: Cambridge University Press, 1960), 181–213; Catherine Glyn Davies, *Conscience as Consciousness: The Idea of Self-Awareness in French Philosophical Writing from Descartes to Diderot* (Oxford: Voltaire Foundation, 1990), 1–21; and Bruce Smith, *The Key of Green: Passion and Perception in Renaissance Culture* (Chicago: University of Chicago Press, 2009), 34–35. For "conscience" as the "internal witness," see Lewis, 187–90; for the "desynonymisation" of "conscience" and "consciousness," see Lewis, 183.

2. See John Denham, *The Poetical Works of Sir John Denham*, ed. Theodore Howard Banks Jr. (New Haven, Conn.: Yale University Press, 1928), 83; and John Milton, *Paradise Lost*, 2nd ed., ed. Alastair Fowler (Harlow, Eng.: Pearson, 2007), 6.521. All references to Milton's Paradise Lost will follow this edition.

3. I follow John Webster, *The Duchess of Malfi*, ed. Brian Gibbons (London: Methuen, 1994); John Donne, *The Songs and Sonets of John Donne*, 2nd ed., ed. Theodore Redpath (Cambridge, Mass.: Harvard University Press, 1983); and Michel de Montaigne, *The Essayes of Michael Lord of Montaigne*, trans. John Florio, ed. Henry Morley (London: Routledge, 1893). In citations of Montaigne here and throughout, the book and essay number of the quotation, in Roman and Arabic numerals respectively, will be followed by the page number in this edition. Quotations from the French original follow *Les Essais*, ed. Jean Balsamo, Michel Magnien, and Catherine Magnien-Simonin (Paris: Gallimard, 2007).

4. For Aristotle's account of the sensitive soul, see his *On the Soul* 2.5–3.3. I follow Aristotle, *On the Soul, Parva Naturalia, On Breath*, trans. W. S. Hett (Cambridge, Mass.: Harvard University Press, 1936).

5. See Charles H. Kahn, "Sensation and Consciousness in Aristotle's Psychology," in *Articles on Aristotle*, ed. Jonathan Barnes, Malcolm Schofield, and Richard Sorabji (London: Duckworth, 1979), vol. 4: 1–31. In *Mirages of the Selfe: Patterns of Personhood in Ancient and Early Modern Europe* (Stanford, Calif.: Stanford University Press, 2003), Timothy Reiss argues that Aristotle's notion of the soul "was tied to a quite different idea and experience of mind and person from anything now familiar to western people. To speak of 'body' *or* 'soul' as *subject* is to distort that notion and experience toward this latter familiarity" (88).

6. Since Jacob Burckhardt, who saw the Italian Renaissance as the moment in which "man became a spiritual *individual*, and recognized himself as such," the claim has taken a range of competing forms: from Catherine Belsey, for whom bourgeois subjectivity "is a product of the second half of the seventeenth century" which denies its foundations in the "range of subject-positions defined by the discourses in which the concrete individual participates," to Katharine Eisaman Maus, who sees the newly intense inwardness of the English Renaissance

as "an almost inevitable result of religious oppression," to Gail Kern Paster's "humoral subjectivity," which is "constituted by the humors coursing through the bloodstream and saturating the flesh." See Jacob Burckhardt, *The Civilization of the Renaissance in Italy* (New York: Harper and Row, 1958), 143; Catherine Belsey, *The Subject of Tragedy: Identity and Difference in Renaissance Drama* (London: Methuen, 1985), 33, 5; Katharine Eisaman Maus, *Inwardness and Theater in the English Renaissance* (Chicago: University of Chicago Press, 1995), 17; and Gail Kern Paster, *Humoring the Body: Emotions and the Shakespearean Stage* (Chicago: University of Chicago Press, 2004), 22. These, however, are just some of the more influential versions of the claim.

7. Burckhardt, *Civilization of the Renaissance*, 143.

8. See Lewis, *Studies in Words*, 189, 211.

9. See Belsey, *Subject of Tragedy*, 35. Maus criticizes the ways in which "'subjectivity' is often treated casually as a unified or coherent concept when, in fact, it is a loose and varied collection of assumptions, intuitions, and practices that do not all logically entail one another and need not appear together at the same cultural moment." Maus, *Inwardness and Theater*, 29.

10. See Brian Cummings and Freya Sierhuis, eds., *Passions and Subjectivity in Early Modern Culture* (London: Ashgate, 2013), 5; Cummings and Sierhuis discuss Belsey on this page as well.

11. Fowler and most other editors gloss "conscious" here as "guilty."

12. William James, *Essays in Psychology* (Cambridge, Mass.: Harvard University Press, 1983), 144.

13. Maurice Merleau-Ponty, *Signs*, trans. Richard C. McCleary (Evanston, Ill.: Northwestern University Press, 1964), 203.

14. The question of whether a concept of consciousness goes back to classical antiquity is a vexed one. For consciousness in Aristotle, see Charles H. Kahn, "Sensation and Consciousness in Aristotle's Psychology," in *Articles on Aristotle*, vol. 4: 1–31, esp. 22–31; and Richard E. Aquila, "On Plotinus and the 'Togetherness' of Consciousness," *Journal of the History of Philosophy* 30, no. 1 (1992): 12n. For notions of consciousness in Plotinus, see Aquila, "On Plotinus"; and Edward W. Warren, "Consciousness in Plotinus," *Phronesis* 9, no. 2 (1964): 83–97. For the argument that Plotinus was the first philosopher to articulate a concept of consciousness in its modern sense of subjective self-awareness, see H.-R. Schwyzer, "'Bewusst' und 'unbewusst' bei Plotin," in *Les Sources de Plotin, Entretiens sur l'antiquité classique* 5 (Vandoeuvres-Genève: Fondation Hardt, 1960).

15. See Gideon Manning, "Mechanizing the Sensitive Soul," in *Matter and Form in Early Modern Science and Philosophy*, ed. Gideon Manning (Leiden: Brill, 2012).

16. René Descartes, *The Philosophical Writings of Descartes*, trans. John Cottingham, Robert Stoothoff, and Dugald Murdoch (Cambridge: Cambridge University Press, 1985), vol. 2: 13.

17. Ibid., 19. Emphasis in original.

18. Descartes, *The Philosophical Writings of Descartes*, vol. 1: 195.

19. Michel Henry, *The Genealogy of Psychoanalysis*, trans. Douglas Brick (Stanford, Calif.: Stanford University Press, 1993), 21.

20. Descartes, *The Philosophical Writings of Descartes*, vol. 2: 171.

21. Quoted in Michel Henry, *The Genealogy of Psychoanalysis*, 21.

22. See Michel Henry, *Material Phenomenology*, trans. Scott Davidson (New York: Fordham University Press, 2008), 81: "A seeing that would only see would be a phenomenological nothing; it would see nothing. There is only seeing if, in an unperceived way, seeing is more than itself. There always acts within it a power other than its own, a power in which it is auto-affected so that it feels its seeing and feels itself seeing. In this way, we should not say that 'we see' (*videmus*) but, like Descartes, 'we feel our seeing' (*sentimus nos videre*). This auto-affection is the original phenomenality, the original givenness as a self-givenness, for example, the self-givenness of seeing to itself."

23. I am here synthesizing and simplifying the complex set of arguments which Henry lays out in *Genealogy of Psychoanalysis*, 18–30.

24. Henry, *Genealogy of Psychoanalysis*, 23.

25. Ibid., 22.

26. For another account of Descartes which reads the cogito in this way, see Lilli Alanen, *Descartes's Concept of Mind* (Cambridge, Mass.: Harvard University Press, 2003).

27. Jean-Luc Marion, *Cartesian Questions: Method and Metaphysics* (Chicago: University of Chicago Press, 1999), 105.

28. See Aristotle, *On the Soul*, 143–45.

29. Daniel Heller-Roazen, *The Inner Touch: Archaeology of a Sensation* (New York: Zone, 2007), 35.

30. Ibid., 49.

31. For Gregory Seigworth and Melissa Greg, "affect, at its most anthropomorphic, is the name we give to those forces—visceral forces beneath, alongside, or generally *other than* conscious knowing, vital forces insisting beyond emotion—that can serve to drive us toward movement, toward thought and extension, that can likewise suspend us (as if in neutral) across a barely registering accretion of force-relations, or that can even leave us overwhelmed by the world's apparent tractability." See Gregory J. Seigworth and Melissa Gregg, eds., *The Affect Theory Reader* (Durham, N.C.: Duke University Press, 2010), 1.

32. Aristotle, *On the Soul*, 67; and Jacques Derrida, *The Animal That Therefore I Am*, trans. David Wills (New York: Fordham University Press, 2008), 49–50. The notion of auto-affection is interrogated by Derrida throughout his writings, starting from his *Speech and Phenomena and Other Essays on Husserl's Theory of Signs*, trans. David B. Allison and Newton Garver (Evanston, Ill.: Northwestern University Press). See especially 78–87.

33. Henry, *Material Phenomenology*, 48.

34. Michel Henry, "Phenomenology of Life," *Angelaki* 8, no. 2 (2003): 97–110, 103.

35. Catherine Malabou, *The New Wounded: From Neurosis to Brain Damage*, trans. Steven Miller (New York: Fordham University Press, 2012), 43. See also Catherine Malabou and Adrian Johnston, *Self and Emotional Life: Philosophy, Psychoanalysis, and Neuroscience* (New York: Columbia University Press, 2013), 48: "We now face two concepts of affects and autoaffection: a traditional one, according to which the subject is affected by an object and by itself first of all; and a different one, according to which affects come before subjectivity as such, as events, points of impact of these events on a surface, like colors on a canvas. If we follow this second line of interpretation, affects and autoaffections are

heteroaffections to the extent that they separate the human subject, the 'I,' from itself."

36. For Damasio's idea of the proto-self, see his *The Feeling of What Happens: Body and Emotion in the Making of Consciousness* (New York: Harcourt, 1999), chap. 6. "The proto-self is an interconnected and temporarily coherent collection of neural patterns which represent the state of the organism, moment by moment, at multiple levels of the brain. We are *not* conscious of the proto-self" (174).

37. Malabou, *Self and Emotional Life*, 34. See also her *The New Wounded*, 45: "the only possible subjective experience of cerebral auto-affection is that of the suffering that follows its damage or interruption." See *Self and Emotional Life*, 31, for her reference to Damasio.

38. Brian Massumi, *Parables for the Virtual: Movement, Affect, Sensation* (Durham, N.C.: Duke University Press, 2002), 36.

39. Paster, *Humoring the Body*, 246.

40. Michael Schoenfeldt, *Bodies and Selves: Physiology and Inwardness in Spenser, Shakespeare, Herbert, and Milton* (Cambridge: Cambridge University Press, 1999), 11.

41. Ibid., 2. For Bruce Smith's notion of "historical phenomenology," see *The Key of Green*, 28–29.

42. Schoenfeldt, *Bodies and Selves*, 3.

43. Paster, *Humoring the Body*, 12.

44. Ibid., 20.

45. Drew Daniel, *The Melancholy Assemblage: Affect and Epistemology in the English Renaissance* (New York: Fordham University Press), 25–26. For a similar critique, see Steven Mullaney, *The Reformation of the Emotions in the Age of Shakespeare* (Chicago: University of Chicago Press, 2015): "Whether an etiological theory is humoral, neurological, or hormonal, it has little to tell us about emotional experience. Does my sadness differ from my daughter's because I think emotions are neurological in their physiology and she has never heard of that? Such contemporaneous theories have a great deal to tell about the history of ideas, but their application to the way things felt—a phenomenology of Elizabethan emotions—seems, to say the least, problematic" (21).

46. See Cummings and Sierhuis, *Passions and Subjectivity*, 5 and 7; and James A. Knapp, "Beyond Materiality in Shakespeare Studies," *Literature Compass* 11, no. 10 (November 2014): 677–90, 684.

47. For a broad account of phenomenology as a methodology applicable to early modern literature, see Kevin Curran and James Kearney, "Introduction," *Criticism* 54, no. 3 (summer 2012): 353–64. For Curran and Kearney, "phenomenology is interested not only in the subject as the necessary lens that apprehends the knowable world, but also in the fact that the apprehending subject is always situated within a scene that necessarily involves other people, other things" (358). Neither they nor the essays collected in this issue address directly the question I am raising here, and indeed, this definition preserves the language of dualism almost intact.

48. See especially the essays gathered in Amanda Bailey and Mario DiGangi, eds., *Affect Theory and Early Modern Texts: Politics, Ecologies, and Form* (New York: Palgrave, 2017).

49. Ibid., 2–3.

50. See Ruth Leys, "The Turn to Affect: A Critique," *Critical Inquiry* 37, no. 3 (spring 2011): 434–72.

51. See Benedict S. Robinson, "Thinking Feeling," in *Affect Theory and Early Modern Texts*, ed. Bailey and DiGangi, 111.

52. For the distinction between "beginning" and "constituted Cartesianism," see Henry, *Genealogy of Psychoanalysis*, 54.

53. Ibid., 52.

54. Garrett Sullivan Jr., *Sleep, Romance, and Human Embodiment: Vitality from Spenser to Milton* (Cambridge: Cambridge University Press, 2012).

55. Ibid., 39

56. Robert Ellrodt, *Shakespeare and Montaigne: The Emergence of Modern Self-Consciousness* (Manchester, Eng.: Manchester University Press, 2015), 84.

57. I follow William Shakespeare, *Measure for Measure*, ed. N. W. Bawcutt (Oxford: Oxford University Press, 1991).

58. It should be obvious that the life I have in mind is primarily *zoe*, "biological life in its repetitive rhythms of consumption, growth, and decay," rather than *bios*, "political life as the practice of public virtue." For this distinction drawn from Aristotle via the work of Giorgio Agamben, see Julia Reinhard Lupton, *Thinking with Shakespeare: Essays on Politics and Life* (Chicago: University of Chicago Press, 2011), 3. In the series of readings that follow, however, Lupton shows just how closely the two forms of life may be entangled. I will return to this important point in my final chapter.

59. For some cogent criticism of reductionist materialism in early modern studies, see Knapp, "Beyond Materiality in Shakespeare Studies": "The claim that everything is ultimately equivalent to the material reality in which human experience occurs must be modified to include something beyond empirical perception, and possibly beyond materiality" (686).

60. Joseph Campana, *The Pain of Reformation: Spenser, Vulnerability, and the Ethics of Masculinity* (New York: Fordham University Press, 2012), 127.

61. Massumi, *Parables for the Virtual*, 14.

62. Catherine Clément, *Syncope: The Philosophy of Rapture*, trans. Sally O'Driscoll and Deirdre M. Mahoney (Minneapolis: University of Minnesota Press, 1994), 5. For Clément's more recent account of trance phenomena, this time from a more purely anthropological perspective, see *The Call of the Trance* (London: Seagull Books, 2014).

63. Clément, *Syncope*, 4, 42.

64. See, for example, Henry, *Material Phenomenology*, 42: "Everything that the Greek phenomenon fails to clarify through its ek-static light. . . . this is what we truly are."

65. Clément, *Syncope*, 15.

66. Plato, *Complete Works*, ed. John M. Cooper (Indianapolis, Ind.: Hackett, 1997), 461 and 402.

67. See, for example, Ficino's *Platonic Theology*, ed. James Hankins, trans. Michael J. B. Allen (Cambridge, Mass.: Harvard University Press, 2003), vol. 3: 12–15: "Contrariwise, when the soul despises corporeals and when the senses have been allayed and the clouds of phantasmata dissipated, and it perceives something on its own, then the intellect discerns truly and is at its brightest. We see this in the case of those who prophesy during the quiet of sleep or some other alienation from

the body." For an account of the "Hermetic trance" as "the supreme Hermetic experience, as described in *Pimander*, in which the soul was transformed into the light of the divine *mens*, in the likeness of which it was created, [and] the body 'slept' during the whole vision, the senses being bound whilst the soul left the body to become divine," see Frances Yates, *Giordano Bruno and the Hermetic Tradition* (Chicago: University of Chicago Press, 1964), 280–81. See also Michael J. B. Allen's chapter on "Poetic Madness" in his *The Platonism of Marsilio Ficino: A Study of His "Phaedrus" Commentary, Its Sources and Genesis* (Berkeley: University of California Press, 1984), 41–67: "Whether Ficino experienced such mystical flights himself is difficult to ascertain, but he certainly believed in the absoluteness of their reality and in the possibility of a few men truly attaining them during this life for however brief a time. He customarily sought and, according to eyewitness accounts, effectively achieved trancelike, enraptured states during his Orphic lyre recitals when he intoned Platonic hymns apparently to the sun" (60).

68. I follow *The English Bible: The King James Version*, ed. Gerald Hammond and Austin Busch (New York: Norton, 2012), vol. 2: 388.

69. For a comprehensive study of *raptus* and the related notion of *excessus mentis* in the Middle Ages, see Barbara Faes de Mottoni, "'Excessus mentis,' 'alienatio mentis,' estasi, 'raptus' nel Medioevo," in *Per una storia del concetto di mente*, ed. Eugenio Canone (Florence: Olschki, 2005), 167–84.

70. I follow Dante Alighieri, *Paradiso*, trans. Robert Hollander and Jean Hollander (New York: Anchor, 2008).

71. Barry Windeatt, "The Art of Swooning in Middle English," in *Medieval Latin and Middle English Literature: Essays in Honour of Jill Mann*, ed. Christopher Cannon and Maura Nolan (Cambridge: D.S. Brewer, 2011), 211–30, 230. See also Judith Weiss, "Modern and Medieval Views on Swooning," in *Medieval Romance, Medieval Contexts*, ed. Rhiannon Purdie and Michael Cichon (London: Boydell and Brewer, 2011), 121–34. In the Middle Ages, Weiss argues, "the phenomenon of fainting by both men and women is well established and is clearly meant to denote an accepted response to strong emotion" (124).

72. Windeatt, "The Art of Swooning," 224.

73. I follow Geoffrey Chaucer, *Troilus and Criseyde*, ed. Stephen Barney (New York: Norton, 2006).

74. "It demonstrates, in the clearest possible way, his subjection to Criseyde and to his love of her, and his dissociation from the idea that she is not still her 'owene womman' " (328). Jill Mann, "Troilus' Swoon," *The Chaucer Review* 14, no. 4 (spring 1980): 319–35.

75. According to *A Dictionary of Stage Directions in English Drama*, ed. Alan Dessen and Leslie Thomson (Cambridge: Cambridge University Press, 2012), in stage directions from 1580 to the shuttering of the theaters in 1642, "*swoon* and its variant spelling *sound* each occur about a dozen times, often combined with *fall*" (223); the entry lists instances ranging from Shakespeare's *Henry IV, Part 2* to Tourneur's *The Atheist's Tragedy* and Fletcher's *The Humorous Lieutenant*. As for stage directions calling for a "faint," at least seventeen are recorded, usually "without embellishment" (87). For faints and fits in Shakespeare, see Kenneth W. Heaton, "Faints, Fits, and Fatalities from Emotion in Shakespeare's Characters: Survey of the Canon," *British Medical Journal* 333, no. 7582 (2006): 1335–38. For an illuminating study of swooning and its gendered dimension in the

Elizabethan prose romance, see Margaret Simon, "Authorial Feints and Affecting Forms in George Gascoigne's *The Adventures of Master F.J.*," in *Renaissance Papers 2013*, ed. Jim Pearce and Joanna Kucinski (Woodbridge, Eng.: Boydell and Brewer, 2013), 43–54.

76. Michael Screech, *Montaigne and Melancholy: The Wisdom of the Essays* (London: Duckworth, 1983), 20.

77. Windeatt, "Art of Swooning," 230.

78. Galen, *Method of Medicine*, ed. and trans. Ian Johnston and G. H. R. Horsley (Cambridge, Mass.: Harvard University Press), vol. 3: 265.

79. Sir Thomas Elyot, *Biblioteca Eliotae* (London, 1542), sig. Kk6v.

80. Philip Barrough, *The Methode of Phisicke* (London, 1583), 74.

81. Sir Philip Sidney, *The Countess of Pembroke's Arcadia*, ed. Albert Feuillerat (Cambridge: Cambridge University Press, 1962–63), vol. 2: 463.

82. Alva Noë, *Out of Our Heads: Why You Are Not Your Brain, and Other Lessons from the Biology of Consciousness* (New York: Hill and Wang, 2010).

83. All references follow Edmund Spenser, *The Faerie Queene*, ed. Thomas P. Roche Jr. (Harmondsworth, Eng.: Penguin, 1978).

84. Ralph Cudworth, *The True Intellectual System of the Universe* (London: Richard Royston, 1678), 160–61.

85. Walter Charleton, *Natural History of Nutrition, Life, and Voluntary Motion* (London: Henry Herringman, 1659), 120.

86. Ibid., 122. For Timothy Harrison's discussion of Charleton see his "Personhood and Impersonal Feeling in Montaigne's 'De l'Exercitation,'" *Modern Philology* 114, no. 2 (November 2016): 226. I am grateful to Harrison's article for bringing this passage to my attention.

87. Margaret Cavendish, *Ground of Natural Philosophy* (London: A. Maxwell, 1668), 100.

88. Ibid., 121.

89. John Locke, *An Essay Concerning Human Understanding*, ed. Alexander Campbell Fraser (New York: Dover, 1959), vol. 1: 138.

90. Ibid., 457.

91. Ibid., 450.

92. Ibid., 131.

93. Montaigne cites the enormous range of theories about the nature of the soul available in the Renaissance as amounting to so much evidence of human ignorance in his "Apologie of Raymond Sebond." For useful overviews of late Renaissance theories of the soul, see Dennis Des Chene, *Life's Form: Late Aristotelian Conceptions of the Soul* (Ithaca, N.Y.: Cornell University Press, 2000); and Fernando Vidal, *The Sciences of the Soul: The Early Modern Origins of Psychology*, trans. Saskia Brown (Chicago: University of Chicago Press, 2011).

94. For a study of Shakespearean theater in the context of early modern questions surrounding the soul, see Donovan Sherman, *Second Death: Theatricalities of the Soul in Shakespeare's Drama* (Edinburgh: Edinburgh University Press, 2016).

Chapter 2

1. See especially Charles Taylor, *Sources of the Self: The Making of the Modern Identity* (Cambridge, Mass.: Harvard University Press, 1989); and Reiss, *Mirages of the Selfe*.

2. For the argument that Montaigne "inaugurates" "the search for the self in order to come to terms with oneself," see Taylor, *Sources of the Self*, 183. For the theme of the self in Montaigne, see also Hugo Friedrich, *Montaigne*, trans. Dawn Eng, ed. Philippe Desan (Berkeley: University of California Press, 1991; original German edition, 1949), 207–58; Richard Regosin, *The Matter of My Book: Montaigne's "Essais" as the Book of the Self* (Berkeley: University of California Press, 1977); and Jean Starobinski, *Montaigne in Motion*, trans. Arthur Goldhammer (Chicago: University of Chicago Press, 1985), 6–14.

3. For the idea that Montaigne's concept of selfhood consists above all in "the constant movement of thought," see Reiss, *Mirages of the Selfe*, 442, and also 458: "the essential character of the universal 'human condition' was its 'perennial seesaw,' in which 'stability itself' was 'nothing but a more languid motion.'" Reiss's account is seconded by Hugh Grady in *Shakespeare, Machiavelli, and Montaigne: Power and Subjectivity from "Richard II" to "Hamlet"* (New York: Oxford University Press, 2002), 109–25, esp. 120, which defines Montaigne's notion of subjectivity in terms of "a private, even withdrawn mental flux which is unfixed and undefined—barely a subject in some of the key traditional senses of the word at all, since it is not an agent in the world" (120). For a contrasting view, see John Lee, "'A Judge That Were No Man': Montaigne, Shakespeare, and Imagination," in *The Shakespearean International Yearbook*, vol. 6 (Aldershot, Eng.: Ashgate, 2006), 37–55. Lee argues that Montaignean selfhood does have a "fixity," not, however, "an essentialist fixity, but rather an achieved, part-literary, construct" (45). Richard Regosin charts a middle course in *The Matter of My Book*, acknowledging that "both the gaze and the self are endlessly moving, evolving" (62), as well as the fact that "some sort of transformation or transference has to occur to provide that self with a degree of unity and, consequently, of entity" (184).

4. See Starobinski, *Montaigne in Motion*; and Géralde Nakam, *Montaigne et son temps* (Paris: Nizet, 1982), 109: "parlant de lui pour la première fois, semble-t-il avec une telle intensité."

5. For one recent answer to these questions, see Johannes Türk, "Approaching Death: Accident, Citation, and Singularity in Montaigne's 'De l'Exercitation,'" *The Yearbook of Comparative Literature* 57 (2011): 230–39. "How can Montaigne, the narrator, give an account and draw conclusions from an experience he did not consciously make," Türk asks, noting that "Montaigne scholarship has only recently shed light on this astonishing fact" (see 236 and n.).

6. Starobinski *Montaigne in Motion*, 143.

7. Ibid., 147.

8. Taylor, *Sources of the Self*, 181; and Friedrich, *Montaigne*, 21. For overviews of Montaigne's concept of *expérience*, see W. G. Moore, "Montaigne's Notion of Experience," in *The French Mind: Essays in Honor of Gustave Rudler*, ed. Will Moore, Rhoda Sutherland, and Enid Starkie (Oxford: Oxford University Press, 1952); and Starobinski, *Montaigne in Motion*, 142–45.

9. Even the most subtle readers of Montaigne have tended to conflate selfhood and experience in his writings. For Jean Starobinski, the two are clearly coterminous: "Here is experience of quite another kind—earlier I called it ethical and ontological—in which one's relation to oneself is primordial. Reflection upon failure constitutes an example that I can call *my own*. In the felt evidence of the present moment . . . what is at issue is my own life" (*Montaigne in Motion*, 155).

See also 11: "time and space are no longer endured as destructive forces but produced from within by the voluntary decision that affirms the *here* and *now* as its own decree."

10. Henry, *Material Phenomenology*, 48.

11. Friedrich, *Montaigne*, 210.

12. Merleau-Ponty, *Signs*, 199. In his reading of "Of Exercise or Practice" Timothy M. Harrison similarly argues that for Montaigne, "the intransitive feeling of life, tethered to the present, can only be felt when we are not there, when our personhood is dissolved and feeling proper is replaced by impersonal feeling" (229). See Harrison, "Personhood and Impersonal Feeling in Montaigne's 'De l'Exercitation.'" However, where Harrison sees in Montaigne "impersonal feelings . . . in the process of becoming personal" (224) and a movement "along a gradation of feeling, from the almost nonexistent impersonal affective state of his swoon, through the varied textures of his awakening, into the deeply felt reflexivity of recovered personhood" (226), I see the trajectory of Montaigne's thought more broadly as moving in the opposite direction—away from the complete personhood aspired to in his youthful stoicism, and toward a broader embrace of "impersonal affective state[s]" in the notion of *expérience*.

13. Giorgio Agamben, Richard Regosin, and Martin Jay have all argued that for Montaigne, experience often seems to verge on the idea of a limit or terminal experience, that is, death. Agamben writes that "Montaigne can formulate the ultimate goal of experience as a nearing to death; that is, man's advance to maturity through an anticipation of death as the extreme limit of experience. But for Montaigne this limit remains something that cannot be experienced, which can only be approached." See Giorgio Agamben, *Infancy and History: Essays on the Destruction of Experience*, trans. Liz Heron (New York: Verso, 1993), 19. Martin Jay writes that "Montaigne revealed an awareness of the unresolvable paradoxes within even the most authentic and fulfilled experience. In this sense, as Richard Regosin has remarked, 'paradoxically, death becomes an emblematic experience' for Montaigne because it signifies the limits of all experience." See Martin Jay, *Songs of Experience: Modern American and European Variations on a Universal Theme* (Berkeley: University of California Press, 2005), 28.

14. See William Hamlin, *Montaigne's English Journey: Reading the "Essays" in Shakespeare's Day* (Oxford: Oxford University Press, 2014), 13. For recent accounts of Shakespeare's philosophical relationship to Montaigne, see, in addition to Hamlin, Hugh Grady, *Shakespeare, Machiavelli, and Montaigne*; Ellrodt, *Montaigne and Shakespeare*; and the essays in *The Shakespearean International Yearbook*, vol. 6 (Aldershot, Eng.: Ashgate, 2006).

15. For a reading of the episode in terms of this problem—death as posing "an insurmountable distance to which all other experiences cannot provide a bridge"—see Türk, "Approaching Death," 232.

16. For Montaigne's stoicism, see Friedrich, *Montaigne*, 60–66. While rejecting any notion of "Montaigne's much discussed 'stoic phase'" (66) on the grounds that Montaigne was never a true stoic, Friedrich nevertheless acknowledges a prevalence of stoic maxims in the earlier essays.

17. As John D. Lyons notes in *Before Imagination: Embodied Thought from Montaigne to Rousseau* (Stanford, Calif.: Stanford University Press, 2005), Montaigne's stoicism here seems to entail a kind of modern perspectivalism: "In many

ways Montaigne is a philosophical pragmatist who would be quite at home in Richard Rorty's intellectual world. He does not make a rigorous and exclusive division between what is objectively true and what is simply false because he recognizes that such a division would not allow an active place for the perceiver. In real life the perceiver actually causes things to become what they are, sometimes simply by perceiving them. This fact is a traditional part of the philosophy of *phantasia* and justifies the Stoic attention to managing perceptions" (46).

18. For a discussion of Montaigne's tasting metaphors, see Starobinski, *Montaigne in Motion*, 165.

19. Harrison, "Personhood and Impersonal Feeling," 221.

20. For a psychoanalytic and deconstructive account of Montaigne's early attitude toward death, see Lawrence Kritzman, *The Fabulous Imagination: On Montaigne's Essays* (New York: Columbia University Press, 2008): "The fear of death is weakened through rhetorical excess. Burying death in a 'writerly shroud' plays the illusory experience of death off against death itself. The dream of eliminating all negative feeling associated with death is the symptom of a will to embrace an aberration of desire" (96). Kritzman sees in Montaigne's language "the desire to transpose death to a locus of pleasure, converting it into a malleable phenomenon" (103).

21. See Henry, *Genealogy of Psychoanalysis*, 13–14: "'Thing,' in the expression 'a thing that thinks,' does not indicate something beyond appearance, in the present of its actualization, as if appearance meant mere appearance, a phenomenon (*Schein, Erscheinung*) that leaves reality behind, revealing it mediately; that is, hiding it. In its self-showing, appearance does not refer to something other, something that does not show itself. On the contrary, 'thinking thing' means what shows itself in self-showing, since what shows itself is not a thing but self-showing itself."

22. See Ellrodt, *Montaigne and Shakespeare*, 4. He continues: "I suggest that it inaugurates a notion of subjectivity more readily associated with the modern and modernity" (4).

23. Marion, *Cartesian Questions*, 105.

24. Quoted in Hamlin, *Montaigne's English Journey*, 17.

25. Lucretius, *De Rerum Natura*, trans. W. H. D. Rouse (Cambridge, Mass.: Harvard University Press, 1924), 227.

26. Michel de Montaigne, *The Complete Essays of Montaigne*, trans. Donald M. Frame (Stanford, Calif.: Stanford University Press, 1958), 270.

27. Ibid., 270; and Michel de Montaigne, *The Complete Essays*, trans. M. A. Screech (New York: Penguin, 1991), 420.

28. See Davies, *Conscience as Consciousness*, 1–2.

29. Reiss, *Mirages of the Selfe*, 459: "For Montaigne, thinking could never be stabilized so as to reflect on its own being and action."

30. Thomas Wright, *The Passions of the Mind in General*, ed. William Webster Newbold (New York: Garland, 1986; originally published 1604), 94.

31. It is no coincidence that Montaigne describes these little movements produced by the body of its own accord—at once active passions and passive actions—in terms of "touch." It has frequently been remarked that, of all the senses, touch is unique in requiring an exchange that is simultaneously active and passive: when I touch another, that other also touches me; and vice versa,

when I am touched, I automatically touch in return. Derrida writes that "touch, *as such*, occupies a median and *ideal* region of effort poised between passivity and activity"; see his *On Touching—Jean-Luc Nancy*, trans. Christine Irizarry (Stanford, Calif.: Stanford University Press, 2005), 155. The autonomous movements of Montaigne's prostrate body do not involve literal touching, of course, but they exemplify precisely the blurring of passivity and activity which for Derrida is so characteristic of this sense. Here, however, the "other" who is touched and touches back is somehow both internal to Montaigne and different from him at once. For the movements are produced by Montaigne's own body—who else could be said to be touching him here?—and yet they touch him as if from without, as if by the agency of another.

32. Derrida, *The Animal That Therefore I Am*, 49.

33. See Henry, *Material Phenomenology*, 48, 93.

34. Compare Regosin, *The Matter of My Book*, 94: "The distance opened between the self as subject and object to create that perspective which makes the painting possible in the first place also serves to alienate the painter from himself, to bring the identity of that self 'out there' into question because it is an 'other.' "

35. Michel Henry discusses the separation between life and its representation in *Material Phenomenology*, 92–93: "But the reality of the transcendent essence of life is not the reality of life itself. The presentation of this essence is not the presentation of life. Quite the contrary, this essence is only the exposure of each one of the characteristics that make up the substance of life before the regard, in such a way that each one of its characteristics undergoes an important modification in this representation."

36. See Türk, "Approaching Death," esp. 236–39. Turk sees the fall as an example of those "accidents and other traumatic events [which] are not available to their protagonists, in spite of the fact that they are intimate and singular events that are more decisive and 'personal' than other experiences. The testimony of the other is the only access to them." The experience of the fall is reconstructed, Türk suggests, on the basis of Montaigne's servants' testimony.

37. For a rich exploration of Montaigne's painting metaphor, see Regosin, *The Matter of My Book*, 170–97.

38. For the swoon as a major turning point in the writing of the *Essais*, see Nakam, *Montaigne et son temps*, 108–10; and Donald Frame, *Montaigne: A Biography* (New York: Harcourt, 1965), 149.

39. Starobinski makes this point in *Montaigne in Motion*, 151–56.

40. For once, Florio has diluted the vividness of the French in this passage: *escouler* means not merely to decline but rather to "flow out." The metaphor is more embodied than "decline": it makes of the mind itself a material substance which is gradually, imperceptibly flowing out of the body, or perhaps with the body. "Escouler," moreover, lacks the negative connotations of "decline," and indeed it is very much Montaigne's purpose, throughout this essay, to characterize such processes as natural events which are good or bad only by virtue of the false constructions imposed on them by thinking.

41. Aristotle, *On the Soul,* 323.

42. Thus for Donne, "melting" in "A Valediction Forbidding Mourning" is above all a metaphor for imperceptibility.

43. Henry, *Material Phenomenology*, 6.

Chapter 3

1. A much earlier version of this chapter appeared as "'And All His Sences Stound': The Physiology of Stupefaction in Spenser's *Faerie Queene*," *English Literary Renaissance* 44, no. 3 (fall 2014): 420–51.

2. Andrew Escobedo, "Daemon Lovers: Will, Personification, Character," in *Spenser Studies* 22 (New York: AMS, 2007), 208; and Andrew Escobedo, "The Sincerity of Rapture," in *Spenser Studies* 24 (New York: AMS, 2009), 187.

3. Escobedo, "Daemon Lovers," 208.

4. Many readers of Spenser have called attention to the abundant moments of stupefaction and astonishment in the poem (although none, to my knowledge, has singled out the notion of the "stound" in particular). In *Reason Diminished: Shakespeare and the Marvelous* (Lincoln: University of Nebraska Press, 1997), Peter Platt defines "a Spenserian moment of wonder" as "characterized by a visual marvel, often an unveiling of something previously unknown or unimagined (a face, an identity, a gender), that renders the observer speechless and cognitively destabilized" (70). To the prevalence of rape in the poem, Katherine Eggert opposes as its complement the "excessive, discombobulating rapture that takes a person away from herself . . . the conspicuous disruption of linear thought" (7–8); see her article "Spenser's Ravishment: Rape and Rapture in *The Faerie Queene*," *Representations* 70 (spring 2000): 1–26. In *The Pain of Reformation*, Joseph Campana argues that "moments of stupefaction also witness a sexual vitality that emerges only as masculinity is disarmed" (144). Kasey Evans discusses "that affective stupor induced by experiences that exceed intellectual comprehension" (46) in her article on "How Temperance Becomes Blood Guiltie in *The Faerie Queene*," *Studies in English Literature 1500–1900* 49 (2009): 35–66. And see Julian Yates's description of Spenserian *otium* as a "state of rest, a zero degree, through which we momentarily return, conscious, but occupied, our agency and awareness turned inside out or shifted to one side": Julian Yates, "Weird Otium," in *Affect Theory and Early Modern Texts*, ed. Bailey and DiGangi, 73.

5. Clément, *Syncope*, 21.

6. Massumi, *Parables for the Virtual*, 28.

7. Ibid., 29. See also Jonathan Goldberg, *The Seeds of Things: Theorizing Sexuality and Materiality in Renaissance Representations* (New York: Fordham University Press, 2009), 91, for his description of the "forward and backward impulses of the divided present (no more, not yet), the space of delay and dilation in which the labor of self-(un)doing occurs."

8. Gilles Deleuze, *Pure Immanence: Essays on a Life*, trans. Anne Boyman (New York: Zone, 2005), 25.

9. For the only major reading of Spenser's poem emphasizing "the phenomenological reality of corporeal experience" (111) over "rational clarity and moral self-possession" (110), see Campana, *The Pain of Reformation*, 107–28. Goldberg's *The Seeds of Things* is arguably even more radical in its insistence on "the fundamentally inhuman nature of sexuality in the poem and its connection to materialized forms of embodiment in which human being is not central" (98), but for Goldberg, Spenserian subjectivity is ultimately constituted by its practices—"the exercises through which the subject transforms itself into an ethical subject" (70)—rather than by its experiences. Meanwhile, in *Open Subjects: English Renaissance Republicans, Modern Selfhoods and the Virtue of Vulnerability*

(Edinburgh: Edinburgh University Press, 2011), James Kuzner explores moments in which "interior existence is emptied out in an ecstatic outpouring of being 'twixt'" (40); in his reading, however, such moments happen primarily in the socially and politically charged context of friendship.

10. Henry, *Genealogy of Psychoanalysis*, 29.

11. All references follow Edmund Spenser, *The Faerie Queene*, ed. Thomas P. Roche Jr. (Harmondsworth, Eng.: Penguin, 1978).

12. Michel Henry, *I Am the Truth: Toward a Philosophy of Christianity* (Stanford, Calif.: Stanford University Press, 1996), 42. See also Henry, *Material Phenomenology*, 95: "I can represent life to myself, and this principle is a part of life. But this possibility must itself be made possible. Paradoxically, this possibility does not reside in representation but in what ultimately founds representation. It resides in the Archi-revelation of the life in which every lived experience 'occurs.'"

13. Petrarch, *Petrarch's Lyric Poems: The "Rime Sparse" and Other Lyrics*, trans. Robert Durling (Cambridge, Mass.: Harvard University Press, 1976), 273.

14. Galen, *On the Doctrines of Hippocrates and Plato*, ed. and trans. Phillip de Lacy (Berlin: Akademie-Verlag, 1980), vol. 2: 469.

15. See Edmund Spenser, *The Faerie Queene*, ed. A.C. Hamilton (London: Longman, 2001), 94n.

16. James, *Essays in Psychology*, 142.

17. Ibid.

18. Darryl Gless also reads Red Crosse's stound as an image of sin: "Red Cross' earlier myopia and hardness of hearing now become total when Orgoglio's blow stupefies him—'all his sences stound' (12.9). The knight can now be seen as an image of spiritual death, humankind's natural condition as Protestants conceived of it." See Gless, *Interpretation and Theology in Spenser* (Cambridge: Cambridge University Press, 1994), 123. What Gless's account does not capture is the way the "stound" represents not merely humankind's natural condition in general, but a moment of crisis brought about by the deepening of that condition—of our immersion in sentient life. See Thomas Bedford's description of a "stound" below.

19. Jean Calvin, *The Institution of Christian Religion*, trans. Thomas Norton (London: Wolfe and Harrison, 1561), fol. 1v.

20. Thomas Bedford, *The Sinne unto Death; or An Ample Discovery of That Fearful Sinne, the Sinne Against the Holy Ghost* (London: William Sheffard, 1621), 7–8.

21. Ibid., 8.

22. For a comprehensive history of the notion of spirit, see Gerard Verbeke, *L'Evolution de la doctrine du pneuma du Stoïcisme à St. Augustin* (Paris, 1945); see also D. P. Walker, "Francis Bacon and *Spiritus*," in *Science, Medicine, and Society in the Renaissance*, ed. Allen G. Debus (London: Heinemann, 1972), vol. 2: 121–30.

23. Galen, *Method of Medicine*, ed. and trans. Ian Johnston and G. H. R. Horsley (Cambridge, Mass.: Harvard University Press), vol. 3: 267–69.

24. Ibid., 265; the Greek is: "kataptosis . . . oxeia dunameos."

25. Helkiah Crooke, *Microcosmographia: A Description of the Body of Man* (London: William Jaggard, 1615), 40.

26. Robert Burton, *Anatomy of Melancholy*, ed. Nicolas K. Kiessling, Thomas C. Faulkner, and Rhonda L. Blair (Oxford: Clarendon, 1989), 141.

27. Avicenna, *The General Principles of Avicenna's Canon of Medicine*, trans. Mazhar H. Shah (Karachi, Pakistan: Naveed Clinic, 1966), 131–32.

28. Ibid., 126.

29. Ibid., 131.

30. Ibid., 126.

31. See Gianfranco Contini, ed., *Poeti del Duecento*, vol. 2 (Milan-Naples: Ricciardi, 1960), 516.

32. Sir Kenelm Digby, *Observations on the 22nd Stanza in the 9th Canto of the 2nd Book of Spencer's "Faery Queene"* (London: Daniel Frere, 1643), 15–16.

33. Donne, *Songs and Sonets*, 220.

34. Avicenna, *Canon of Medicine*, 132

35. See, for example, Paster, *Humoring the Body*, 30–43; and Smith, *The Key of Green*, 29–31.

36. For Galen's description of the spirits as the soul's *organon* rather than as constituting the soul itself, see *On the Doctrines of Hippocrates and Plato*, vol. 2: 445. The definition of the spirits as the soul's "instrument" was widespread in early modern English medicine.

37. See Walker, "Francis Bacon and *Spiritus*," 126.

38. For Melanchthon and Servetus's identification of spirits and soul, see Walker, "Francis Bacon and *Spiritus*," 125.

39. Schoenfeldt, *Bodies and Selves*, 3.

40. Ibid., 3.

41. Drew Daniel, "Self-Killing and the Matter of Affect in Bacon and Spinoza," in *Affect Theory and Early Modern Texts*, ed. Bailey and DiGangi, 94

42. See Henry, *Genealogy of Psychoanalysis*, 59.

43. Hugh MacLachlan, "The Death of Guyon and the Elizabethan Book of Homilies," in *Spenser Studies* 4 (1983): 93–114, 97. Maclachlan provides a useful bibliography of readings of the faint to that date. Foremost among these are Harry Berger Jr., *The Allegorical Temper: Vision and Reality in Book II of Spenser's "Faerie Queene"* (New Haven, Conn.: Yale University Press, 1957), to which I will come shortly; and Paul Alpers, *The Poetry of the "Faerie Queene"* (Princeton, N.J.: Princeton University Press, 1967), 274: "it is the result of the inherent strains of knowing an evil." Berger and Alpers established something of a consensus that, in Alpers's words, the faint is not a "moral judgment against Guyon" but rather "due to man's nature, and it is the inevitable result of the trial Guyon has endured," a view which more recent readings have tended to confirm: see Schoenfeldt, *Bodies and Selves*, 51 (the episode reminds us "of the organism's dependence on just the digestive and defecatory processes that are detailed in the house of Alma"); and Christopher Tilmouth, *Passion's Triumph over Reason: A History of the Moral Imagination from Spenser to Rochester* (Oxford: Oxford University Press, 2007), 63 ("Guyon, it transpires, is no match for the most basic frailties of human nature"). Recently, however, Garrett Sullivan Jr. has offered a post-human account of the scene by thinking critically about its implications for the way humanity overlaps with animal and vegetal life; see his *Sleep, Romance, and Human Embodiment*, 43–45.

44. Galen, *Method of Medicine*, 269–71.

45. Ibid., 273.

46. James Norhnberg, *Analogy of the Faerie Queene* (Princeton, N.J.: Princeton University Press, 1976), 299.

47. For a reading of the episode in terms of the "constitutive nature of self-discipline," see Schoenfeldt, *Bodies and Selves*, 73. For this theme more broadly, see also Tilmouth, *Passion's Triumph over Reason*.

48. For a reading of Guyon's swoon as one of several moments in book 2 revealing a vitality that blurs the lines between vegetal, animal, and human, in which "life [is] construed from the perspective of sleep and the passions" (39), see Sullivan, *Sleep, Romance, and Human Embodiment*. For "the intimation of a world bristling with vitality" in *The Faerie Queene*, see Joseph Campana, "Spenser's Inhumanity," *Spenser Studies* 30 (New York: AMS, 2015), 294.

49. Gordon Teskey, "Death in an Allegory," in *Imagining Death in Spenser and Milton*, ed. Elizabeth Bellamy, Patrick Cheney, and Michael Schoenfeldt (New York: Palgrave Macmillan, 2003), 65–77, 75.

50. See Henry, *Genealogy of Psychoanalysis*, 8.

51. Charleton, *Natural History of Nutrition*, 120.

52. Goldberg, *The Seeds of Things*, 102.

53. Timothy Harrison uses this phrase in reference to Adam's awakening in *Paradise Lost*. See his "Adamic Awakening and the Feeling of Being Alive in *Paradise Lost*," *Milton Studies* 54 (2013): 29–58, 42.

54. While Schoenfeldt acknowledges the Aristotelian distinction between temperance as "a static virtue, a physiological and psychological *state* achieved through proper humoral balance" and continence as "a dynamic and ethical program demanding unending vigilance" (see his *Bodies and Selves*, 43), his reading of the House of Alma and book 2 in general consistently privileges the importance of "rigorous self-control" and the "heroic human labor of regulations" (41). And yet it is less "the moral job of the upright self . . . to police these necessary thresholds between the outside world and the inner self" (50) than it is a feature that the temperate body exhibits in and of itself. For Harry Berger Jr., by contrast, Guyon is temperate rather than continent, displaying "a natural, aristocratic virtue rendering its possessor immune to inner struggle and temptation." See *The Allegorical Temper*, 62. This virtue belongs to a "certainty of instinct" (62) rather than to conscious choice; correspondingly, "what we are shown" in the House of Alma "is an image of instinctive purpose, the wisdom of the body operating according to its own laws even in the lowest regions of the human body" (74).

55. Compare Berger, *The Allegorical Temper*, 8: "If we assume the castle to represent the being of each knight, a much more basic process of self-discovery is going on, and it is not really a conscious self-discovery, for the knights only see themselves as guests in a strange and wonderful castle."

56. Berger, *The Allegorical Temper*, 80.

57. Susanne Lindgren Wofford, *The Choice of Achilles: The Ideology of Figure in the Epic* (Stanford, Calif.: Stanford University Press, 1992), 219–94. For the notion that Spenser's characters "do not know they are in an allegory, and cannot and do not 'read' the signs of their world as figurative pointers to another arena of understanding," see 220.

58. For Berger, "if the first half of Book II is a study of the hero's conscious. . . . the second half is a study of his unconscious" (64). Even the three figures in the turret occupy a level "beneath conscious activity" (83). See his *The Allegorical Temper*.

59. Henry, *Material Phenomenology*, 6.

60. See *Spenser Studies* 24 (New York: AMS, 2009). Again, the major exceptions are Campana's *Pain of Reformation* and Goldberg's *The Seeds of Things*. Goldberg himself critiques the conservative and Platonizing tendencies of Spenser criticism at 119.

61. Berger, *The Allegorical Temper*, 29.

Chapter 4

1. For the only sustained critical discussion of Othello's epilepsy, see Stephanie Moss, "Transformation and Degeneration: The Paracelsan/Galenic Body in *Othello*," in *Disease, Diagnosis, and Cure on the Early Modern Stage*, ed. Kaara L. Peterson (London: Routledge, 2004). For the tradition of omitting the swoon from performances of the play, see Marvin Rosenberg, "The 'Refinement' of *Othello* in the Eighteenth-Century British Theatre," *Studies in Philology* 51, no. 1 (1954): 75–94.

2. William Shakespeare, *Othello*, ed. Michael Neill (New York: Oxford University Press, 2006). All references to the play follow this edition.

3. Stanley Cavell, *Disowning Knowledge* (Cambridge: Cambridge University Press, 1987), 133.

4. Reading *Othello* in the context of Elizabethan witchcraft and treason trials, Katharine Maus interprets the play as evoking a "hidden, inward realm [which] remains . . . incompletely revealed in the theater" (126), so that "the same mechanisms which seem to break down the boundaries between self and other simultaneously reinforce boundaries that can never really be eliminated" (126–27). See Maus, *Inwardness and Theater in the English Renaissance*, 126–27. In *Issues of Death: Mortality and Identity in English Renaissance Tragedy* (New York: Oxford University Press, 1999), Michael Neill sees Iago as responsible for a "systematic opening of Othello" (145) and his "violent induction into [a] new discourse of interiority" (162). John Bayley writes that "Othello is the most unexpected hero to . . . live in the mind." See his *Shakespeare and Tragedy* (London: Routledge, 1981), 200. For a contrasting reading of Othello's interiority in terms of "the natural facticity of the emotions and the body as the source, site, and means of the emotions' occurrence" (70), see Paster, *Humoring the Body*, 60–76.

5. Paster, *Humoring the Body*, 63.

6. François Tonneau, "Consciousness Outside the Head," *Behavior and Philosophy* 32 (2004): 97–123, 107.

7. For the account which follows I am heavily indebted to Owsei Temkin's authoritative history of epilepsy, *The Falling Sickness: A History of Epilepsy from the Greeks to the Beginnings of Modern Neurology* (Baltimore, Md.: Johns Hopkins University Press, 1994).

8. Hippocrates, *The Sacred Disease*, ed. and trans. W. H. S. Jones (London: Heinemann, 1923), 139.

9. Ibid., 157.

10. Galen, *On the Affected Parts*, trans. Rudolph E. Siegel (New York: S. Karger, 1976), 86.

11. Ibid., 87.

12. Ibid., 86.

13. Paracelsus, "The Diseases That Deprive Man of His Reason," in *Paracelsus: Four Treatises*, ed. Henry E. Sigerist (Baltimore, Md.: Johns Hopkins University Press, 1941), 144–45.

14. Paracelsus, *De Spiritu Vitae* 1.3:229, quoted in Andrew Weeks, *Paracelsus: Speculative Theory and the Crisis of the Early Reformation* (Albany: SUNY Press, 1997), 109.

15. Paracelsus, "The Diseases That Deprive Man," 145.

16. Ibid., 145.

17. Paracelsus, "Von den hinfallenden siechtagen," in *Sämtliche Werke*, ed. Karl Sudhoff (Munich: Barth, 1922–33), vol. 8: 274. All translations of this text are my own.

18. Ibid., 273–74.

19. Ibid., 275.

20. Ibid., 275–76.

21. Ibid., 276.

22. Ibid., 276.

23. Ibid., 282.

24. John Donne, *Devotions vpon Emergent Occasions and Seuerall Steps in My Sicknes* (London: Thomas Jones, 1624), 5–7. Emphases in original.

25. Paracelsus, "The Diseases That Deprive Man," 144.

26. Paracelsus, "Von den hinfallenden," 281. Emphasis mine.

27. Galen, *On the Affected Parts*, 86.

28. Ibid., 281–82. Emphasis in original.

29. Andreas Vesalius, *A Compendious Declaration of the Excellent Uertues of a Certain Lately Inuented Oile, Called for the Worthiness Thereof Oile Imperial*, trans. Thomas Rainold (Venice: Gryphius, 1551), sigs. F3r-v.

30. Ibid., sig. F4r.

31. Ibid., sig. F4r.

32. Damasio, *The Feeling of What Happens*, 16.

33. All quotations follow William Shakespeare, *All's Well That Ends Well*, ed. Susan Snyder (New York: Oxford University Press, 1993).

34. For a comprehensive overview of Paracelsus's reception in early modern England, see Allen G. Debus, *The English Paracelsians* (London: Oldbourne, 1965), chaps. 2 and 3. Debus describes a compromise position in which "the great majority of English physicians and surgeons . . . . readily accepted those of the new remedies which proved their worth, but very few of them concerned themselves with the deeper and more occult aspects of Paracelsian thought" (80). See also Charles Webster, "Alchemical and Paracelsian Medicine," in *Health, Medicine and Mortality in the Sixteenth Century*, ed. Charles Webster (Cambridge: Cambridge University Press, 1979), 301–34. Webster finds evidence that Paracelsus had "a by-no-means insubstantial impact, especially during the last twenty-five years of the sixteenth century" (319); he argues that "it can be assumed that Paracelsus was virtually unknown in England in 1560, but that his ideas had been largely assimilated by 1600" (323).

35. Like my reading, Moss's reading also connects Paracelsus and modern phenomenology, in contrast to Galenic objectivity: both "posit that perception and the surroundings that one perceives are ineluctably interconnected, and the body, although distinct from the world it inhabits, is not separate from it. The Galenic body and its counterpart in medical phenomenology both imply the objectivity of 'thinking' about the body rather than the subjectivity of 'feeling' inside it." See "Transformation and Degeneration," 158. For Moss, however, "Othello's

degeneration following his collapse can be investigated as a shift from a Paracelsan to a Galenic body, from a subject to an object" (153).

36. Paster, *Humoring the Body*, 9.

37. For a valuable account of bodily awareness in both its conscious and unconscious dimensions, see José Bermúdez, "Bodily Awareness and Self-Consciousness," in *The Oxford Handbook of Self*, ed. Shaun Gallagher (Oxford: Oxford University Press, 2011). See especially his account of proprioreception and the vestibular system at 158–61: "the vestibular system, which monitors balance and spatial orientation, is typically non-conscious (although disturbances of the vestibular system, such as motion sickness, certainly make their presence felt within consciousness)" (159).

38. Fredric Jameson, *The Political Unconscious: Narrative as a Socially Symbolic Act* (Ithaca, N.Y.: Cornell University Press, 1981), 112.

39. Donne, *Devotions*, 233–34.

40. Charleton, "Natural History of Nutrition," 122.

41. See G. Wilson Knight's chapter on *Othello* in his *The Wheel of Fire* (London: Oxford University Press, 1930).

42. See, respectively, Marjorie Garber, *Shakespeare After All* (New York: Pantheon, 2004), 111; Stephen Greenblatt, *Renaissance Self-Fashioning: From More to Shakespeare* (Chicago: University of Chicago Press, 1980), 244; and Edward Pechter, *Othello and Interpretive Traditions* (Iowa City: University of Iowa Press, 1999), 102.

43. Michael Witmore, "Shakespeare, Sensation, and Renaissance Existentialism," *Criticism* 54, no. 3 (2012): 419–26, 421. In terms very similar to mine, Witmore argues that "Shakespearean characters frequently draw attention to the sensed fact of affect in the moment as it ripples through the body or overtakes the soul—and this announced fact is often dramatically just as important as the qualities which characterize that affect" (420).

44. Othello's swoon thus anticipates the trance-state in which he strangles Desdemona. See James Kuzner's account of that state in *Shakespeare as a Way of Life: Skeptical Practice and the Politics of Weakness* (New York: Fordham University Press, 2016), 62: "Caught in absolute but contradictory framings of love, Othello can only reconcile the frames for an instant, can only possess Desdemona completely by claiming that he is absolutely possessed, that he is not death's agent; complete denial of self-control allows complete control over Desdemona."

45. Again, compare James Kuzner in *Shakespeare as a Way of Life*, 50: "Love becomes fatal when Othello assumes sovereignty not only over Desdemona, but also over an experience that ought to have overmatched him."

46. See Rosenberg, "The 'Refinement' of *Othello*."

47. William Shakespeare, *Hamlet*, ed. G. R. Hibbard (Oxford: Oxford University Press, 2008). All references follow this edition.

48. For the anonymous ode on Burbage from which this passage is taken, see Tobias Döring, "Writing Performance: How to Elegize Elizabethan Actors," *Shakespeare Survey* 58 (2005): 60–71, 67.

49. Michael Witmore, *Shakespearean Metaphysics* (London: Continuum, 2008), 8.

50. B. L. Joseph, *Elizabethan Acting*, 2nd ed. (London: Oxford University Press, 1964), 3. In Joseph's view, "personation" is for all intents and purposes the

same as modern "method acting" as formulated by Stanislavski. Accordingly, in the player's performance, "what Stanislavski calls the magic 'if' has allowed the actor really to feel moved by [Hecuba's] imagined agony. His 'whole function'—voice, face, attitude, gesture—expresses what he feels" (3). See also Meredith Anne Skura, *Shakespeare the Actor and the Purposes of Playing* (Chicago: University of Chicago Press, 1993), 49–52. She largely agrees with Joseph, suggesting that "we should be careful not to overestimate the differences between 'personating' then and now. . . . The fact that a player used stereotyped gestures does not preclude his identifying with the feelings believed to motivate such external signs of emotion" (49). For the opposing view, against the idea that Elizabethan acting involved "acting, in its now-commonplace sense of self-transference" (328), see Peter Thomson, "Rogues and Rhetoricians: Acting Styles in Early English Drama," in *A New History of Early English Drama*, ed. John D. Cox and David Scott Kastan (New York: Columbia University Press, 1997), 321–36. Thomson thus reads Hamlet's commendation of the player very differently: "It is the imitation of grief, not the imitation of Aeneas, that astounds Hamlet. Indeed, real grief would look and sound very different from this histrionic representation" (323).

51. For Shakespeare's "metaphysics of immanence," see Thomas Heywood, *An Apology for Actors* (London: Nicholas Okes, 1612), sigs. C3v–C4r.

52. Ibid., sig. C4r.

53. Jonathan Gil Harris, "'Look Not Big, Nor Stamp, Nor Stare': Acting Up in *The Taming of the Shrew* and the Coventry Herod Plays," *Comparative Drama* 34, no. 4 (winter 2000–2001): 365–98.

54. See Charles Lille, ed., *Original and Genuine Letters Sent to the Tatler and Spectator* (London: R. Harbin, 1725).

55. For a closely related argument, see Garrett A. Sullivan Jr.'s chapter on "Descartes and the Romance Episode in Dryden" in his *Sleep, Romance, and Human Embodiment*, 139: "What was once associated with horizontal vitality is now aligned with Antony's poetic (and prone) meditations upon his resemblance to other forms of life; what were once ontological connections derived from Aristotelian thought appear here as fanciful connections drawn from the human imagination."

Chapter 5

1. Teresa Brennan writes: "I am using the term 'transmission of affect' to capture a process that is social in origin but biological and physical in effect. The origin of transmitted affects is social in that these affects do not only arise within a particular person but also come from without. They come via interaction with other people and an environment." See Brennan, *The Transmission of Affect* (Ithaca, N.Y.: Cornell University Press, 2004), 3. What Stephen Greenblatt calls "the circulation of social energy" is arguably a description of the same phenomenon. It is, he writes, "associated with repeatable forms of pleasure and interest, with the capacity to arouse disquiet, pain, fear, the beating of the heart, pity, laughter, tension, relief, wonder. In its aesthetic range, social energy must have a minimal predictability. . . . enough to reach out beyond a single creator or consumer to some community." See Greenblatt, *Shakespearean Negotiations: The Circulation of Social Energy in Renaissance England* (Berkeley: University of California Press, 1988), 6. See also Jacqueline T. Miller, "The Passion Signified:

Imitation and the Construction of Emotions in Sidney and Wroth," *Criticism* 43, no. 4 (2001): 407–21: "the passions are not so much our own, and do not so much always emerge from within, but rather get transferred from one person to another" (412). See also Evelyn Tribble, "Affective Contagion on the Early Modern Stage," in *Affect Theory and Early Modern Texts,* ed. Bailey and DiGangi, 195–212.

2. Wright, *Passions of the Mind*, 148.

3. Agrippa von Nettesheim, *Three Books of Occult Philosophy Written by Henry Cornelius Agrippa of Nettesheim* (London: R.W. for Gregory Moule, 1651), 141.

4. Mary Floyd-Wilson, *Occult Knowledge, Science, and Gender on the Shakespearean Stage* (Cambridge: Cambridge University Press, 2013), 47. Crucially, in contrast to the modern notion of sympathetic empathy which "presumes individuated boundaries between the subject and object," in the early modern period "sympathy was . . . a somatic feeling that breached the boundaries of individual bodies" (9).

5. See Hobgood's *Passionate Playgoing in Early Modern England* (Cambridge: Cambridge University Press, 2014), 2.

6. In her essay on "Affective Contagion on the Early Modern Stage," Tribble also tries to move beyond binaries that separate consciousness from affective transmission: "Human beings are not pre-existing individuals suddenly and mysteriously infected with affect; rather, humans are inherently social and permeable, liable to consciously and unconsciously imitate and entrain; moreover, they come to particular places and events with pre-formed conceptions of the affective exchanges they might expect" (201–2).

7. Though Brennan herself would perhaps not accept this way of talking about transmission, one of the two major categories into which she divides it is defined by asymmetry: "There is transmission by which people become alike and transmission in which they take up opposing positions in relation to a common affective thread (the angry and the depressed; the loved and the lover)." See *The Transmission of Affect*, 9. Brennan herself cites Montaigne (though not this particular passage) as an early theorist of affective transmission (16).

8. In a reading that is similar to my own, Hannah Chapelle Wojciehowski argues that *The Winter's Tale* helps us to "conceptualise a kind of arousal that exists prior to the religious meanings that a viewer might attach to that experience." See Wojciehowski, "Statues That Move: Vitality Effects in *The Winter's Tale*," *Literature and Theology* 28, no. 3 (September 2014): 308. For a reading of how the play "relates to the entanglements of faith and a distinctively emerging discourse of skepticism" (328), see Walter S. H. Lim, "Knowledge and Belief in *The Winter's Tale*," *Studies in English Literature 1500–1900* 41, no. 2 (2001): 317–44. For discussions of the play's theology, see Julia Lupton's chapter on "'The Winter's Tale and the Gods," in *Afterlives of the Saints: Hagiography, Typology, and Renaissance Literature* (Stanford, Calif.: Stanford University Press, 1996). See also Huston Diehl, "'Strike All That Look Upon with Marvel': Theatrical and Theological Wonder in *The Winter's Tale*," in *Rematerializing Shakespeare: Authority and Representation on the Early Modern English Stage*, ed. Bryan Reynolds and William West (London: Palgrave, 2005), 19–34; and Jennifer Waldron, "Of Stones and Stony Hearts: Desdemona, Hermione, and

Post-Reformation Theater," in *The Indistinct Human in Renaissance Literature*, ed. Jean E. Feerick and Vin Nardizzi (Basingstoke, Eng.: Palgrave, 2012), 205–27. For the epistemology of skepticism in *The Winter's Tale*, see below, note 14.

9. There is no consensus over whether or not Hermione simply falls into a sixteen-year coma, or actually dies and is resurrected—or, for that matter, over whether Shakespeare himself was clear on the question. Ruth Nevo writes that "there is, of course, no miracle at all. Hermione, never dead, is not resurrected." See *Shakespeare's Other Language* (London: Methuen, 1987). Lupton writes that "unlike the Ovidian metamorphosis, Hermione was alive all along" (217). However, in his introduction to the Oxford edition of *The Winter's Tale*, Stephen Orgel treats Hermione's death as one of the play's "hard facts" (36), though he goes on to point out that "Shakespearean drama does not create a consistent world." See *The Winter's Tale*, ed. Stephen Orgel (Oxford: Oxford University Press, 1996). Susan Snyder, in her introduction to *The New Cambridge Shakespeare* edition, suggests that "Shakespeare seems to want it both ways: as marvel and as something that can be explained in human terms." See William Shakespeare, *The Winter's Tale*, ed. Susan Snyder and Deborah T. Curren-Aquino (Cambridge: Cambridge University Press, 2007).

10. Brennan, *Transmission of Affect*, 25. For a recent reading of how political, social, and biological conceptions of life are all intertwined by the play's staging of the risks inherent in hospitality, see Lupton, *Thinking with Shakespeare*, chap. 5.

11. Henry, *Material Phenomenology*, 121.

12. I follow William Shakespeare, *The Winter's Tale*, ed. Stephen Orgel.

13. For the priority of feeling and smelling over vision as modes of affective transmission, see Brennan, *Transmission of Affect*, 10–11. For an account which captures well what happens to Leontes in this opening scene, see 77: "both affect and motion . . . are responding to a third factor altogether: the social environment, whose air can be thick with anxiety-provoking pheromones."

14. Stanley Cavell's reading of Leontes as "a portrait of the skeptic at the moment of the world's withdrawal from his grasp" has been the starting point for many of the most significant recent readings of the play. See *Disowning Knowledge*, 206. Sarah Beckwith sees the play as depicting "the costs of the denial of creatureliness," resolved only at the end of the play in a resurrection of "flesh and blood." See her *Shakespeare and the Grammar of Forgiveness* (Ithaca, N.Y.: Cornell University Press, 2011), 134, 128. Elaborating on Cavell's "portrait of the skeptic," David Hillman argues that Leontes is also "a portrait of a repudiation of the contents of both the other's and the sceptic's own corporeal interior." See *Shakespeare's Entrails: Belief, Scepticism and the Interior of the Body* (Basingstoke, Eng.: Palgrave, 2007), 155. James Kuzner, meanwhile,"trace[s] another skeptical practice that inflects the play, one that enjoins being absorbed and transported by a distinctively Pauline law of faith." See *Shakespeare as a Way of Life*, 82.

15. As Mary Floyd-Wilson suggests, early modern scenes of "emotional contagion" should be understood in "literal rather than metaphorical terms": Floyd-Wilson, *Occult Knowledge*, 54.

16. For a discussion of the passage's editorial history, see William Shakespeare, *The Winter's Tale*, ed. J. H. P Pafford (London: Methuen, 1963), 165–67; and Stephen Orgel, "The Poetics of Incomprehensibility," *Shakespeaere Quarterly* 42, no. 4 (1991): 431–37. I have followed Orgel's own punctuation in the Oxford

edition, but as he notes, "most editions since Rowe's time have adopted his equally radical repointing, whereby 'may't be—' stands alone, and 'Affection,' no longer a predicate nominative in the simple question 'may't be Affection?', is now the vocative subject of a new sentence, 'Affection, thy intention stabs the centre'" (433–34). Orgel notes "how little attention the editorial tradition has paid to the fact of a drama that speaks in this way," and indeed as I see it, the slipperiness of the syntax here in fact expresses quite precisely the blurring of the boundaries—which for Leontes is intolerable—between one's own "affection" and that of others. Lupton is the only reader I know of for whom both meanings of "affection" are active in the passage: she reads "the two faces of 'affection' as aspects of idolatry, linking the prohibition against adultery on the second tablet to its counterpart on the first tablet." See Lupton, *Afterlives of the Saints*, 193. See also Hillman, *Shakespeare's Entrails*, 159.

17. Several critics have called attention to Leontes's uncannily perspicacious observation of his own cognitive processes. Ruth Nevo notes "the degree of unaware awareness with which [the play's] characters are endowed. We have already heard Leontes struggling, half-knowingly, with his own conflicting modes of cognition." See Nevo, *Shakespeare's Other Language*, 115. James Kuzner describes this speech as a "moment of accurate observation and acute self-awareness." See *Shakespeare as a Way of Life*, 89.

18. I differ here from Hillman, who reads "the apparent afterthought—'nor my brows'" as expressing "the displacement upward from bosom to head." See *Shakespeare's Entrails*, 157. For an account of the face in Shakespeare more broadly, see James A. Knapp, ed., *Shakespeare and the Power of the Face* (London: Routledge, 2015): "Shakespeare's invitation to look past the face and find the inner character is not an invitation to seek the static text beneath the external image. Rather, the invitation is to experience the power of the face to initiate reflection, judgment, and action" (6–7).

19. See Massumi, *Parables for the Virtual*, 29.

20. Lupton, *Afterlives of the Saints*, 196. For Deleuze's account of the close-up, see his *Cinema 1*, trans. Hugh Tomlinson and Barbara Habberjam (Minneapolis: University of Minnesota Press, 1986), 87–88.

21. See Levinus Lemnius, *The Touchstone of Complexions*, trans. Thomas Newton (London: Thomas Marsh, 1576), fol. 90r. Lemnius's account uses both senses of "complexion" interchangeably, making it clear that the face is not merely an outward expression of humoral life, but a place where such life actively takes place: "There is no surer way (sayth *Galene*) certainly to knowe the humours and iuyce in a Creature, then by the colour and outward complexion." See also Paster, *Humoring the Body*, 36–37.

22. Deleuze, *Cinema 1*, 88–89.

23. For example, by J. H. P. Pafford in the Arden edition of *The Winter's Tale*.

24. See Daniel, *Melancholy Assemblage*, 7. Or as David Hillman puts it, "the mutual accessibility of the interior of the body, the visceral connection Montaigne describes is, in a sense, the source of Leontes' problem." See *Shakespeare's Entrails*, 156.

25. Brennan, *Transmission of Affect*, 15

26. Compare Drew Daniel's account of Biron thumping his chest to indicate the location of his melancholy in *Love's Labour's Lost*: "By shifting from oaths

made with proverbial, received expression . . . to an ostensive gesture towards *this* paper and *this* body, Biron tries to drive some kind of barrier between the instability and potential falsehood of promissory language and the ontological bedrock of thingly existence . . . . the ontological security with which the breast can be thumped upon and pointed at is meant to secure an epistemological security about the emotions which supposedly reside there." Daniel, *Melancholy Assemblage*, 83.

27. I follow the edition given in appendix A of *The Winter's Tale*, ed. Pafford, 198.

28. Hillman notes Leontes's "ability to diagnose the interior condition of his wife's 'infected' (1.2.304) body as a mirroring of his own interior affliction." See *Shakespeare's Entrails*, 159.

29. For an overview of this tradition in painting and a careful study of the theological questions surrounding it, see Harvey E. Hamburgh, "The Problem of *Lo Spasimo* of the Virgin in *Cinquecento* Paintings of the Descent from the Cross," *The Sixteenth Century Journal* 12, no. 4 (winter 1981): 45–75.

30. Thomas Lodge, *Prosopopeia* (London: Printed for E. White, 1596), sig. H7v.

31. See Aemilia Lanyer, *The Poems of Aemilia Lanyer: Salve Deus Rex Judaeorum*, ed. Susanne Woods (New York: Oxford University Press, 1993), 94. For Lodge, Lanyer, and *lo spasimo* in early modern England, see "Aemilia Lanyer and the Virgin's Swoon: Theology and Iconography in *Salve Deus Rex Judaeorum*," *English Literary Renaissance* 37, no. 1 (2007): 47–73.

32. Quoted and translated in Hamburgh, "The Problem of *Lo Spasimo*," 46.

33. Ibid., 54

34. See Gary Waller, *The Virgin Mary in Late Medieval and Early Modern English Literature and Popular Culture* (Cambridge: Cambridge University Press, 2012), 180. For Hermione as the Virgin Mary, see also Lupton, *Afterlives of the Saints*, 213–14.

35. See Jacques Rancière, *The Politics of Aesthetics*, trans. Gabriel Rockhill (New York: Continuum, 2006), 12. Rancière defines the distribution of the sensible as "the system of self-evident facts of sense perception that simultaneously discloses the existence of something in common and the delimitations that define the respective parts and positions within it. A distribution of the sensible therefore establishes at one and the same time something common that is shared and exclusive parts. This apportionment of parts and positions is based on a distribution of spaces, times, and forms of activity that determines the very manner in which something in common lends itself to participation and in what way various individuals have a part in this distribution."

36. Brennan, *Transmission of Affect*, 60.

37. Henry, *Material Phenomenology*, 128. Brennan too draws on hypnosis as an example of how "transmissions affect the subject's intentionality" (*Transmission of Affect*, 76).

38. Wojciehowski, "Vitality Effects in *The Winter's Tale*," 303.

39. In Lupton's most recent reading of the play, in *Thinking with Shakespeare*, the sociopolitical emerges out of the biological here, *bios* out of *zoe*: "the living statue that now reaches out her trembling hand to the quaking king extends the chance for a new drafting of the politico-domestic space, a marital *politeia* that

might cultivate the inoperative latency of virtue in order that life might once more become political on its own terms" (179).

40. James Kuzner reads the ending of the play in a similar way in *Shakespeare as a Way of Life*: "In this, the play suggests that it is better to be below the level of discourse—better for Leontes to have *tremor cordis* upon him and be faithful to it—than to formulate a propositional belief ('Hermione is unfaithful') that would justify the *tremor cordis*; better, too, in his experience at the end, not to try to assign Hermione a copulative as to whether she is resurrected. It is better that he embrace being overwhelmed by her stirring, that he allow his fidelity to consist in being so overwhelmed" (99).

41. For the idea that the end of the play emphasizes separateness, see Cavell, *Disowning Knowledge*, 220: "Then let us emphasize that this ceremony of union takes the form of a ceremony of separation, thus declaring that the question of two becoming one is just half the problem; the other half is how one becomes two. It is separation that Leontes' participation in parturition grants—that Hermione has, that there is, a life beyond his, and that she can create a life beyond his and hers, and beyond plenitude and nothingness."

42. The play, in other words, moves beyond the subject/object dichotomy altogether and in doing so repudiates the model on which sensation is based. David Hillman concludes: "We might think of Shakespeare's choice to make Hermione return as a statue as reaching towards a reconceptualization of the whole question of inner and outer. . . . Perhaps 'joy' is precisely that: the transcendence of the whole apparent dichotomy between the outward and the inward." See *Shakespeare's Entrails*, 171.

43. See Henry, *Material Phenomenology*, 101–34.

INDEX